'This is a wonderful book that affirms the importance of DDP in the relationships of children in and out of home care. It also explores the beautiful themes that shape the identity and capacities of children – love, trust, shame. It offers direct applications of DDP for practitioners in this context. Kim Golding and her colleagues reflect on how relationships have the power to transform childhood pain and trauma into meaning that heals.'
– *Dr Joe Tucci, CEO of the Australian Childhood Foundation*

'This book will be of great value not only in residential care but anywhere where DDP is practised. Based on the authors' wealth of experience, this book is full of conversations and stories that beautifully illustrate DDP principles to practise, whilst providing safety and new knowledge of self and other.'
– *Dan Hughes, Ph.D., Founder of DDP*

'Grant, Thompson, and Golding present an innovative exploration in *Working with Relational Trauma in Children's Residential Care*, skilfully uncovering the transformative impact of DDP on the lives of children in residential care. This timely and accessible book seamlessly blends DDP with insights from contemporary neuroscience, providing a fresh perspective on applying these principles to therapeutic environments for children with profound trauma experiences. The authors showcase the remarkable effectiveness of the DDP approach, cultivating a therapeutic atmosphere that warmly and playfully invites children into a realm of safety. Through co-regulation and a "symmetry" of presence with the child, their approach encourages children to process their trauma-related experiences, creating an environment where they can securely embark on a journey of emotional healing and growth.'
– *Stephen W. Porges, Ph.D., Founding Director of the Traumatic Stress Research Consortium*

'If you care about children, please take this book with you wherever you go and devour it. You'll learn that residential treatment is not a place of last resort; it can be a place that gives rise to hope.'
– *Jonathan Baylin, co-author of* Attachment-Focused Therapy

'This is a must-have for any residential setting that is looking to embed or introduce therapeutic care. This is wonderfully written by Kim, Edwina, and George who have a wealth of expertise that enriches each ~~pter and creates a f~~ ~~ui~~de for all practitioners.'
– *Anthony Small, Registered Manager*

T0385254

Also in this series

Working with Relational Trauma in Schools
An Educator's Guide to Using Dyadic Developmental Practice
Kim S. Golding, Sian Phillips and Louise Michelle Bombèr
Foreword by Dan Hughes
ISBN 978 1 78775 219 1
eISBN 978 1 78775 220 7
Guides to Working with Relational Trauma Using DDP

Working with Relational Trauma in Children's Social Care
A Practitioner's Guide to Using Dyadic Developmental Practice
Alison Keith and Andrew Lister
Foreword by Kim S. Golding
ISBN 978 1 78775 274 0
eISBN 978 1 78775 275 7
Guides to Working with Relational Trauma Using DDP

of related interest

Making Connections with Vulnerable Children and Families
Creative Tools and Resources for Practice
Jan Horwath
Illustrated by Stevie Wilkinson
ISBN 978 1 78775 794 3
eISBN 978 1 78775 795 0

The Adverse Childhood Experiences Card Deck
**Tools to Open Conversations, Identify Support and Pro-
mote Resilience with Adolescents and Adults**
Dr Warren Larkin
Illustrated by Jon Dorsett
ISBN 978 1 83997 142 6

D.I.V.E.R.S.I.T.Y.
A Guide to Working with Diversity and Developing Cultural Sensitivity
Vivian Okeze-Tirado
ISBN 978 1 83997 631 5
eISBN 978 1 83997 632 2

Working with Relational Trauma in Children's Residential Care

A GUIDE TO USING DYADIC DEVELOPMENTAL PRACTICE

Edwina M. Grant,
George S. Thompson
and Kim S. Golding

Foreword by Kim S. Golding

Jessica Kingsley Publishers
London and Philadelphia

First published in Great Britain in 2024 by Jessica Kingsley Publishers
An imprint of John Murray Press

3

Copyright © Edwina M. Grant, George S. Thompson and Kim S. Golding 2024
Chapter 9 copyright © Rachel Swann 2024

A CIP catalogue record for this title is available from the
British Library and the Library of Congress

ISBN 978 1 78775 559 8
eISBN 978 1 78775 560 4

Printed and bound by CPI Group (UK) Ltd, Croydon, CR0 4YY

Jessica Kingsley Publishers' policy is to use papers that are natural,
renewable and recyclable products and made from wood grown in sus-
tainable forests. The logging and manufacturing processes are expected to
conform to the environmental regulations of the country of origin.

Jessica Kingsley Publishers
Carmelite House
50 Victoria Embankment
London EC4Y 0DZ

www.jkp.com

John Murray Press
Part of Hodder & Stoughton Ltd
An Hachette Company

We dedicate this book to the children and young people in residential care who have experienced relational trauma and to the adults who offer them what they need and deserve: safety and trust, joy, love, and hope. We thank them all for the learning they have offered us. We honour them for trusting us to walk with them as they have travelled their heroic journeys.

Contents

Part 2: HOW WE APPLY DDP INTERVENTIONS IN RESIDENTIAL SETTINGS

Part 3: HOW WE EMBED AND EMBODY DDP PRINCIPLES IN RESIDENTIAL SETTINGS

Series Editor's Foreword

KIM S. GOLDING

This book is part of a series exploring the application of Dyadic Developmental Practice, Psychotherapy and Parenting (DDP) to different settings and with different populations. Written by experienced DDP clinicians, these books provide an exploration of how DDP is being applied to facilitate open and engaged, emotionally connected relationships, supporting children and young people with experience of developmental trauma to heal and grow emotionally.

In this volume, I am joined by Edwina Grant and George Thompson to explore DDP within residential care. Residential care is often seen as a last resort when other care situations have failed. This is not our view. Residential care is a positive choice, used proactively as a resource when the road gets rocky. Residential care can support children and their parents, whether by birth, kin, foster care, or adoption, preserving these relationships into the child's future.

Edwina, George, and I offer stories and reflections as context for exploring what the DDP model can offer to residential care and education. The overall style is of sharing stories and reflections while providing theory, description, and experience of DDP within residential care.

Part 1 introduces the DDP model.

Chapter 1 introduces the DDP model of intervention while Chapter 2 explores the underlying theory.

We end this section with Chapter 3, an exploration of why young people come into residential care, illustrated with the fictional story of Bill.

Part 2 explores DDP as a model of practice that can be applied to the care and education of children living within residential settings. The DDP principles provide structure and regulation for the young people, helping them to experience trust in relationships.

As we explore in Chapter 4, the building of trust begins in the conversations we have with the young people.

Trust is also embedded in children's positive experience of love. In Chapter 5, we explore the meaning of love and experience of shame for children who have experienced developmental trauma. We consider the importance of providing love through our care and discipline, embedded within two hands of parenting.

In Chapter 6, we take a step back to explore the support that the adults caring for the children need. This considers the importance of embedding the DDP principles within teams, management, and leadership.

We end this section in Chapter 7 with a consideration of emotional pain as an integral part of residential care which needs to be approached with PACE (playfulness, acceptance, curiosity, and empathy), co-regulation, and the co-creation of new narratives.

In Part 3, we move on to consider how DDP principles can be embedded and embodied within residential care.

Chapter 8 begins this exploration with a consideration of the impact of caring for children who have experienced developmental trauma and the hope and despair that the adults can carry.

The experience of despair and need for hope may be at its most vivid when caring for children who are locked up for their own safety. In Chapter 9, guest author Rachel Swann helps us to understand how DDP principles are applied to the care of young people who are living in secure settings.

The attitude of PACE is referred to throughout this book. In Chapter 10, we invite you to consider how a cascade of PACE can provide a culture of support, building regulation and reflection for all.

Finally, in Chapter 11, we return to the story of Bill, his experience of residential care and the support it provides him while he finds the parenting he needs and deserves.

Additional to this book, we are excited to let you know that we have written three bonus chapters. These explore the top and tail of residential care. At one end is the recruitment and induction of residential carers and at the other is the partnership necessary for working with those supporting the children beyond the residential setting walls. These chapters are available, along with some additional resources that we think you will find helpful, on the DDP website (DDPnetwork.org). They are also available as downloadable PDFs from https://library.jkp.com/redeem using the code NUWCKKZ

Throughout this exploration of DDP in residential care, attention is given to the context within which interventions are provided. This takes account of what the staff, young people, and families bring to the intervention in terms of their upbringing, culture, identity, and experience. Unfortunately, marginalization, oppression, and discrimination are familiar experiences to many young people and families who need residential care support; this is also true for some of the residential staff providing this support. Adapting DDP interventions that are socially just and racially equitable is an important goal. With these adaptations, attention needs to be given to the intersections of race, sexuality, gender, religion, disability, neurodiversity, class, and physical appearance.

A word about our culture and identity

Edwina, George, and I are white, privileged, heterosexual, cisgender, and able-bodied DDP practitioners living in Scotland, England, and America. This book is infused with the values that we have internalized from our cultures, identity, and experience. We respect that these may be different within other cultures for those of differing identity and with different experience from ours. Much of what we have written will be helpful to residential care practitioners of all cultures, identity, and experience. We also invite you to reflect on your own experience; how this has informed your identity, cultural beliefs, and values; and how these can fit within DDP practice in residential care.

Acknowledgements

This book about DDP in residential care would not have been written if it had not been for Kim Golding, who patiently nurtured, mentored, and supported us throughout the writing journey. Of course, without Dan Hughes's curiosity, determination, and innovation (now over 30 years ago) about how to support the healing of children who have been harmed through relationships, no books about Dyadic Developmental Psychotherapy, parenting, and practice (DDP) would have been written! Dan is an inspiring teacher, guide, and friend. The authors waited with bated breath for Dan's feedback on the final draft of the book and were absolutely delighted when Dan said he loved the book. He thinks 'it will be of great value for residential care but also for anywhere where DDP is known and practiced'. We hope it is.

Back to the beginning of the writing journey. This book was commissioned by Jessica Kingsley Publishers (JKP) as part of a series exploring the application of DDP to different settings and different populations. Kim is the series editor. It has been three years in the writing as opposed to the originally agreed one year! We have to thank Steve Jones, publishing director at JKP, for his patience both with our missed deadlines and for extending the book's word count. Once we got going, we couldn't stop!

Many thanks to Rachel Swann whose powerful chapter, 'Behind the Walls', tells compelling stories of how she applies DDP principles to secure care settings. Gratitude to those individuals who have given their valuable time to read the draft manuscript, both feeding back their positive views and making suggestions for change: Julie Hudson, Evie Orr-Campbell, Dr Kelly-Marie Peel-Wainwright and the STARLAC team, Anthony Small, Emma Simpson, Dr Jon Baylin, Jan Moore, Julia Fishman, Dr Louise Packard, Karen Willey, and Tara Thompson-Glodich. Many thanks to Caryn Mirriam-Goldberg for her editorial sculpting that brought to light gems we may have otherwise buried.

Thank you, also, to John Adair, Ruth Emond, Andrew Burns, and Scottish Attachment in Action (particularly David Woodier, and the late Dave Lettice), all of whom gave us permission to use aspects of their published work in the book.

Edwina M. Grant and George S. Thompson

I started my DDP journey in 2003. Having been inspired by level one DDP training with Dan at Family Futures in London, I, somewhat impetuously, emailed Dan to come to train in Scotland. He said yes! As an independent practitioner, I had no infrastructure to organize training and approached two organizations that I was working with – Crossreach Children's Services and Aberlour Child Care Trust – to help me. With the support and shared enthusiasm of these organizations, the journey of DDP principles-to-practice in residential care in Scotland started in 2004. I am grateful to all the residential care services I have worked with who have shared my passion for DDP. Particular thanks to those organizations who were with me at the start of the journey. They are Crossreach, Seamab, and Moore House Care and Education. The key figures who need particular acknowledgement in supporting and trusting me are Chris McNaught, Paul Gilroy, Martin Walsh, Kyle Fleming, Pat Sheridan, Stephen Drysdale, Moira Greentree, Joanna McCreadie, and Gary Gallacher.

My main coauthor, George Thompson, and I have held hands across the pond from Scotland to Kansas in writing this book. We have shared our hearts and minds. We were writing (or trying to!) during the COVID-19 pandemic, which presented many challenges for us both personally and professionally. It has been my honour to get to know George. George and my husband, Ian, have gotten to know each other on Zoom, sharing stories and corny jokes! We have never met in person. When we do, which we will, an enormous hug is well overdue.

The DDP community is one in which PACEful support is always available. We laugh and cry together! Particular individuals are my anchors and, alongside Dan and Kim, have been my teachers: Sez Morse, Julie Hudson, Betty Brouwer – thank you.

My family have been absolutely central to writing this book. My husband, Ian, and our adult children, Sarah, Rachel, and Michael. They are the centre of my world and my universe. They have offered me love and PACEful support through this whole process. They have tolerated my 'I can't do that right now; I am writing this book!' (sometimes with an expletive before the word 'book').

There are many, many children, young people, parents, carers, and practitioners who work in residential care who have contributed to my learning and hence to this book. A massive thank you to all of you.

Edwina M. Grant

I am grateful to Edwina for her companionship over the past nine years. Her presence is a wonderful infusion of warm-hearted kindness, playful irreverence, and wisdom that comes from deep experience with DDP in residential settings. She has become my sister in creating a better world for our children.

Like Edwina, I owe a tremendous debt of gratitude to Dan Hughes for his 13 years of generous mentorship. From 2012 to 2019, Dan and Grey McKellar guided the KidsTLC team to embed and embody a PACEful, relational approach to our work, culminating in KidsTLC's certification as a DDP organization. Through Dan, I met other DDP trainers who were equally generous in their support, in particular Sian Phillips, Courtney Rennicke, Betty Brouwer, Mervin Maier, and Julie Hudson.

At KidsTLC, my residential treatment home for 12 years, I was blessed to have genuinely good-natured and caring colleagues. Brandon Mock and Mark Siegmund shared a passionate vision for grappling with the ravages of developmental trauma. They, along with our other clinical leadership, Roy Rotz, Renee Azzouz, Cindy Whitney, Kelly English, Rebecca Toy, and Dan Lash, met weekly to build a programme that truly helped traumatized children and their families. I hold dear the clinical team I worked most closely with, especially Jan Moore, Mitchell Cloud, Mary Eibes, Jordan Carroll, Scott Smith, Sarah Heffron, Cassie Barrett, Navia Syrie, Amanda Harlow, Mallory McKim, Ren Andersen, Paul Perrini, Brad Link, Isaac Henges, Sandy Chu, and Lauren Hentchel. I value the collaboration with Kansas leaders Gary Henault, Commissioner Andy Brown, and Secretary Laura Howard. Dr Sosunmolu Shoyinka has been a trusted friend and counsellor throughout these years as well.

Finally, it has been a great privilege to work with the young people whose lives started out so harshly. The courage they display in regaining the humanity which life has tried to wrest from them never ceases to amaze and inspire me. I am honoured that they and their families have trusted me to accompany them through hellish realms on their healing quests.

George S. Thompson

Introduction

How Did DDP Find Its Way into Residential Care?

Welcome to our book. There is much excellent writing by Dan Hughes, Jon Baylin, Kim Golding, Louise Bomber, Sian Phillips, and others about DDP in family and education contexts; there is very little written specifically about DDP practice in residential settings.

However, if you are looking for the definitive guide to DDP in residential care, then this is not it! Let us explain. Residential care settings, like any human endeavour, are quite unique with their own, if you will, personalities, attachment styles, and often a cast of many, many characters, adults, and children. Our hope is that this book will stimulate thinking and provide guidance that can be used flexibly and adapted to the unique needs of each residential setting.

As Kim comments in the Foreword, the authors are all white, privileged, heterosexual, cisgender, and able-bodied DDP practitioners living in Scotland, England, and America. We are aware that although all of us have worked with children and adults from a diverse range of backgrounds, experience, and identity this book may be limited by our lack of experience working outside of these countries. However, we hope that our DDP experiences and knowledge are transferable to other parts of the world. We also know that legislation, policy, and procedures vary widely in different countries and potentially impacts on how DDP can be embedded into practice. We offer this guide and trust in the knowledge and creativity of those reading it to adapt it to suit their own unique needs, always with the relational needs of the children in mind.

What is this book then?

This book is the story of how DDP, initially a family-focused attachment therapy originated by Dan Hughes, found its way into residential care in the UK and US. It explores the application of the DDP principles in residential settings across all relationships. It is important to us that this book, the knowledge and experiences we describe, is accessible to you. In short, we hope you will come on a learning journey with us that will be educational, emotional, and enjoyable.

What do we mean by residential care settings?

For the purposes of this book, we have in mind all residential care settings for children and young people who have experienced developmental trauma. The authors' direct experience is in group care settings, including care only, care and education, psychiatric residential treatment, and secure accommodation. The age span of the children is from 5 to 21 years. All of the residential care settings we describe use DDP principles to guide and inform the care and, when available onsite, education of the children. Some of the settings also have DDP therapy available.

Storytelling

One of the essences of DDP is storytelling. Here, Edwina, George, Kim, and our guest author Rachel offer you the stories of how we found our way to DDP and became passionate about supporting the embedding of DDP in residential care.

Edwina's story

I live in Scotland. Way back in the 1980s, I was a residential childcare worker and manager in what was termed a therapeutic community (care and education) for children. All of the children had experienced relational trauma within family in their early years, and all had experienced multiple transitions from birth family to foster care, back to birth family, to children's homes. You will know the story as it is unfortunately still too common. The therapeutic community was viewed as a 'last gasp' potentially before secure accommodation when all else was deemed to have failed.

I knew nothing of attachment theory (out of 'favour' at the time), intersubjectivity (in its infancy), developmental trauma (unheard of), or neuroscience (non-existent with respect to understanding child development). However, I was qualified as an educational psychologist; this offered me a theoretical (psychodynamic at the time) understanding of what were termed 'maladjusted' children. I understood that the children's dysregulated behaviours were symptoms of distress not intrinsic, they were not born 'bad, mad, or sad'. This theoretical knowledge helped me understand that what felt like a daily personal onslaught from the young people was a result of distress and defensiveness, not personally intended – well, sometimes it was personal, and it was intentional! Also, being a therapeutic community, there was a philosophy of care which promoted recovery and healing through relationships. It astounds me now that there were 20 children in our care and only four adults looking after them at any one time!

Nothing could have prepared me for the intensity of mixed emotions that engulfed me! Joy and fun were in abundance and also anxiety, anger, despair, and, at times, shame: a mirroring, of course, of the children's 'big feelings' and, as I now know, an inevitable consequence of trying to build safe and trustworthy relationships with children who were terrified of relational closeness and highly resistant to discovering that maybe they were likeable or even lovable.

I left residential care in the 1990s with some unanswered questions. I had learned much about myself and my relational capacity from the children and young people and from the adults I worked alongside. The ethos of the therapeutic community was: *no matter what you do we will still care for and about you.* I had experienced this being effective in changing some of the children's life trajectories. When the children started to think and feel *'maybe I am likeable, maybe I am lovable'*, that possibility was potentially enough to change their life course from destruction to construction. What puzzled me was why some of the children started to consider themselves as likeable, to be proud of their achievements, to take some control over their emotional thermostats, to trust, to take responsibility, and other young people couldn't, no matter what we tried. Some of the children who made use of safe adult relationships went on to live different, more positive lives than the lives they would have had without our residential care. I know this because I remain in touch with them, and we have talked about what made the difference. But I attended far too many funerals of young people who died through suicide, violence, and drugs. As I write this, I see their faces and feel so sad for them.

In 2003, I undertook DDP level one training with Dan Hughes, and the light bulbs flashed on. Now I understood why the young people who died could not trust or accept adult care, and I also understood what might have helped them stay alive and start to recover. It became my passion to offer an understanding of DDP in practice in Scotland, including to residential care settings.

Forward the clock to the present. In my capacity as DDP practitioner, consultant, and trainer, I offer training and consultancy to residential establishments. Much of what I offer is based on what I and that initial residential team needed. DDP is now firmly rooted in my practice. I am privileged to have Dan as my guide and mentor on my DDP journey, with Kim and others who are passionate about DDP supporting me.

It is not a cliché to say that the children and young people I have cared for and worked with, both in residential care and in families, have taught me what they needed to be able to live, love, and learn successfully.

I am still learning!

George's story

I live in the middle of the US in what we call the heartland. In 2010, I was searching for answers to two things of great importance. My four-year-old adopted daughter was having big blow ups and struggling to let her mother and me make decisions for her. At the KidsTLC psychiatric residential treatment facility where I was medical director, there were a significant number of young people who weren't getting better. For help with our daughter, we were referred to a DDP therapist. Though my wife and I were both interested in trauma, we had not heard of Dan Hughes or the therapeutic approach he had developed. When I read Dan's book *Building the Bonds of Attachment*, light bulbs started going off in my head. As we followed the therapist's advice, our daughter opened up in response to our PACEful attitude, letting us provide comfort when disappointment threatened to overwhelm her.

At the same time, Dan's book explained why certain group of kids in the residential treatment facility didn't get better. For them, connection was dangerous, and controlling people meant safety. Even when a part of the child wanted to trust our bids for relationship, it was as if another part screamed, 'Don't do it! Don't trust them! It's a trick and a trap!'

Their developmental trauma had led to the blocked trust we describe in this book. So, we began to introduce this understanding in our work, to prioritize building safe relationships instead of focusing so much on the child's behaviour. By accepting and empathizing with their experiences, we showed the children we were safe, trustworthy, and interested in them as unique human beings. We were building bonds of attachment, and those bonds were more motivating to the children than any reward we had dreamed up for our behavioural modification system.

Both the therapy with my daughter and the work at KidsTLC reminded me of two formative experiences from my own childhood. Around the age of 12, I read *Dibs in Search of Self* by Virginia Axline (1964), a story about therapy with a young boy locked in his own world, a world which he defended with episodes of rage. I was moved by the compassion of the therapist and her care with the boy's humanity. Even though a child myself, I knew I wanted to touch people with that kind of care someday. Then, when I was 15, I saw a child psychiatrist for two sessions of psychotherapy, to help with feelings about my parents' divorce. Dr Hal Boylston listened thoughtfully to what I was going through with a warm and empathic curiosity that Dan Hughes would have recognized. That experience also moved me deeply, and it was only years later, after I had finished my own child psychiatry training, that I realized I had followed in Dr Boylston's footsteps, even attending the same training programme where he had trained.

In the autumn of 2011, I contacted Dan Hughes to ask for assistance in applying DDP principles to our residential programme, and in January 2012, I attended a DDP training with Dan Hughes in Annville, Pennsylvania, in the US, along with Brandon Mock, my primary companion in introducing DDP to KidsTLC. The evening of the first day, Brandon and I each called home and tried out what we were learning with our children. We were both amazed. The training had brought the concepts off the page and brought a PACE attitude into our lives. We returned to KidsTLC inspired to broaden and deepen the relational approach we had already developed. Over the next seven years, we continued to train ourselves and our staff to embed and embody DDP principles in our work. If you would like to discover more about the story of KidsTLC's journey to become a certified DDP organization, we have included this in the bonus material on the DDP network website (https://ddpnetwork. org). This material is also available as downloadable PDFs from https:// library.jkp.com/redeem using the code NUWCKKZ

I can clearly picture the faces of many young people who were written off by clinicians and social services alike. They gradually responded to the DDP approach, eventually relaxing their guard enough to trust our intention to help them stay emotionally regulated, build meaningful relationships, and see themselves in a whole new light. DDP principles and practices turned out to be powerful and humane, able to transform grim realities into hopeful futures full of courage, warmth, and joy. A boy who for several years couldn't live outside the structure of a residential treatment facility now sleeps over at his friend's house. A girl who couldn't tolerate being around other young people now mentors younger girls in school. The work with them has been an honour and a gift, conveying to me an absolute certainty that kids like them can and do get better when they are kept safe within the structure of a residential treatment facility by staff who have become adept at PACEful interaction and Dyadic Developmental Practice.

Kim's story

My first experience of residential care was the large hospitals common in the 1980s which provided people with severe learning disabilities a place to live. I was employed as psychology assistant and the work was very behavioural. One important lesson that experience gave me was to look behind the behaviour and discover the person. Behaviours which could be quite daunting became easier to manage when you knew it was just Bob in urgent need of a cup of tea and a little company.

During clinical training, I became interested in working with children and families. Behavioural, and the newer cognitive behavioural, models equipped us for our lives as clinical psychologists. These were the models that guided me in my post-qualifying positions, first with preschool children born with learning disabilities and then with children who experienced mental health difficulties.

I felt fairly confident working with younger children and involving the parents in 'parent training'. I was much less confident when required to provide therapy for older children, especially those living in children's homes who had suffered early trauma and loss of multiple families. The expectation was that the 'worker' would bring these children for their therapy appointments, returning in an hour to collect them. I was not at all sure what I was going to do for that hour. The children were often polite but wary. They feigned disinterest but I suspect this was to cover the sense of threat they were experiencing. I was lucky if I got monosyllabic answers to my questions. I was not sure what they were expecting from me, nor what they would like to achieve by attending this series of appointments. As they left, I felt particularly unskilled at my job. I was not sure what therapy the children would benefit from, and the care staff parenting them felt remote and inaccessible.

Nearly ten years later, with a little more experience under my belt, I was involved in setting up a service supporting foster and residential carers. While I felt more confident in engaging these carers, I still needed to find a way to make a difference for the children. I needed something additional to the traditional approaches I learned during my training.

Fortunately, I met Dan Hughes and learned about Dyadic Developmental Psychotherapy. This provided me with a different way of working with the children, young people, and their parents. Nowhere was this more important than in the consultation I provided to the staff working in the children's homes. I would no longer expect to offer therapeutic support to the young people, without also working collaboratively with the care staff. Together, we would find ways to reach these young people, offering healing relationships with therapy only a small part of this.

Often the staff experienced unreasonable expectations of what they could achieve with the young people. Children who had not yet experienced safe dependency were being pushed to independence. Some of the most satisfying work I did in these homes was supporting the children and their residential parents to discover healthy relationships and safety in dependence, trusting in their carers' nurture and support. And therapy? It didn't look like therapy when I sat with a young person, watching their favourite TV programme or we went out for a walk together. We chatted and I discovered that the relaxed, informal connections helped them to explore many things with me. Within these informal connections, we would touch on the past as it linked to their current experiences. We would involve their key worker in a way and at a pace that they were ready for. Sometimes, an informal connection would move into a more typical DDP therapy session, but always DDP was my guide for the 'what, when and how' of working both with these children who had experienced such challenges in their life and with the residential parents trying their best to secure better futures for them.

Rachel's story

Once upon a time a long time ago (2011), a family of clinicians working in the National Health Service (NHS) mental health services for Children in Care in the Southeast of England invited some wizards to our kingdom. The wizards were Dan Hughes, Julie Hudson, and, later, Kim Golding. Here is where my DDP story began – in a journey which has included moments of awe (the resilience of children who have had such difficult starts to their life), heartbreak (when DDP was not enough and a child-carer relationship we were so invested in came to an end), joy (touching moments of intimacy between a child and carer each previously fearful of such connection), trepidation (uncertainty about what I was doing and digging deep to 'trust the process'), and celebration (to witness what a difference it has made to many of those I have worked with).

It was a privilege and a treat to work with our wizards. In the early days of making sense of and stepping into DDP, I would find myself seeking to channel internalized nuggets of Dan – his 'let's work it out' announcement to the child and carer always made me smile, whether it was he or I saying it. It offered such confidence to the child and carer about what could be achieved together. The model intuitively felt right, although not accompanied by a manual and the skills are nuanced. You don't do PACE, you embody it. It is who you become. It is understanding your strengths and your weaknesses. For me, particularly noticing what happens to my (and others) curiosity when working with children and systems in which there are powerful conscious and unconscious projections to 'not go there!'. Anther nugget that I held onto in the early days when being supported to trust the process was Dan speaking about how as a therapist you have to find something you like in the person you are seeking to help. This is where you start. The young person/carer/system needs to feel your genuine interest and appreciation for who they are. This alongside a genuine belief that everybody is doing their best – albeit hard at times to hold on to – has allowed me to find compassion for individuals and systems whose adaptive behaviours at times seek to create distance, to split, and to repel. I have learned to be curious rather than critical, and to never forget that it all rests on our collective sense of safety.

As I write this, I am surprised to realize that I don't use the 'let's work it out' nugget so much anymore; I am finding my own sense of PACE. I shan't pretend I now wander through life being PACEful all the time – my family will attest to this not being the case! – but I am certainly acutely aware when I am not. I'm still practising.

Working with young people (10–17 years) who have been deprived of their liberty in secure accommodation has been the biggest challenge to my DDP story yet. The secure environment is an extremely intense place for staff to work in and for the young people to live in. Emotions run high among the young people and the staff teams supporting them. Moments of threat, frustration, exhaustion, vulnerability, comfort, hope, and joy tumble around within and between individuals, dyads, groups, and systems. DDP's focus on relational safety and support as the container for these experiences complements the focus of the Integrated Framework of Practice for Children and Young People in the Secure Estate (England and Wales). This proposes the 24/7 relationships for young people as one of the key drivers for change. Yet these are the young people who have been repeatedly let down by relationships across their life. Described as young people who are high risk/high vulnerability/high complexity/high need, they are also a cohort of young people understandably highly mistrustful of the next person in a long line of professionals who proclaim to be there to help them, should they even be of the opinion that help is what they need. If we cannot create safety and trust in relationships with us, we are just 'holding' environments, trying to keep the young person safe for a moment through physical structure and boundaries. If we are to support a real change of trajectory for these young people, we must create relationships that are safe, trustworthy, and meaningful. The relationship of each to the other must be genuine and must matter. This is true not only in our relationships with the young people, but also in relationships of trust among staff and within and between teams and agencies. DDP for me offers the best chance of us getting there together.

What do our stories say about what DDP has to offer residential care?

Children are placed in a residential care setting when living in a family is not working for one reason or another. This is often because they have been harmed through relationships with adults, parents, or parenting figures whose responsibility it was to love and protect them. It is our view that healing and recovery first and foremost come through relationships that offer them the comfort and joy that was lacking in their early experiences of being parented. To learn in their hearts and minds that relationships with adults can be safe and trustworthy. Often, of course, they also must learn new, more prosocial ways of behaving rather than trying to control everyone and everything in any way possible. It is our view that this heart and head learning is not achieved by rewards and sanctions. It is done through the experience of relationships that are loving, that strive to keep them safe, and that are trustworthy.

As Kim comments in the Foreword, residential care and education are often seen as a last resort when other care situations have failed. This is not our view. Many children who have experienced relational harm in their families and are now in foster care, kinship care, or adoptive homes have emotional and behavioural challenges on their journey to recovery, particularly in their teenage years. Family living can become unsafe, particularly when children become aggressive or a risk to themselves. Both the children and their carers need a break while support is given to both parties to make sense of what is happening. This can lead to repair of family ruptures and often to the child's ability to live safely in the family again. In our view, residential care could and should be used proactively to provide this break and support the repair. Residential care should not be a last resort in which everyone feels they have failed – the child, the carers, and involved professionals. Used proactively as a resource when the road gets rocky, residential care can be a positive choice.

Residential settings need a theoretical and research base supporting an understanding of why the children behave as they do; a philosophy of care; and a practice model underpinned by theory and research. All of these elements create a shared understanding, a shared way of working, a shared value base, and a shared language. These elements are enacted by the adults who work with the children, with each other, with parents and carers, and with other professionals. This book tells the story of why and how the DDP practice model can inform best practice for children in residential care.

How to use this book

There are several ways to read this book. Of course, you can simply proceed from start to finish, an approach that will give you a coherent sense of how we go about embedding DDP principles into residential settings. You could also read a single chapter to get more insight into the material the chapter addresses. Or, if a supervisor wants to support an individual staff member or group of staff members to develop their knowledge and skills in a certain area, they could study the corresponding section or chapter together. Finally, the book can be shared with policy- and decision-makers who oversee resources and systems for children who have experienced developmental trauma to guide their understanding, prioritization, and strategies for action.

A residential home might use the book as part of their training curriculum. For example, they could convene a study group to read and discuss a chapter every few weeks. One facility we know asked their service leaders to read and discuss a DDP book to create a train-the-trainer programme. Each month, one of the leaders would examine a chapter in detail, then guide the other leaders through a discussion of that chapter. As a group, the leaders developed ideas for how to assist their staff in applying that chapter's concepts. During the following month, each leader trained their staff using the ideas they had developed together. In their next monthly meeting, before discussing the next chapter, the leaders debriefed on the training they had just completed. At the end of 12 months, readers and staff members had explored material from the whole book. They had also developed a training programme that they could use going forward.

Notes on terms and language

- DDP is a dyadic, developmental model for psychotherapy, parenting, and practice. Throughout this book, the term *DDP* is used for all three of these. When referring to one of these areas of intervention specifically, we indicate this.

- In recognition of the non-binary nature of gender, we use the terms *they* and *their* rather than *he* or *she*, except where gender is clearly indicated.

- We use the term *parent* to describe those who have a parenting role towards the children in their care, whether they are biological, step, adoptive, foster, kinship, or residential parents. This term is used interchangeably with *residential carer* and *caregiver.*

- Unless indicated, case examples and dialogues are fictional, composite case stories inspired by the many young people, families, residential homes, and practitioners that we have worked with. The stories depict the situation we are describing while protecting the privacy of the individual children and families with whom we work.

- We use the terms *child*, *children*, and *young people*. These words refer to children from birth to 18 years of age.

- The authors are English, Scottish, and American. We have decided to 'keep it real' in terms of the language and terms that are used in the UK and in America. We thought the reader might appreciate some explanation of terms that may be unfamiliar to them:

  - *Key adult/worker/teacher:* These terms are often used in the UK for a designated adult whose responsibility it is to build a primary relationship with a particular child or children. This adult also has responsibility for liaison with the child's family and other professionals in the team around the child; to report on the child's views and progress; and to ensure the child's health needs are monitored and addressed.

  - *Residential treatment facility:* In the US, a residential treatment facility, sometimes referred to as a residential programme, provides intensive, round-the-clock supervision and mental health services to people whose emotional and behavioural issues prevent them from living safely in the community. They are considered medical facilities which conduct psychiatric and other assessments and deliver medication management; social and life skills training; educational services; and individual, group, and family therapy. The multidisciplinary team usually includes psychiatrists, psychologists, social workers, nurses, therapists, direct care staff, and teachers.

  - *Residential care:* In the UK, this term is used for group care homes for children who are 'looked after'. This may be arranged under a statutory care order or a voluntary accommodation arrangement. Some group homes provide education as well as care; some employ therapists; and some are secure settings. In the US, a residential care home is usually referred to as a *group home*.

– *Looked after child:* In the UK, this term means a child who has been in the care of their local authority for more than 24 hours. In the US, a looked after child is known as a child who is in state custody or in foster care.

PART 1

THE CONTEXT AND FOUNDATIONS OF DDP IN RESIDENTIAL SETTINGS AND WHY WE NEED IT

CHAPTER 1

Introduction to the Dyadic Developmental Psychotherapy Model of Intervention

Dyadic Developmental Psychotherapy (DDP) was developed by American clinical psychologist Dan Hughes as a way of working with children living in and adopted from care who had early experience of developmental trauma (Hughes, 2007, 2009, 2011; Hughes *et al.*, 2019). Dan recognizes the importance of providing interventions that pay attention to the attachment needs of children. This involves the parents before, during, and after the therapeutic work with the children.

Dan has led and supports the ongoing development of DDP into a practice model. This expands the use of the DDP principles into working within school environments, social care settings, supervisory and management relationships, and, of course, residential care.

What is DDP?

DDP is a model of intervention for children who have experienced developmental trauma (also called *relational trauma*) early in life, many of whom are growing up in care or adopted from care. The model is grounded in relationship theory, neuroscience, and an understanding of the impact of relational trauma on a child's development and functioning (Hughes *et al.*, 2019).

DDP is a model that has grown out of Western psychology. While many of the understandings gained in the Western world have universal applicability, attention also needs to be given to how DDP can adapt and grow to encompass learning from the global majority in the non-Western world. The importance of human social connection is one example of areas in which adaptation and growth of the model is needed. This is work in progress and is paving the way for exciting developments as DDP continues to evolve (Hughes & Golding, 2024).

DDP is based on an understanding that:

- children need healthy reciprocal relationships in order to thrive

- children with developmental trauma have learned to avoid these relationships because of their previous traumatic experience.

This is particularly true of young people living in residential care. Often these young people have also experienced multiple caregivers, and the loss of each of these has further eroded trust in parents and adults in general. Moving into residential care can be challenging for children and their families, particularly if it is against their wishes. However, it can also provide a sense of relief from the intimacy of family living.

DDP interventions offer children the opportunity for the new relational experiences necessary for healthy development. Children are invited into reciprocal relationships modelled on healthy parent-child relationships. The children's reluctance to take these invitations is met with acceptance and empathy. Curiosity helps the child to discover who they are and to experience open and engaged relationships with adults that are interested in them and all they experience. Playfulness represents a way adults can interact with children that demonstrates their enjoyment in their relationship with the child. This offers the child the opportunity to build relationships with safe adults within which the child can experience fun and laughter. The child discovers the other's interest in them and experiences joy in these relationships.

Through this attitude of PACE (playfulness, acceptance, curiosity, and empathy), the child is offered the safety needed to manage some gentle challenge. The child is challenged to experience a different way of being. The child is helped to feel safe when open and engaged in the relationship, a move away from the defensive ways of being that have become so much a part of who they are. As social engagement increases and vulnerability decreases, opportunities for emotional growth arise.

DDP enables children who have experienced relational trauma to feel safe, often for the first time in their lives – safe to be sad and safe to seek and experience reciprocal joy. In DDP, children learn too that they may develop their unique sense of autonomy while at the same time maintaining a close relationship with someone who will keep them safe and assist them in their development. (Hughes *et al.*, 2019, p. 6)

Children who have experienced relational traumas in the form of abuse, neglect, loss, and exposure to frightening environments without parental protection are often left in states of shame and terror. This in turn distorts the developing self-identity and expectations of others. This experience can be enacted within the residential home, often in very challenging ways.

The children need different relationships within which they can learn about themselves and others, not distorted by past experiences. This reduces shame and terror and opens the children to relationships which offer comfort and joy. The children receive healthy developmental experience within which emotional states are identified, regulated, and expressed. Reflective capacities to understand self and other, not distorted by past learning, increase. Children discover that they can seek comfort, resolve conflicts, and engage in relationship repair without the gnawing fear of abandonment and loss that they have been anticipating for so long.

The development of DDP

DDP is a therapy model which has its roots in a range of theoretical and clinical knowledge based on Western psychology models. The model developed from eclectic beginnings, drawing from our understanding of healthy therapist-client relationships and healthy parent-child relationships. The increase in neuroscientific understanding has also contributed, with increased knowledge about the impact of abusive and neglectful parent relationships on children. DDP is therefore an integrative psychotherapy.

DDP is a product of its time and, as is evident below, has been influenced in the majority by white, male researchers, psychologists, and psychiatrists. DDP, however, is a model that continues to grow and develop. Its ongoing development also encompasses non-Western ways of being, adding to its flexibility and strength (Hughes & Golding, 2024).

Healthy therapist-client relationships

Clinical inspiration was drawn by Dan Hughes from clinicians and researchers working primarily with adults. For example, the work of Milton Erikson, Carl Rogers, and Diana Fosha (Hughes, 2007). He adapted the work of these clinicians and researchers to provide a relationship-focused therapy for children and families. This included careful consideration of healthy parent-child relationships. Erikson's stance of accepting and utilizing his client's presence to achieve therapeutic change; Rogers's person-centred therapy with the therapeutic stance of unconditional positive regard (acceptance), congruence (genuineness), and warmth (empathy); and Fosha's attention to developing coherent autobiographical narrative by integrating affect and cognition are all echoed in the DDP principles guiding the interventions.

Healthy parent-child relationships

Dan Hughes (2007) integrated understanding of the attachment relationship experience articulated by John Bowlby (1998) with the intersubjective relationship experience articulated by Colwyn Trevarthen (2001).

Attachment theory focuses on the parents' role in helping children to feel safe and to regulate strong emotions. These attachment connections offer a secure base for exploration and learning about self, other, and the world.

Intersubjectivity theory provides a detailed understanding of the reciprocal relationship experience children need with their parents. Within this relationship children develop a sense of who they and their parents are.

Within DDP, these theories are applied to interventions which can recreate this experience, attending to both the attachment and intersubjective needs of the child.

Alongside this, several other researchers have influenced the development of DDP, including:

- the work of Stern on understanding attunement and the importance of affect matching the vitality of the child's expression (Stern, 2000)

- Schore's insights on the integration of right and left hemispheric brain functioning for communication, with the telling of the story seen as important as the content of the story for developing a successful relationship (Schore, 2012)

- Siegel's attention to integration and coherence of brain functioning assisted through the child experiencing intersubjective engagement with the adult's brain (Siegel, 1999).

DDP-trained therapists are guided towards a relational approach to working with child and parent. The therapist provides the child with a healing and integrative relational experience based on meeting attachment and intersubjective needs and supporting integrated brain functioning and healthy neurodevelopment. Working with the parents, including residential caregivers, separately and involving them in the therapy sessions ensures that this relational experience includes these attachment figures. This also ensures that the same experience is provided in day-to-day living and learning.

Abusive and neglectful parent-child relationships

Growth in the understanding of neuroscience has further strengthened the DDP model.

Many studies have demonstrated the interpersonal nature of the human nervous system. Research by Stephen Porges (2017), Allan Schore (2012), Daniel Siegel (1999), Ed Tronick (2007), and others is guiding our understanding of the role and importance of relationship in human development. This gives increased insights into what goes wrong in abusive and neglectful parent-child relationships and the impact of challenging parenting upon children. This provides a road map for what children need to recover from the harmful impact of this experience.

A more detailed discussion of this theoretical body of knowledge and its influence on the practice of DDP can be found in Chapter 2.

Dyadic Developmental Psychotherapy

The DDP model integrates understanding of what works in therapist-client relationships with an understanding of healthy and unhealthy parent-child relationships. Attachment theory describes how human beings are born relational. When parents are not able to sufficiently attune to their baby's needs, and/or are actively harmful, the child fears and withdraws from such relational experiences. An important goal of therapy is to help the child to become open to relationship experience again, overcoming the trauma of early frightening relationships. The therapist provides here and now intersubjective experiences with the child and facilitates these between the child and parents.

The parenting role in the residential setting is provided by the residential care workers, each of whom are likely to have 'key worker' responsibilities for a particular child or children. Within a DDP approach, this key adult is modelled on a healthy parent. The adult pays attention to the building of a positive, in-depth relationship with the child. This facilitates other positive relationships within the team of adults and children. The key worker is a dependable relationship, providing a secure base and the safety needed for the child to start to trust in adult co-regulation and care. This parenting relationship provides the platform for the child to develop a more secure attachment.

This secure base provides room for exploration. Therapist, parents, and child explore the child's current experience and better understand the defences that have enabled that child to survive difficult past experiences. Defences described by Stephen Porges as heroic, in honour of the role they have played in the child's life (Porges, 2017). Trauma narratives of fear and terror are thus understood, and, from these, new narratives of hope and healing are co-created.

Dyadic Developmental Parenting

DDP, and its central attitude of PACE, provides the relational 'surround sound' in residential care. The child is immersed in a therapeutic environment offering emotional connection alongside structure, supervision, and boundaries to keep them safe. While not all children need DDP therapy, this can be a helpful additional provision within residential care.

A central part of the DDP model is the involvement of parents in the therapy and in providing a DDP-informed approach to parenting. Residential carers have the role of parent to children living in residential homes. While not all residential carers are comfortable considering themselves parent figures, it is a central belief within DDP that all children need secure parental care. Within residential care, this parenting is adjusted and matched to what the child can tolerate. For example, the level of closeness and degree of empathy matches what the child can handle with a little gentle challenge to extend their tolerance.

In residential settings, therapy can also be extended to include a parent who the child will return to in the future. This might be a birth parent or a previous foster, adoptive, or kinship parent.

The involvement of parenting figures in DDP interventions recognizes that if the child cannot seek some security of attachment to current parents, they remain stuck in the past, relying on defences that served them well but have reached their sell-by date. Increased safety and security provide the fertile soil needed for developmental and emotional growth as the child discovers a way of being beyond their defences. This relies on the parent providing emotional connection as well as guidance and discipline (Golding, 2017a).

The attitude of PACE is central within DDP:

Playfulness expresses joy in the relationship.

Acceptance is of the child's inner world.

Curiosity is held about the meaning underneath the behaviour.

Empathy is for the child's emotional state.

PACE is a parenting attitude, a way of being that facilitates emotional connection between parent and child (Golding & Hughes, 2012; Hughes, 2009). PACE increases security for the child, reducing shame and opening new possibilities for the self and for relationships with others.

PACE is a universal part of DDP interventions, with all those caring and supporting the child encouraged to adopt this way of being. PACE is also context specific; the demonstration of playfulness, acceptance, curiosity, and empathy differs within and between cultures. For example, it is influenced by differences in:

- the social hierarchy and status of children within the community

- expectations of independence or interdependence

- the value placed on autonomy, relatedness, moral obligations, and respect

- the value placed on play and on participation in household chores

- the role of emotion in relation to self and other

- the use of dyadic or polyadic communication within nuclear or extended households

- how love is expressed in words and facial expressions and through acts of care and doing things for others.

(Harwood et al., 1995; Keller, 2022; Lancy, 2017)

The DDP practitioner considers these differences, collaboratively working with parents to figure out how PACE can be a culturally relevant way of being for them. This has an additional complexity when working with young people living in residential care as they are interacting with multiple caregivers, each of whom has their own cultural roots and are comfortable with PACE in different ways.

Parenting children with experience of developmental trauma can be a challenge. Parents are touched by the child's trauma, sometimes colliding with their own past traumatic experiences. They are hurt by the child's need to control and the rejection of the nurture they are offering. They are exhausted by the overwhelming emotional demands made upon them. They are worried by a bewildering array of difficulties and symptoms displayed by the child, and by the search for answers to what is wrong and how it can be put right. And, of course, they still have the range of practical and emotional tasks that all children require of their parents. Within residential care, many of these tasks are shared by teams of caregivers. Outside of residential care, they are coupled with the added necessity for good communication and a shared understanding of what they are aiming to achieve for the young people. Asking parents to additionally play a pivotal role in the child's therapy and to support this with a style of parenting which is often different from how they were raised is a lot to ask. For this reason, DDP interventions involve a high level of support for the parents. This support provides the parents with someone who can:

- guide them around the best time to introduce therapy to the child, help them to understand what is happening in therapy, and how to carry out their role in therapy

- guide them in their parenting of the children, helping them to understand the DDP model and to apply this to their unique child or children

- provide emotional support when this feels too hard and overwhelming

- encourage them to seek social support and to engage in self-care

- recognize for them when they have moved into blocked care, temporarily losing their capacity to provide empathic, attuned caregiving because of physiological changes in the brain linked to the impact of the child (Hughes & Baylin, 2012). The therapist provides relational support, which helps the parent to move out of blocked care again

- help them to understand the impact the child is having on them, understanding the triggers and how to manage them. This involves jointly understanding the parents' attachment and past relationship experience

- advocate for them and their child while also helping them to find their voice in the network surrounding the child and family.

Providing a consistent parenting approach within residential care encourages teams of caregivers to work closely together with shared aims, values, and ways of being that can provide the young people with a more coherent sense of being cared for.

Dyadic Developmental Practice: The development of DDP as a practice model

DDP aims to heal relational trauma for children who have been exposed to abusive, neglectful, and frightening parenting. With this healing, children can benefit from healthy parenting, supporting neurodevelopment and emotional well-being. This parenting is described as therapeutic. It needs to be good enough to provide a healthy environment for the child to grow up in. It also needs to provide conditions within which children can benefit from different healthy relationship experience, facilitating healing from trauma. While challenges might remain because of neurodevelopmental difficulties resulting from environmental experience combined with genetic influences, providing the children with good enough therapeutic parenting gives them the best chance in life to grow emotionally and cognitively and thus to fulfil their potential.

Therapy and parenting has the best chance of succeeding if it is supported by networks also informed by the DDP principles. Dyadic Developmental Practice describes a way of applying the DDP principles throughout the residential setting, influencing the parenting of the young people and supporting the close team of education and care staff caring for them. It also extends to guide a way of working with the wider team involved with the young person and their family and can influence the running of the organization and the systems supporting it.

Trauma tends to have an organizing influence on organizations and systems. They become defensive in their activities and responses. To avoid this, the organizations need to become informed about the trauma of the people they are supporting (Bloom, 2013). Trauma-informed organizations are less defensive and more able to support individuals at all levels of the organization to stay open and engaged to each other and to their clients. Open and engaged states promote healthy growth, exploration, and learning.

The DDP model provides a set of principles that can be used by all staff, supervisors, and managers, supported by DDP-trained practitioners, to facilitate these open and engaged states within organizations. Dyadic Developmental Practice describes a model in which the DDP principles are being applied at all levels (see Figure 1.1).

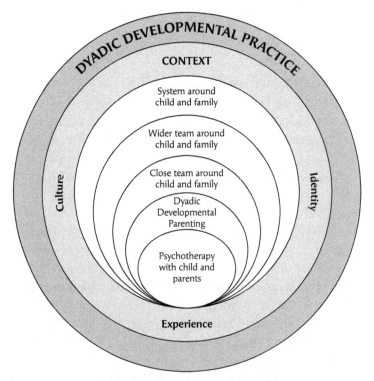

Figure 1.1: The DDP Practice Model

ADAPTED FROM HEALING RELATIONAL TRAUMA WORKBOOK BY DANIEL A.
HUGHES AND KIM S. GOLDING. COPYRIGHT © 2024 BY DANIEL A. HUGHES AND
KIM S. GOLDING. USED BY PERMISSION OF W. W. NORTON & COMPANY, INC.

This model illustrates how the DDP principles can be applied to increase safety for the child in all aspects of their life, within the therapy room and outside of it. This includes home, school, the community, professional relationships (e.g. social care, health, educational, and community practitioners), and the systems within which these practitioners work. This DDP practice is collaborative and embedded within the context the family brings, including their culture, identity, and experience.

Evidence base for DDP

The DDP community is active in developing an evidence base, supporting single case studies, evaluation with outcome measures, waiting list comparison studies, and qualitative studies. A research base is growing with qualitative and quantitative research demonstrating the efficacy of the DDP model as a therapy, as a parenting approach, and as applied in school environments (Hughes & Golding, 2024; Hughes *et al.*, 2019). Practitioners are offered support to develop an evaluative approach to their work. Trainee and student doctoral and masters research is also supported. Additionally, pilot and feasibility work has been carried out, and, at the time of writing, a randomized control trial (the RIGHT trial) is underway (Turner-Halliday *et al.*, 2014).

CHAPTER 2

Understanding the Theory Informing DDP Interventions

This chapter provides a brief overview of the models and theory that have guided the development of DDP.

It is important to note that these psychological models and theories are informed by research with Western, middle-class participants. Henrich and colleagues (2010) describe Western populations as Western, Educated, Industrialized, Rich, and Democratic – a WEIRD world. This represents less than 12 per cent of the world population (Arnett, 2008) and therefore is not the global majority. Additionally, Henrich (2021) describes these populations as being psychologically and behaviourally unusual. Cross-cultural data puts Western samples at an extreme end of the distribution on many dimensions, such as spatial reasoning, memory, attention, patience, risk-taking, fairness, and executive function.

An understanding of socio-emotional development has been dominated by this WEIRD psychology with an emphasis on cognitive models, such as mentalization, and a focus on the mind (Kinouani, 2021). As we open to the influence of the global majority, our theories and models become richer and our interventions more globally applicable.

Developmental trauma

Complex trauma results from multiple or chronic exposure to adverse experiences (Cook *et al.*, 2005). Many of the families whose children experience developmental trauma have been exposed to their own complex trauma and/or been impacted by intergenerational trauma experienced by their ancestors.

Developmental (or relational) trauma results from the experience of complex trauma from within the family early in life (van der Kolk, 2005).

The experience of developmental trauma can lead to:

- a lack of safety – the parent is a potential source of safety while also causing, or not protecting, the child from trauma

- disorganized controlling attachment patterns

- resistance to entering reciprocal relationships offering intersubjective experiences.

This foundation for the children's development leads to a range of difficulties (Cook *et al.*, 2005). These are:

- biological

- social

- emotional

- cognitive

- behavioural.

Fragmented and negative self-identities occur alongside the above difficulties. In order to cope with lack of safety, developmentally traumatized children develop defensive patterns of relating, which impact on future relationships.

- They do not trust others, including new parents, to keep them safe.

- They behave based on expectations derived from past experiences.

- Highly controlling behaviours leave little room to discover that their expectations are no longer valid.

- The children continue to defend against a threat that is part of their past.

As children grow, they continue to live in a constant sense of threat leading to:

- emotional growth being hampered: The children's developmental age is younger than their chronological age

- a negative sense of self: The children believe that they are unlovable and that others will hurt or abandon them

- chronic feelings of shame, which further reinforces defensive responding to current experiences

- highly controlling, rejecting, and hurtful behaviours, which impact on the parents' resilience to remain open and available to the child. When the parents become defensive in turn, the child's negative sense of self is confirmed.

Within DDP interventions

The child is supported to heal from early traumatic experience through the current regulating relationships they are experiencing. Feelings of terror and shame reduce, leading to emotional growth and reduced defensiveness as the child learns new ways of being within close relationships.

This helps the child to:

- relax and become open to new experiences

- seek comfort when needed

- experience the joy of being in a relationship

- be curious and open to exploration and learning.

The child develops a revised sense of identity, one within which the possibility of being lovable opens.

Relationships

Infant research demonstrates that, although born immature, infants are remarkably well equipped to engage with others (Field, 2007). For example, infants look more at faces than objects and display conversational skills: they take turns; the parent talks and the infant 'talks' back.

As the infant matures and becomes more mobile, they use an intersubjective experience known as social referencing. The child looks to the parents for clues about what they should do. For example, the visual cliff experiment demonstrates that infants will crawl over a transparent floor, stopping when the ground appears to drop away (the cliff). They will, however, continue to crawl when encouraged by a parent (Field, 2007).

Infants therefore use their early abilities to interact with parents, experiencing a contingent, reciprocal relationship.

- They thrive when parents respond to them in ways which are linked to the infant's behaviours – the infant calls and the parent responds.

- Parents and infants are mutually responsive to each other, and research has shown that they are in synchrony with matching affective, behavioural, and physiological states.

The importance of these interactions is revealed in the still face experiment. The infant becomes visibly distressed when the still face, representing a non-contingent response, appears. While these infants quickly recover as the parent repairs the rupture in the relationship, the memory can remain. Toddlers have been shown to react negatively to strangers who they received a still face from just once as an infant (Field, 2007).

All of this research demonstrates how well-equipped infants are for relationship from birth. This is no accident of evolution. Infants need relationships in order to survive.

There are two aspects to this relationship experience that are essential for children to thrive.

1. *Attachment* (Bowlby, 1998). Safety and security arise because infants and young children can turn to their caregivers for support when experiencing distress. All children need a secure base for protection, nurture, and comfort. The provision of this secure base is culturally influenced, depending upon the social community within which the child is living. In some cultures, the norm is a nuclear family, while for others it is extended social networks. This early attachment experience impacts on the child's continuing and later relationships through the development of attachment patterns. These are also culturally influenced. For example, in Western cultures where there is an emphasis on individuality, an open expression of emotion is encouraged. Societies with a more communal orientation encourage emotional reserve and neutrality (Keller, 2022). This impacts how they express their attachment needs. Children are socialized into these norms from infancy, helping them to fit into their communities.

2. *Intersubjectivity* (Trevarthen, 2001). A central goal of the attachment system is to ensure that infants and children can attain and maintain a sense of safety. This safety is a necessary condition for exploration. Attachment and intersubjectivity are complementary. When the child is unsettled, the attachment system is activated and they seek comfort. Once the child is soothed, the exploratory system motivates them to explore the world, beginning with the social-emotional world of relationships. Just as with the expression of attachment needs, children engage in exploration in line with the norms of their culture and the context within which they are living. For example, if the environment is dangerous, exploration for young children is restricted. The Aché Indians of Paraguay carry infants until they are two years of age without allowing them to touch the ground (Keller, 2022).

The attachment relationship

DDP interventions aim to increase security of attachment for the children. A universal repertoire of attachment behaviours may exist among children across cultures. The selection, shaping, and interpretation of these behaviours are culturally patterned (Harwood *et al.*, 1995). DDP interventions need to consider these differences. It is therefore important to have an understanding of the culture of the families the children are growing up in, including the residential family, so that interventions are tailored appropriately. We need to think beyond a dyadic perspective of attachment and consider the value of extended family, kinship network, culture, and community (Fejo-King, 2017). For example, Keller (2022) discusses differences between polyadic communication (more than two people communicating with each other at the same time), which is typical within the larger social networks in sociocentric societies, and the dyadic communication more commonly seen in individualistic societies.

As we explore attachment theory from a Western perspective, we need to bear in mind that while helpful for guiding DDP interventions, we need to have a better understanding of the development globally for these interventions to become more nuanced and culturally sensitive.

Secure attachment develops with the experience of sensitive parenting, including:

- recognizing the child's needs for comfort or exploration

- accepting these needs as reflecting the child's current state

- acting to meet these needs.

Through a process of co-regulation with a secure attachment figure, the child develops:

- emotional understanding and regulation. Allan Schore describes attachment as a regulatory system that prevents us from becoming overwhelmed by the stresses of life (Schore & Schore, 2014)

- social cognition, which allows them to develop an understanding about other people and themselves in relation to others

- a positive sense of self

- good reflective functioning, that is, the ability to understand why things happen and why people behave as they do. This occurs alongside the development of mentalization abilities, being able to understand, and consider, the mental state of another person, that is, what they are thinking and feeling (Fonagy *et al.*, 2016)

- an internal working model of self as lovable and successful and of others as loving and able to meet their needs. This model acts as a template for future relationships (Bowlby, 1998). A positive internal working model allows children to grow into adults who are independent and can also seek help from others when needed.

All parents are insensitive to their children some of the time, causing microruptures to the relationship. The attuned parent notices the ruptures and seeks to repair them. This experience of relationship rupture (stress) and repair (resolution of stress) builds stress regulation and resilience (Tronick & DiCorcia, 2015).

Attachment insecurity develops with the experience of insensitive parenting in which the parent does not:

- attend to the signals that the child gives or does not accept that the child has the needs being signalled (misattunement)

- meet the need, causing a relationship rupture

- attend to the relationship, so that there is no repair which would re-establish a state of attunement.

From a young age, children learn to adapt to this relationship experience by learning patterns of behaviour that reduce the stress of this misattunement. These are called insecure attachment patterns and include:

- *Avoidant attachment patterns:* Children learn to minimize their attachment needs because their parent is least available or most mis-attuned when their child is emotionally needy of them. They develop patterns of emotional self-reliance and compliance to maintain some sense of safety when parental availability is most threatened.

- *Ambivalent attachment patterns:* Children learn to maximize their attachment needs (whether or not they are experiencing distress) and to resist being soothed in order to maintain the attention of unpredictable parents. These are coercive, attention-needing strategies.

Within both the avoidant and ambivalent patterns, children have learned to miscue their attachment needs based on their expectations of parents rather than their internal state of comfort or discomfort. Mary Dozier (2003) describes this as a pattern of hidden and expressed needs. Only attending to the expressed need leaves the child in a state of emotional distress and reinforces the learned attachment pattern. Children who move into alternative homes, including residential care, draw their new parenting figures into patterns of responding that are reminiscent of their early attachment experiences. Only when the parent can meet expressed and hidden needs will the child discover that this relationship might be different from those previously experienced.

Children with developmental trauma have experienced parenting that is not just insensitive but also frightening and/or neglectful.

- *Disorganized controlling attachment patterns:* Children's instinctive need to seek security and protection from parents when feeling threatened is overridden because the source of threat is coming from these same parents. This experience is highly disorganizing emotionally, cognitively, and behaviourally. Children develop behaviours organized around a need to control. This is achieved through extreme use of the avoidant and ambivalent strategies.

These strategies move with the child. The child expresses a need to control new caregivers and hides a need for relationship. This is experienced as rejecting, and parents can withdraw from or become equally controlling of the relationship because of the hurt they are experiencing. The child is left in a state of fear.

Within DDP interventions

DDP practitioners work with the children and their attachment figures. The parents are supported to:

- provide the child with sensitive but also gently challenging parenting, that can demonstrate the difference from previous relationships

- read the miscuing from the child so that they can attend to the hidden as well as expressed needs.

As the children experience the availability of the parent and therapist, they learn to rely on them to co-regulate their emotional states.

As emotional needs are met, the children can:

- experience a different relationship, allowing moments of comfort and joy instead of guarding against anticipated terror

- develop curiosity. Therapist and parents work together with the child to discover and make sense of the children's stories of terror and shame, developing a coherent narrative of this experience. They help the children to discover new stories of hope and belonging.

The intersubjective relationship

The theory of intersubjectivity is also a theory of exploration within social relationships. As mentioned earlier, there is a cultural dimension to this exploration which gives us a context for providing intersubjective experiences to children and families. A predisposition for exploration is universal, while the context and culture determine how exploration is encouraged or discouraged. For example, in many Asian and African cultures, children do not touch or manipulate objects but rather explore visually through observation (Keller, 2022). Understanding the cultural practices of the families and caregivers we are working with helps our DDP interventions to be culturally sensitive.

Trevarthen (2001) describes intersubjectivity as a process within which experiences are shared, each person influencing the other in making sense of these experiences. This is a reciprocal influence as each is open to the influence of the other. These shared experiences provide:

- *primary intersubjectivity:* We learn about ourselves

- *secondary intersubjectivity:* We learn about others and the world around us.

Three components are needed for intersubjective connections:

1. *Matched affect:* Affect describes the way the body expresses an emotion. When the adult matches the child's affective expression, the child feels understood. This provides co-regulation, allowing the child to stay regulated while experiencing strong emotion.

2. *Shared attention:* The adult and child are both attending to the same object, event, or experience.

3. *Complementary intention:* The intentions of adult and child within the interaction are complementary to each other. The adult seeks to understand the child's experience, while the child seeks to be understood.

Through these intersubjective connections:

- negative emotions are soothed and calmed

- positive emotions are amplified. Imagine a parent and child jumping in puddles together, there is more laughter and fun than either of them would experience if they were doing this alone.

Intersubjectivity – An example
A parent arrives home stressed from work. The child experiences their parent as abrupt and misattuned. The child is left feeling unsettled and worried. The other parent maintains an intersubjective relationship with the child. Through this connection, this parent can help the child to understand that the first parent is cross

with work, and it is not the child's fault. Intersubjectively, the child is helped to make sense of the experience, and, in the process, is soothed and comforted, also strengthening the attachment system.

The first parent could not enter an intersubjective relationship with their child as they were preoccupied with their day. They needed to take care of themselves first. This meant the three components needed for intersubjective connections were missing:

1. *No matched affect:* The parents' affect, the bodily experience of their emotional state, is influenced by the difficult day and they are tired and irritable. The child is not soothed by this as the parents' affect does not match their own experience of being worried.

2. *No shared attention:* The parents' attention is still on the events of the day. They cannot share the child's attention, which is a vigilance to the parent's mood.

3. *No complementary intention:* At this point each has a different, non-complementary intention. The parent's intention is to absorb the stresses of the day, the child to monitor safety.

The lack of matched affect, shared attention, or complementary intention means that for the time being they are not intersubjectively connected.

The other parent, in a more relaxed state, can compensate for this:

- *Matched affect:* They notice the child's discomfort and match the affect being expressed.

- *Shared attention:* Both parent and child are attending to the child's worries.

- *Complementary intention:* The parent does the soothing and the child receives it.

The child experiences safety as their emotion is regulated. This helps them to make sense of the experience and a joint narrative is created about the parent's day at work. This helps the child to understand their experience without developing any associated shame that can come from a misattunement with the parent.

To complete the story, the first parent was able to take care of themselves, and, later, attend to their relationship with their child, repairing the rupture that had inadvertently been caused by the bad mood. The child goes to bed feeling safe and loved, knowing that things can go wrong and be put right again, and it is not their fault.

The child with developmental trauma

Children who have experienced developmental trauma have experienced parenting environments where they received no intersubjective experiences or where these experiences were filled with fear and terror. They are likely to have a very different relationship with their parents compared to the securely attached child.

Intersubjectivity – An example reimagined

A parent arrives home from work stressed and angry. This is taken out on both the other parent and the child.

The parent is hit because dinner is not on the table.

The child is shouted at for staring and being in the way.

- *No matched affect:* Neither parent can be intersubjectively present for the child whose affect is left unsoothed.

- *No shared attention:* The parents' attention is on each other, one in order to vent frustration and the other to placate in order to protect themselves and the child. Neither attend to the child's fear and vigilance.

- *No complementary intention:* The child's need for soothing is not met by either parent.

The child is left in a stressed state. The misattunement is experienced by the child as shame, an inner sense that somehow this is all their fault. The shame is left unregulated, and the child's narrative is a confusion of fear, terror, and blame. Many experiences like this become built into the child's identity of feeling not good enough.

These children are often anxious and vigilant, continuously monitoring the environment for signs of threat. This does not allow them to enter the open and engaged state of deep interest and curiosity about the world of the non-traumatized child.

While as infants developmentally traumatized children are born open to intersubjective connection, this is quickly lost as the children withdraw from reciprocal interactions. They take charge of their own safety by developing non-reciprocal, controlling relationships.

Children who have experienced developmental trauma hold onto their controlling patterns of behaviour when they move into healthier parenting environments. They are reluctant to test whether things are different now. Parents experience their nurture and intersubjective presence as rejected by the child. This can be a deeply painful experience and these parents may eventually withdraw from the reciprocal aspects of the relationship as well, a condition described as blocked care by Hughes and Baylin (2012).

Within DDP interventions

Offering intersubjective experiences is a central part of the therapeutic stance that the therapist takes. The therapist:

- strives to get into a connection with the child, allowing a rhythm to develop between them as the therapist becomes interested in what the child is interested in

- shows a deep interest in the child, expressed through a storytelling tone of voice, PACE attitude, and attention to the relationship.

At times, the child might offer a theme to the therapist, something of significance that is occupying their attention at that time. The therapist:

- follows this theme, maintaining the same intersubjective stance and storytelling attitude.

The child continues to experience themselves to be of interest to the therapist, and the safety that this establishes can allow them to be led into a deeper exploration of the theme. If the child begins to struggle with this, or their attention moves elsewhere, the therapist:

- follows the child, maintaining the intersubjective connection, and then gently leads the child back to the theme when they are ready to attend to it again.

This relational approach represents a slowing down in therapy, allowing attention to the relationship at all moments.

Initially, the parent is largely witness to this process, offering insights when helpful. Later, the therapist invites the parent into the process, often by talking about the child and the story they have been discovering together or helping the child to tell this story to the parent in their own words. If a child struggles to find the words, the therapist might 'talk for them', always checking that the words the therapist chooses resonates with the child and fits with their sense of the story. The parent, helped by the therapist, responds with PACE, and the intersubjective relationship becomes shared between all present. The child is helped to experience safe intersubjective connections which are very different from those they experienced in the past and those they expect in the present.

Shame and the development of identity

The development of shame and guilt are important stages of child development (Tangney & Dearing, 2002).

Shame develops first as part of the socialization process (see Figure 2.1).

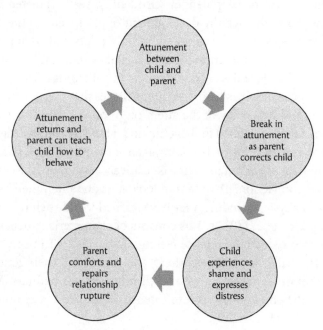

Figure 2.1: Attunement – Shame – Attunement Cycle

The degree of shame a child experiences is determined by the degree of threat the parent is experiencing. The greater the threat, the bigger the response from the parent and thus a higher level of shame for the child. Kim remembers reading about Inuit societies in which the whole community joins in the shaming of a young child who has stepped onto thin ice. Differentiating between thick and thin ice is a lesson learned early.

As the child matures, the lessons from these experiences of shame are learned and the child internalizes the rules and values of the parents. Transgression of these rules leads to feelings of guilt instead of shame. In guilt, remorse is experienced and amends can be made.

The child with developmental trauma

When children have experienced developmental trauma, they have not had healthy socialization experiences. Times of attunement with parents are scarce and breaks too many. In addition, the parental repair which allows shame to be regulated doesn't happen. These children have too many shaming experiences without support to regulate the intense emotion generated. They experience toxic levels of shame, and the development of guilt is disrupted. These experiences of shame and guilt influence the development of self-identity. Well-regulated shame experiences and the healthy development of guilt leads to the development of a sense of self as good. The child understands that they are a good person who sometimes makes mistakes that can be repaired. Unregulated shame and weak development of guilt leads to the development of a sense of self as bad. The child believes that they are no good, unlovable, and unworthy of the attention of others. They expect that others will be disappointed in them but find it hard to acknowledge this, consumed as they are with defending against their own sense of failure.

Recognizing children in shame is relatively easy. These are children who avoid connection. They cannot look at us and often they hide. In addition to physically hiding, they have learned to hide behind a shield (Golding & Hughes, 2012). This consists of characteristic behaviours developed to reduce the intense feelings associated with unregulated shame. The child lies, blames others, and minimizes their actions to defend themselves from an overwhelming sense of badness. When these fail, the child collapses into intense rages directed at others or themselves (see Figure 2.3).

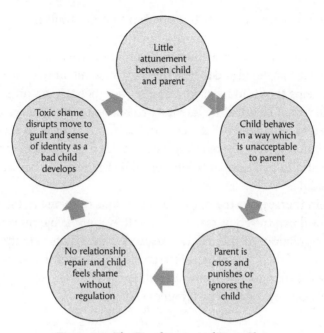

Figure 2.2: The Development of Toxic Shame

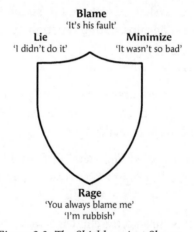

Figure 2.3: The Shield against Shame

Within DDP interventions

As with other negative emotions, a child in shame needs co-regulation. DDP-informed interventions regulate shame by offering the child inter-subjective relationships. The adult encourages the child to trust their support. The child's feelings of shame are accepted, conveyed through the tone of voice and storytelling rhythm that the adult is using. The adult uses their presence to demonstrate that they care enough to support the child, even at these most difficult times. There is time later to explore what happened and to help the child to repair any damage done.

This helps the child to make sense of their behaviours differently. The child recognizes that they are not bad but had some strong feelings which led to behaviours that were not helpful. As the child develops a less shame-based sense of self, they are able to experience guilt and remorse and to make amends, supported by the relationship with the trusted adult.

Within therapy, the therapist is alert to signs of shame in the child. They slow down the conversation so that they and the parent can provide co-regulation. As the shame is regulated, the adults help the child make sense of their experience. Narratives of pain and shame become narratives of strength and resilience within the intersubjective connections provided by the therapy (Hughes *et al.*, 2019).

Neuroscience

The human nervous system has evolved to be interpersonal, designed to thrive within relationships, and to function optimally in conditions of safety.

At times of increased stress or threat:

- the nervous system draws upon more primitive defences – this represents a vigilant state – with increased alertness to signs of physical or interpersonal danger

- the child is triggered into states of fight, flight, and shutdown; this is designed to support survival and, in the short term, can be helpful

- when threat is chronic, the child experiences little sense of safety; the defensive system then becomes habitual

- the child moves into a state of perpetual vigilance, ignoring signs of safety and withdrawing from curious exploration.

In developmental trauma where much of the threat is interpersonal, a state of blocked trust develops as is illustrated in Figure 2.4 (Baylin & Hughes, 2016).

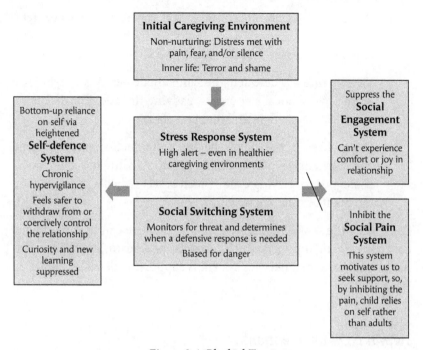

Figure 2.4: Blocked Trust

When nervous systems are connected, the child can use the adult's more mature nervous system, especially the higher cognitive function located in the cortex, to provide regulation, thus restoring equilibrium. The child's immature brain 'borrows' the adult's brain to provide the physiological support needed. This process is described as social, or parental, buffering (Gunnar *et al.*, 2015). Without this, the child is left in a defensive state, relying on an immature nervous system with well-developed defensive structures but with a less well-developed cortex. This is like driving a car with an accelerator but no brake. The child is left responding to threat with no means of calming and soothing the threat system when the danger is past or has been misperceived.

Stephen Porges (2017) has been researching the role of the vagal system in understanding social defence and social engagement. This involves neurobiological systems within the brain and extending throughout the body. Porges's polyvagal theory explores how the autonomic nervous system operates under conditions of threat and safety based on a process of neuroception. This is a process of detecting safety, danger, or life threat that is outside of conscious awareness, triggering different physiological states.

- When safety is detected, the ventral vagal social engagement system activates, and we can relax (immobilize in safety) and engage with others and the world (mobilize in safety).

- When a threat is detected, the sympathetic nervous system provides physiological responses, readying the body for defensive mobilization via fight and flight responses.

- In situations of life threat, the parasympathetic nervous system has a defensive immobilizing function allowing shutdown, analogous to 'playing dead', which is seen when a predator is at the point of catching prey.

Only when the social engagement system is active can the autonomic nervous system support health, growth, and restoration. In other states, the autonomic nervous system is supporting defence (Porges & Dana, 2018).

Within DDP interventions

DDP interventions aim to move children out of defensive states and into socially engaged states, allowing them to heal and grow.

Differing states tend to synchronize when individuals interact; two people in a social interaction cannot stay in opposing states of defence and engagement. Commonly, because priority is given to safety, when one person is defensive, it evokes a defensive response in the other.

If, however, one of the dyad can remain open and engaged, they eventually lead the other person to move into this state also.

Children who have experienced developmental trauma are frequently in a defensive state, evoking defensiveness in the parents and therapists they are relating to. Within DDP, therapists and parents strive to maintain an open and engaged state or to move back to this state when they are becoming defensive. This allows the child to become more open and engaged, at least for a time. With repeated experience of relationships supporting the child to move out of defensive states, the child begins to feel safer, and the bias to danger built into their nervous systems starts to change.

Noticing a tendency to become defensive, learning to inhibit this, and maintaining an open and engaged state is therefore a crucial part of DDP practice for therapists, parents, and anyone supporting children who have experienced developmental trauma.

Conclusion

In this chapter, we have provided a brief overview of the theories and models that have guided the development of DDP. We have paid particular attention to how children develop relationships and the impact on these relationships of the experience of developmental trauma. DDP interventions provide the child with different relational experience, increasing safety and facilitating the exploration of trauma stories and offering alternative narratives.

CHAPTER 3

Our Kids: Who Needs Residential Care and Why?

Bill, A Story of Trauma and Survival, Part 1

Children develop optimally within reciprocal, attuned parent-child relationships that impart a sense of safety. A safe and secure attachment in turn offers a firm foundation from which children can explore and learn. Children whose early life is filled with frighteningly abusive and neglectful parental relationships often develop disorganized controlling attachment patterns and reject potential new relationships that could help them heal. These are coping strategies to manage their traumatic experiences, but these strategies are maladaptive and pose problems as they get older.

To better understand these concepts, let's look at Bill,[1] a seven-year-old boy in the US, whose traumatic early life led to disordered emotions and behaviour. This is a story that gives voice to the children and families with whom we work and the kinds of traumas and malad-aptations that bring them to residential care. As we tell Bill's story, we make connections to the research, theory, and DDP practice model we wrote about in Chapters 1 and 2.

But first, in the spirit of care for you, the reader, we want to advise you that reading this book may evoke unpleasant reactions. We describe the abuse of children as well as the aftermath of that abuse. We assume since you have picked up this book, you care about children, their heal-ing, and their well-being. Therefore, these descriptions can lead you to feel sad, angry, outraged, and even hopeless. We urge you to notice

---

1   Please note, Bill's story is a composite case study, created by incorporating details of different children's stories into an integrated whole.

these reactions, as self-awareness is ultimately our ally in doing this work. We also urge you to slow down and care for yourself if you find yourself getting stirred up. As we describe in Chapter 8, our well-being and hopefulness are resources we all call on in doing this work.

We appreciate your willingness to learn about childhood trauma and how Dyadic Developmental Practice can provide a path to healing. Thank you for your courage in embarking on this exploration.

BACKGROUND

Bill and his sister, Olivia, who are of dual heritage, spent their first few years with their mother and father, Adina, a dual heritage woman, and Elijah, a white man. However, as is often the case for children who come to residential care, Bill's story starts long before he was born, when his parents were children, and most likely in the generations that preceded them as well. The trauma that Adina and Elijah endured as children influenced how they treated Bill and Olivia.

Adina's father, a Black man, was an alcoholic and would hit her mother, a white woman, when drinking made him hostile and belligerent. To make matters worse, Adina was sexually abused for several years by her mother's brother, while he lived with the family. When Adina disclosed the abuse to another girl at school, her friend told the school counsellor, who reported it to child protective services. This resulted in Adina being placed in four different foster care homes from ages six to nine. Foster care added to her trauma. In one of the homes, the family forced Adina to clean different parts of the house, something they didn't require of the other children who were all white. Furthermore, it wasn't unusual for Adina to be called racial names at whatever school she was attending. Adina was eventually reunited with her mother who used drugs on and off until, when Adina was 17, she was imprisoned for cocaine possession. Adina, rather than return to foster care, ran away and found shelter in a friend's home.

Following the departure of his mother when Elijah was three years old, Elijah was raised by a neglectful and rageful alcoholic father. His father soon dated a woman who moved in with them. They went on to have two children together. Elijah felt that his dad's girlfriend was a mostly friendly presence, and he tried to protect her when Elijah's father screamed at her and broke things. When Elijah was 12, the girlfriend gathered her courage and moved out, taking Elijah's two half-siblings with her. This was devastating to Elijah, as was living alone with his father. Elijah did worse in school and started stealing from stores. By the time he was 15, he would fight back when his father was drunk and then leave home for several days. When he turned 18, he dropped out of high school and moved into an apartment with some older guys. He made money at odd jobs and sometimes by selling drugs.

Though the stories of Adina and Elijah are dramatic, they are not unusual for the staff who work in residential settings. In a typical scenario, the staff hear how the parent was thoughtless, cruel, or violent toward their child. As a result, the staff can feel judgemental or angry toward the parent. When the staff discover that this parent has endured the same or even worse treatment in their own childhood, judgement turns to compassion as the legacy of trauma passed from generation to generation becomes clear. Abuse early in childhood impairs attachment security and the ability to regulate affect and modulate stress. When an abused child grows up and has children of their own, those impairments form the basis for the intergenerational trans-mission of trauma (Schore, 2002). That was the case with Adina and Elijah. One implication of these observations is that, when a child is admitted to a residential setting, it is often imperative to address the parents' burden of trauma as well as the child's.

Returning to Adina, she lived with a friend for a year and, at a certain point, began hooking up with Elijah, whom she knew from the fast-food restaurant where she worked. After several months, Adina realized she was pregnant, and she and Elijah moved into a place of their own. This was a relatively good time for Adina and Elijah. They had hope and were planning for a better life than either of them had experienced as kids. They were both working, paying their bills, and partying with their friends on weekends. Though they would get pretty drunk at times, it didn't turn violent, and they considered themselves to be pretty stable.

_____

_____

BILL AND OLIVIA

Adina quit work when Bill was born, and the first months were fairly smooth. She liked holding him, feeding him, and dressing him. It did bother her when he cried, but she could mostly get him to calm down. When he began to crawl, things got rockier. She no longer felt that she knew what he needed and resented him for what she perceived were demands she couldn't meet. When he continued crying in spite of her efforts to soothe him by feeding or changing him, she would yell at him and lock him in the bedroom where he cried himself to sleep. She found herself lonely and miserable. To escape, she started smoking marijuana with Elijah when he came home from work. A few months later, she found she was pregnant again. Olivia was born before Bill turned two.

Trauma impairs important abilities developed in childhood, such as being able to tolerate frustration, to be curious, and to name the emotions and sensations one experiences inside. These abilities are crucial for successful parenting. Adina's troubled early life didn't leave her with much ability to manage the emotional challenges of raising babies. The psychological, emotional, and sexual abuse she experienced as a child had left its mark. She blew up when she couldn't handle things any longer and would scream at Elijah and the kids. She lost interest in trying to understand what Bill and Olivia might be experiencing and provided for their physical needs without emotional warmth. Her self-esteem, which had always been fragile, now plummeted, and she considered herself a failure as a parent.

Fast forward two years, and the stress of raising children was debilitating to Adina and Elijah. They had migrated from marijuana to opiate use, and sometimes left the kids at home to fend for themselves while they partied with friends for one, two, or even three nights at a time. A new neighbour at the apartment complex saw Bill, who was now four, foraging in the dumpster and asked where he lived. Discovering that Olivia was the only one at home, the neighbour called the police, who took Bill and Oliva into custody. After an emergency court hearing, they were placed in foster care and assigned a caseworker, who began piecing together what life had been like for the two children.

As hard as it was for his caseworker to believe, it was apparent that Bill had been taking care of Olivia for quite some time. Bill made sure she was warm, had water to drink, and had enough to eat. When his parents left no food in the house, he climbed in the dumpster in the alley behind their apartment to see what he could find. In addition to neglecting the children, the caseworker discovered that Adina and Elijah would often terrify the children by yelling at them and at each other. One night, when they were both drunk, Elijah had started throwing the living room furniture out of the apartment while he cursed out Adina at the top of his lungs. On another occasion, when Elijah found Bill taking some money from his wallet, he grabbed Bill by the ankles and held him over the balcony, threatening to throw him off if he ever stole from him again.

Needless to say, the children were often in states of fight-or-flight, with adrenalin causing their hearts to beat faster, their little bodies to tense up and shake, and their pupils to dilate wide. When the stress became overwhelming, they would go into a state of physiological shutdown, they would become emotionally numb and disconnected from what was happening around them.

In very real ways, our nervous systems are wired to constantly scan our environment for signs of danger and safety. As discussed in Chapter 2, Stephen Porges, developer of polyvagal theory, calls this threat surveillance process *neuroception*, which happens outside our conscious awareness. When the nervous system neurocepts signals of danger, it activates the neurophysiologically defensive states of fight-or-flight, while neuroception of life-threatening danger causes shutdown. Neurocept enough safety, however, and the child's nervous system lets its guard down to become open and engaged. Understanding that traumatic experiences predispose the child's neuroception to over-respond to situations as if they are dangerous helps us to change how we think about a child's 'bad behaviours'. Therapist, author, and parent educator Claire Wilson offers language that reframes disruptive behaviours that are triggered by threat. She calls them 'survival make-myself-safe behaviours' (2018).

Clearly, Adina, Elijah, Bill, and Olivia have all experienced developmental trauma, as described in Chapter 2. They have each been neglected, emotionally abused, and terrorized by one or more parents. As psychiatrist, author, researcher, and educator Bessel van der Kolk points out, developmental trauma (also known as relational or interpersonal trauma) not only includes physical abuse, but can be comprised of 'separation from caregivers, traumatic loss, and inappropriate sexual behavior', which show up in Bill's family's history as well (2005, p. 406). Furthermore, it is not uncommon for developmental trauma to intersect with traumatic experiences of racism, such as Adina experienced.

In addition to causing emotional dysregulation, developmental trauma causes dysfunction in multiple other systems as well (Cook *et al*,. 2005; van der Kolk, 2005). When Bill moved into foster care, his foster parents noticed that he didn't sleep well, didn't know when he was hungry, and couldn't tell when he needed to have a bowel movement, which often led to 'accidents'. These are all signs that the trauma had caused physiological dysregulation. Like his parents, Bill could go into a rage when frustrated or ashamed. He was unable to regulate his intense feelings and couldn't think before he did things, that is, he had poor impulse control. Because his parents could act so differently depending on the day, Bill's sense of self was fragmented, and he could feel like a very different boy from one day to the next. Bill frequently experienced self-loathing. Furthermore, relational trauma impaired his cognitive development as well. He couldn't pay attention for as long as other four-year-olds, and his vocabulary was not as robust.

THE FOSTER HOME

When Bill and Olivia arrived at the foster home, their foster parents were confused and disturbed by Bill's behaviour because they hadn't yet learned that children who experience developmental trauma are often left with disorganized controlling attachment patterns. Instead of developing behaviours that arise from a secure attachment to parents who are responsive, reciprocal, and nurturing, Bill's behaviour was chaotic and unpredictable. He often had meltdowns when he seemed to want something but couldn't tell the foster parents what it was. He would play with a toy contentedly for a bit, then would break it, saying, 'I'm so stupid!'

Bill did other strange things that his foster parents couldn't explain. For example, one day when they were on the porch, he ran across the yard and hit a woman who was walking by. As infants and toddlers, children with a disorganized pattern can look anxious and helpless, but as they move toward preschool, they can become harsh, threatening, and controlling (Bureau *et al.*, 2009). At four years old, Bill frequently told the foster parents what to do and would scream at them when they didn't comply.

The foster parents did the best they could to use the parenting skills that had worked for other children, and after several weeks Bill did calm down. He still had blow ups (meltdowns) fairly frequently, but they weren't as intense as when he first arrived. At that point, the foster parents, who were kind-hearted and gentle, were most bothered by how Bill rejected the care they so wanted to give him. Rather than accept their help, Bill wanted to do everything for himself. One night he screamed 'I don't need your help!' when they tried to cut the pork chop they served for dinner. Bill picked it up with his fingers and ate it rather than allow them to cut it for him. Bill also tried to control how the foster parents treated Olivia, mostly wanting to take care of her himself. When they did things for Olivia, he watched them carefully, as if to make sure they didn't harm her.

As discussed in Chapter 2, the traumatized child's symptoms and experiences cause them to value mistrust, hyper-independence, manipulation, and control instead of interdependent and trusting relationships that can nurture and support their developmental needs. They push adults away to feel safe, a condition which Baylin and Hughes (2016) call blocked trust (see Figure 2.4). The problem is that, even after the trauma is over and the child has been moved to the safety of relatives, foster homes, or adoptive parents, the momentum of these self-protective mechanisms prevents the child from relaxing and letting their new caregivers take care of them. The new caregivers may be available and willing to provide the nurture the child desperately needs, but the child's blocked trust won't allow them to accept it. Caregivers seek out therapists for support, but the child's avoidance of connection can even defeat the therapist's best efforts. Medication from a child psychiatrist may be helpful to decrease the intensity of anger, lessen depression, or improve impulse control and attention, but often the child pushes away medical assistance as well.

During the year Bill and his sister spent in foster care, Adina and Elijah tried to follow their reintegration plan to get the children back. The plan asked them to stop using drugs, attend counselling sessions and substance use groups regularly, and maintain their employment. No matter how hard they tried, they just couldn't do it. They would get sober for a few weeks, then go back to using. They wouldn't show up for work during their binges and would lose their jobs. Each blamed the other for their failures, and they eventually split up.

When it became clear that Adina and Elijah would not be able to achieve stability in any sort of timely fashion, social services started looking for extended family members who might be able to foster or even adopt the children. The social services office had recently completed training in 'family finding' (Holmes *et al.*, 2020) and were eager to see if there were relatives who might be willing and able to care for the children. In one session, Adina casually told the worker, 'I'm not even sure if Elijah is Bill's father. I was sleeping with this other guy named José at the time.' Adina helped the social worker track down José, and the worker called him up to see if she could meet with him. She told José she wanted to talk with him about something important without saying what it was.

———————————

———————————

A NEW FATHER

The social worker scheduled to meet José at home after work. She explained that José might have a son who was five years old and had been in foster care since he was four. This, of course, was shocking news for José. It took a bit to sink in, and the worker gave him time to process it. Then she continued, asking: 'If you are the boy's biological father, would you be interested in raising Bill?' José was understandably ambivalent about this proposal. He told the worker he needed to talk with his mother, with whom he was close. A day later, he decided that, if he was the boy's father, he wanted to take responsibility for him. He phoned the social worker to tell her of his decision.

The paternity test indeed showed that José was Bill's biological father. Elijah had also taken a paternity test which showed he was Olivia's biological father. Olivia was placed with Adina's aunt.

José, who was dual heritage, had a history that was quite different from Adina and Elijah's. He was raised by his Puerto Rican mother, who had had diabetes for many years but was otherwise pretty stable. He never knew his white father, who left before he was born. José's mother considered herself lucky that José's father had left because 'he was nothing but trouble'. José had been a quiet child who stuck close to home. His aunt had helped take care of him growing up, but she left the state when José was 10, when her husband was transferred. José dropped out of school when he was 16 because 'school was not his thing'. He did get his GED (high school equivalency exam) the next year. He started out stacking groceries, then moved on to fast food. That's where he met Adina. Adina liked this quiet boy, and they would sometimes go back to José's mother's house to have sex while José's mother was at work. Though Adina was hooking up with Elijah at the same time, she never mentioned this to José. When Adina moved in with Elijah, she abruptly cut off contact with José.

José tired of working in fast food after a couple of years and went back to working in the grocery store where he gradually took on more responsibility. At 24, he was in charge of the produce section, and he took pride in keeping the fruits and vegetables looking fresh. He had not had a girlfriend since Adina and had only thought about her a few times in the previous five years. He had a few friends from the store, mostly older guys with families with whom he sometimes drank a beer after work.

Bill was five when he moved in with José. It was explained that José was his biological father, though Bill wasn't really sure what that meant. Bill had spent the past year with the foster family and felt relief to be leaving them. As Dan Hughes (2017) points out, a child who has experienced developmental trauma often doesn't mind moving to a new home. They don't really connect with their foster parents but instead see them mostly as a way to meet their physical needs. Bill had seen his foster parents that way and had come to feel that they weren't really good at meeting his needs anyway. He did feel a bit of curiosity about a biological father, but mostly was just glad to be leaving the foster family. What caused him more anxiety was leaving his sister, and he worried about how she would do without him.

DEVELOPMENTAL TRAUMA FOLLOWS A CHILD TO THE NEXT HOME

Bill had many of the same behaviours with José that he had with the foster family. He would ignore José's requests and, when angry, would break one of his toys or even break something valuable that belonged to José. He would try to control José and would threaten him if José didn't do what he said. He sometimes wanted his bath water hot and sometimes tepid. He would tell José he couldn't do things right. At other times, José would find Bill curled up in a ball, sucking his thumb and rocking back and forth. José would try to talk to him then, but Bill would just keep rocking. José didn't know it, but Bill was locked in his own world of wordless anguish during these times. He wouldn't have been able to tell José what he was feeling even if he had been connected enough to speak.

Bill was often unpredictable, doing things that confused José because they seemed to come out of the blue. José didn't have the same reactions that the foster family had though, and this puzzled Bill. José had told Bill that he was going to keep living with him, that the judge had said that was the plan, and that José was going to be his father forever now. Bill thought to himself, 'I don't need a father. I can take care of myself.' Truth be told, there was something about the matter-of-fact manner in which José related this news that caught Bill's attention. On the other hand, Bill also had a deep sense that he himself was the only one he could count on and that would never change. Bill's disorganized controlling attachment pattern, his blocked trust, and his states of shutdown kept him mired in suffering.

José had gone through a 4-hour training on trauma in children that were getting adopted. He had read some of the reports about what Bill had experienced and felt a lot of compassion for him. He knew enough to not set the expectation that Bill would see him as his father right away. He also knew that it would be important for Bill to get treatment that could help him get past what happened to him. José took Bill for an intake at the community mental health centre. He was assigned to a therapist who would see him for an hour every two weeks and to a case manager who would meet with him in the community for an hour on each of the two intervening weeks. The therapist was concerned that Bill had foetal alcohol syndrome because Adina drank while pregnant. The assessment the therapist requested showed that Bill did have a mild case that might improve over time.

José was naturally curious about Bill, about this little person that had his genes and had come, in part, from his own body. He hadn't been around

75

children much but wasn't nervous around them. When children came to his store with their parents, José enjoyed helping the child and their caregiver find what they were looking for. José also had an innate interest in people in general. Maybe it came from his relationship with his mother, who was always intrigued by what he had learned in school, what he had dreamed the night before, or his questions about why the world was the way it was. José liked telling her what he was thinking and liked the questions she asked him in return. As discussed in Chapter 2, these shared experiences are known as intersubjectivity and can take the form of emotional connections within which the dyad experiences shared attention, matched affect, and complementary intention. By sharing each of these aspects of his experience, José's mother entered his world fully, and he felt a sense of togetherness with her.

Because Bill lacked the shared intersubjective experiences that characterized José and his mother's relationship, he was not comfortable with José's curiosity about what he was thinking and feeling. He would often turn away when Bill wondered what was going on with him. Sometimes, he would make fun of José's efforts to get to know him better. Bill didn't understand why José asked him those questions. Nevertheless, every now and then, something José would say would get through to Bill and Bill would feel a momentary twinge of connection. He felt that José had truly seen him, and, while part of him liked this, another part of him was terrified that José would get rid of him if he knew him well enough.

Sometimes, when Bill made a mistake, he suffered with an intense feeling of shame that burned his cheeks and caused him to turn his back on anyone within eyesight. He felt that he was loathsome, though he didn't know that word. If José tried to make eye contact, Bill would yell, 'Don't look at me! Leave me alone!' José, feeling the best thing to do was to give Bill space, would go into the next room. Often afterwards, Bill would minimize what had happened, saying it didn't matter or didn't even happen. Rage and minimizing are two of the behaviours described in Chapter 2 that shield a child like Bill against the burning shame that can overwhelm him (see Figure 2.3) (Golding & Hughes, 2012). Lying and blaming are the other two aspects of a child's shield against shame, and Bill used these strategies to divert from feeling shame also.

_____

SOME CONDITIONS DON'T IMPROVE
IN THE COMMUNITY

For the next two years, Bill and José limped along. Things didn't get a lot better, but neither did they get much worse. José felt he was able to endure Bill's rages and hoped that one day they would reduce. Instead, when Bill was seven, his outbursts got progressively more intense, to the point where he stayed enraged for an hour or more each time. It wasn't clear to anyone why this change had happened. Bill would pummel José with his fists, and, though this did not injure José, it was emotionally exhausting. One night, José was quite disturbed to wake at 3:00 a.m. and find Bill standing over him. It made him worry that Bill might hurt him while he slept. On several occasions Bill ran out of the house and across a busy street. He didn't seem to be trying to hurt himself, but he was out of control and it was dangerous. José called the police to help find Bill on three occasions, and on two other occasions Bill was taken to an acute inpatient psychiatric unit. Due to Bill's out-of-control behaviour, José was increasingly worried that he couldn't keep Bill or himself safe at home.

Bill's blocked trust, shield against shame, disorganized controlling attachment pattern, and aversion to intersubjective experience all sabotaged his outpatient treatment. An hour a week simply wasn't enough time to build the trust, connection, and skills needed for Bill to thrive in the community with José. He needed more intensive treatment to support these changes and a more structured setting to keep him safe. Bill's therapist recommended that Bill spend some time in a residential setting, and the case manager helped José make an application for admission. Fortunately for Bill, there was a residential setting that had embedded and embodied Dyadic Developmental Practice located nearby that was willing to take him.

This ends the story of Bill for now. For those of you who can't wait to find out how he does in residential care, you will find the rest of his story in Chapter 11. Bill's story raises questions central to children's recovery from developmental trauma:

- How do we help children who feel safest when they are pushing adults away?

- How do we navigate blocked trust and the toxic shame that keep children rageful and alone?

- Is it possible to help children move from a disorganized controlling attachment pattern to a more secure attachment?

- How do we enter the children's world and create a sense of togetherness, like that enjoyed by José and his mother?

We cannot underestimate the challenges that these questions present. At the same time, we need to know that there is hope as we address each challenge in turn, persevere, and watch for subtle signs of progress. In residential settings informed by Dyadic Developmental Practice in the US, the UK, and elsewhere, staff have answered these questions one interaction at a time until the child has been relieved of enough of the burden of trauma that they are able to experience safe and engaged relationships with their caregivers who share in their comfort and joy. We describe how that is achieved in the chapters that follow.

PART 2

HOW WE APPLY DDP INTERVENTIONS IN RESIDENTIAL SETTINGS

CHAPTER 4

Opening Pandora's Box

Conversations the DDP Way

In this chapter, we begin to explore how DDP theory and principles are applied to children like Bill, who arrive in residential care. This starts with DDP-informed conversations. Conversations with children can open up the future for them as they become more able to stay regulated in relationships, building connections that help them to process and integrate their experiences.

We include day-to-day light chats, conversations initiated by child or adult, and the longer, more planned conversations that build deep connections with the child. These help the child make sense of their behaviour within and beyond residential settings. We also focus on the central role of PACE and storytelling within these DDP conversations.

At the heart of DDP conversations is the story which helps the child discover and explore a narrative about their inner emotional world and linking this to current and past experience. As Louis Cozolino tells us:

> Having a conscious narrative of our experience helps us remember where we have come from, where we are, and where we are going. In other words, our stories ground us in the present, within the flow of our histories, and provide a direction for the future. (2016, p. 241)

Why do we need DDP-informed conversations with children living in residential care?

We believe that all children would benefit from conversations informed by the DDP principles. They are especially important for children who have experienced disrupted care and past developmental trauma. Children living in residential care have generally not had enough life experiences to know how to talk about how they feel and what they have been doing. So often these children:

- have not had relationships in which they have experienced deep interest in themselves from another

- have not discovered that others can help them make sense of their experience, good or bad

- cannot put words to their emotional experiences or to the experience of others.

Emotional worlds can be a closed book when children have not had relationships to help them open the book and read what is inside. They may not know that there is a book to read, that they have an emotional world to explore. They may be frightened of opening the book because their emotional world is full of worries and fears about their own sense of badness and unlovability and their lack of belief that others might see them differently.

You may ask: Why bother opening the book? Isn't it enough to love, feed, clothe, and shelter the children? Why explore the pain of emotional worlds that they have already lived through?

Humans are born storytellers. We begin life being told stories. We learn to tell these stories back, and then we develop our own stories. The initial storytelling from a baby is not in words. The parent reads the infant's non-verbal communications and provides words to describe this experience. The parent's non-verbal communication along with these words co-regulates this experience so that the infant is not overwhelmed by their emotions.

Let's think about the importance of storytelling in the development of a secure attachment relationship between a parent and child, Adam and Luciana.

Adam hears his eight-week-old baby daughter, Luciana, crying. She's been sleeping and now needs a cuddle and food. He goes to her cot. 'Hello, my sweet Luciana. You were a sleepy girl and there you are awake, your beautiful brown eyes wide open. I think you need a cuddle.' He lifts her into his arms, gently rocking and singing to her.

Luciana, soothed, looks into her dad's eyes and smiles. Adam is enchanted. 'Oh my, look at you with that beautiful smile. I think you're really enjoying our cuddle, and so am I.' Luciana coos, still looking at her dad and smiling. 'Are you telling me a story, sweetheart?' her dad asks quietly. 'You're so beautiful, and you look so happy with that lovely smile.' Luciana gurgles back to her dad. 'Are you telling me that you love me too or maybe what you've been dreaming about? Come on, let's get that nappy changed.'

Adam changes Luciana's nappy as they continue to 'chat' together. Suddenly, Luciana's face wrinkles and she starts to cry. 'Oh, my goodness, sweetheart, you're not so happy now! Is your tummy rumbling? I think you're hungry. Let's go and get you some milk.' Luciana is crying harder now. Adam scoops her up, still chatting to her and rocking her gently up and down. He feeds her; she calms and sucks at her bottle contentedly. 'You were a hungry girl indeed!'

As the infant grows into toddlerhood, they discover words for themselves and can enter into joint storytelling with their parent.

Luciana is now three years old. She and her mum, Giorgia, are sitting on the floor with an unopened box – a new jungle jigsaw. Luciana loves jigsaws. She's excited, and her mum is excited with her. 'Okay, Luciana, are we ready to open this box? It's so exciting, isn't it?' Luciana laughs. 'There are monkeys!' she exclaims, standing up and pretending to be a monkey. 'And lions! Grrrr,' she growls. Giorgia joins her in imitating the monkey and in growling. They laugh together. 'And big snakes! I don't like snakes – they're scary!' Her face drops, and she looks worried. Giorgia sees her scared face. 'It's okay, Luciana, I see you're a bit scared – it's just a picture of a snake; it can't come out of the jigsaw or I would be worried too!' She gives Luciana a reassuring cuddle.

This sort of storytelling helps children learn to regulate their emotional experience. They can notice and attend to their emotional world and are able to put this into words. They discover their stories verbally and non-verbally. They also learn that other people have their own stories which can be shared. The child is learning about reciprocal relationships. Discovering and sharing the stories of our experience is at the heart of relationships.

Luciana is now six years old. It's a sunny day, and she and her dad are in the car on the way to the beach. She's excited. 'Dad, Dad, when will we get there?' (for the tenth time!). Adam sighs and smiles. 'Not long now, Luciana, I promise. Look out for the sea.' Luciana is peering out of the car window. 'Dad, last time we went to the beach Mum came too.' Her words come tumbling out. 'We made a *huge* sandcastle, the biggest on the beach; I buried you and Mum in the sand and then you buried me!' Laughing, she says, 'We got sand all over ourselves – we looked like sand monsters – so we had to go in the sea to wash it off.'

This sharing of stories helps us to:

- understand ourselves and others (reflection)

- manage the emotional experience that goes alongside this (experience the affective)

- develop empathy for ourselves and others.

Within DDP, we call this an affective-reflective conversation. The child is developing capacities that help them to regulate, to reflect, and ultimately to have successful relationships.

Children who have experienced developmental trauma miss out on a lot of this early experience. They may not be talked to, or the words they hear may be harsh and cruel. These words are often paired with actions which are hurtful and harmful. Alongside this, they may not have anyone making sense of their experience for them, verbally or non-verbally. Alternatively, they might have someone making sense of it in a way that leaves them feeling bad and unlovable.

Remember, we learn about ourselves through intersubjective connections with our caregivers. For many children with developmental trauma, these intersubjective experiences are painful, denigrating, and shaming. These are the origins of blocked trust. Within a state of blocked trust, children are either too scared to notice or trust others with their emotional worlds and/or are unable to find a way to communicate this experience through words. They are left with big feelings and no words to express them, or they have only the words that they heard through their traumatic childhood. If a parent told them they were stupid and ungrateful, or if they heard their parents being verbally abusive to each other, these experiences echo through their thoughts about themselves and interactions with others. The children show us these big feelings of sadness, shame, fear, and worry via a range of challenging and largely dysregulated behaviours rooted in a place without words.

In residential care, there are opportunities to provide children with different relationship experiences that in time give them the words to make sense of their experiences and to be able to tell the story of what has happened to them. Residential caregivers can help these children discover and trust in the words and stories that describe their experiences and to trust the other to make sense of this with them. They start to learn how to communicate their current experiences through words rather than actions. Helping children to know what their story is helps them to develop mental well-being and physical health. The paradigm shift from 'what is wrong with you?' to 'what happened to you?' is essential (Bloom, 1994, p. 476).

The complexity of conversations when teams of adults support the children

Talking with children living in residential homes has a layer of complexity not found in family homes because of the increased numbers of adults in a parenting and teaching role. Children may also choose to talk with someone, such as a cook, gardener, administrator, or the taxi driver who takes them to school.

Each child has a different relationship with each adult. Children are astute at knowing who to talk to, who to annoy, and who to ignore. These interactions arise out of a need to feel safe, and children exhibit a range of ways of managing their safety, not always along the lines desired by the adults. Often these behaviours are highly controlling, and the adults need to feel confident to respond in ways that ultimately open up conversations rather than close them down.

DDP: Some helpful principles for talking with children

In Chapter 1, we outlined the parenting and therapeutic attitude of PACE. This attitude provides a way of being for all the adults supporting the child. This includes those in the role of carer, teacher, cook, gardener, or administrator. Everyone needs to know how to respond to the children, whether these children are communicating through words or behaviour.

DDP conversations have a rhythm to them. Often, they begin with some connect and chat, gently helping the child move into an emotionally connected, intersubjective relationship. These can be light and playful. They often focus on what the child is currently thinking about or interested in. As the conversation develops, the adult maintains the rhythm and cadence of this chatting as they move into a theme or topic that is potentially harder for the child. Even if the connect and chat does not happen – for example, because the child has initiated a conversation around a significant theme – this rhythm and cadence is still important.

PACE, held as a way of being, facilitates the adult in using a set of DDP principles.

- *Connect and chat:* Not all conversations are deep and meaningful. In life, many of our conversations are light, in which we express curiosity about current experience and provide an opportunity for sharing interests. These lighter conversations provide children an opportunity to enter intersubjective experiences with their carers that do not feel threatening because they are not touching on past or current pain and hurt. These conversations can be playful, allowing the children to smile, laugh, and discover fun in relationships. Conversing in gentle, safe, and playful ways helps children discover safety and practise trust in intersubjective relationships.

- *Safety:* We have seen how connect and chat can start to help children feel safe within relationships. Unless children feel safe, there is no point trying to engage them in the more difficult conversations about past or current experiences. We need to build safety and return to establishing this safety on the many occasions when it is lost. As we do this, we are helping children to develop trust where they had mistrust and to build confidence in the relationships they are engaging with. Only when this is in place are they ready for deeper conversations which touch on areas of sadness, shame, fear, and danger, all supported by the care worker.

- *Co-regulation:* As the caregiver relates to the child, either chatting about light themes or more difficult ones, they notice the verbal and non-verbal communications from the child. This enables the carer to know when the child is becoming anxious. At these times the caregiver shifts from the conversation to a focus on co-regulation. This helps the child regulate their increasing emotion, re-establish safety, and, in time, continue with the conversation.

To provide co-regulation, the carer ensures that they are matching the affect of the child. If the child is becoming sad, the carer talks to them quietly, with lower energy and a gentle rhythm. If, on the other hand, the child is becoming angry, the carer talks with more energy and urgency. Notice that the carer is matching affect and not emotion. The carer does not get sad or angry but uses their words combined with tone and rhythm to convey that they get it. This allows the child to regulate these rising emotions.

Let's see how these principles work in action by considering an angry teenager in conversation with his key worker.

Rudra is 14 years old. He has just attended a review meeting with his key worker, Stephen. He desperately wants to return to live with his family and did a really good job of advocating for himself with Stephen's support. However, the meeting decision was that Rudra needs to remain in residential care. Weekends spent with his family have been going well. There are concerns that this would not be sustained if Rudra lived with them all week.

When asked to do anything he doesn't want to do, Rudra becomes verbally abusive and aggressive. He has done damage by punching and kicking walls, including severely bruising himself. It was agreed in the meeting that more work needs to be done with Rudra and with his family to figure out why this is happening and how to support them all. Although Stephen helped Rudra advocate to go home in the meeting, he is of the opinion that Rudra needs to stay in care. Rudra knew that Stephen was of this view – Stephen had showed him the report he had written – but Rudra hoped that Stephen would change his mind in the meeting.

When the decision is made, Rudra can't contain himself. He storms out of the meeting, shouting obscenities, slams the door, and stomps off.

Stephen has developed a trusting relationship with Rudra and has been his key worker for two years. They have been through a lot of fun and challenge together. When Rudra leaves the meeting, Stephen excuses himself and hurriedly follows Rudra. Stephen knows how desperately Rudra wants to return to his family – he feels for him and is proud of him for advocating so well for himself. He knows Rudra is furious with him. Stephen prepares himself for what's to come, knowing that he and Rudra will get through this as they have many times. He checks himself. He drops his shoulders, relaxes his pace, and says to himself 'open and engaged'.

Rudra turns, aware that Stephen is behind him. He rushes towards Stephen, enraged and with fists clenched.

'You bastard, I hate you, I hate this place – I hope you and your family all die!'

Stephen keeps walking towards Rudra. He feels the adrenalin pumping but is remaining as relaxed as he can. Arms outstretched, palms open and towards Rudra, face serious, voice animated, matching the high energy and pace of Rudra's voice but not bellowing and not angry, he says, 'Rudra, I know how desperately you want to go home – of course you do! I know you don't want to be here anymore, and I absolutely get that you hate me!'

Rudra stops an arm's length away from Stephen. Still bellowing and kicking the ground, he says, 'It's all your fault. You told me I could go home. You told me you would help me, but you're just like all the rest. All f****** talk and no f****** action. I'll never trust you again, bastard!'

Stephen maintains his open and engaged stance, his voice remaining energetic as he says, 'I get that! Why would you trust me if I've lied to you, if it's my fault you can't go home, if I haven't helped you?'

Rudra is still angry, but his voice and body language have come down a notch or two as he says, 'I *want to go home*, and you're stopping me!!'

Stephen notices Rudra's decreased rage and quietens to match his decreasing affect as he says, 'I know you do, and I want that too. That's what you and I have been working towards for two years, and I'm so proud of how hard you've worked. It has to be safe for you to go home – you don't want to come back here! And it has to be safe for your family, because they don't want you to come back here either!'

Rudra, calmer, voice quieter, as he feels 'heard', says, 'So why did you agree with the rest of those bastards, but you helped me say what I wanted to say?'

Stephen says, 'Good question. Do you remember we talked about this? I said I would help you say what you wanted to say, but I couldn't agree to you going home because I don't think you or your family are ready yet. I know that's confusing. It must seem like I'm against you. I'd have been lying if I had said I thought you and your family are ready. We've *all* got work to do so when you do go home it works and it's safe.'

Rudra, now disgruntled but calm, says, 'What work?'

Stephen says, 'Great you asked and happy to talk about that now if you're ready – or we can wait. Either way, can we go and get a cup of something in the house?'

Rudra says, 'Suppose so.'

Stephen puts his arm around Rudra's shoulder. Rudra shrugs him off, but Stephen knows Rudra well enough to know that the repair needed in their relationship is done. Rudra decides not to talk anymore today – he's exhausted – but they have a drink and snack in the house and a general chat about what's happening that evening. Stephen lets Rudra know that they need to let the adults coming on shift know that Rudra has had a challenging day so that they can support him. Stephen and Rudra do this together, and Stephen lets the adults know in front of Rudra that he is proud of Rudra for how he has handled the situation. Stephen and Rudra agree to talk the following day. Rudra allows an arm around the shoulders before Stephen leaves for the day. Stephen leaves hoping that Rudra will remain settled.

- - -

- As we can see, during this process, the adult gives the child some control over what happens next. It is important that the adult accepts resistance from the child, allowing the child to control timing, pace, and content of these conversations.

- From the story about Rudra and Stephen, you can see that we are not talking about only verbally co-regulating with the child. Accompanying this are a range of soothing and calming actions from the carer to facilitate this co-regulation. Soothing can be done by voice and also by touch that is acceptable to the child. A hand on the shoulder or, for some children, a cuddle can help them to calm and, in the process, to deepen their trust in their caregiver. When dysregulation escalates despite our best efforts, more active ways of co-regulating might be needed, such as taking a walk, having a drink and snack, or any of a range of calming activities that are known to work for the particular child.

Reflection
What could have happened if Stephen had become angry and frustrated with Rudra?

- *Co-creation:* Children who feel safe and accept co-regulation can build trust with the caregiver. Now they are more open to those safe, intersubjective experiences that they missed out on in early life. This means giving up some of the control that they learned to survive and becoming open to the influence of the caregiver. These children are expert at influencing (we call this controlling), and only with trust and safety can the children open up to being influenced intersubjectively. They are now able to join in the co-creation of their story, including the difficult experiences that they are encountering. Generally, we would expect to begin with current experience before trying to make sense of past experience. For example, a child might have fallen out with a friend at school. The carer and child together can figure out what happened and how it impacted the child. This is not about finding solutions, although that might come later. It is about helping the child to trust in the process of making sense of things, which in turn helps them to start to feel supported and less alone.

There may come a time when the child signals that they are ready to also think about the impact of their past experience. This may come from the child offering some insight about what happened to them.

Let's think about Melanie who is tripped to the hurt she experienced in the past, from her mother, by a comment from another child.

Melanie is 12 years old. She was removed from the care of her birth mother when she was ten due to physical and emotional neglect, the result of her mum's mental health and addiction issues. Melanie goes to gymnastics. She loves it and does it well, and the gymnastics club has 'claimed her'. It's a safe, successful space for Melanie where she can purposely bounce off some of her energy!

It's Monday evening – gymnastic club evening. Melanie is ready to go and hopping about excitedly. She had a haircut on Saturday. This is a big change of style, going from long hair to short, to look, she says, 'more grown-up'. She loves her new look and is desperate to go to the club and show her coach and her friends. Shari, her key worker, drives her there. When they arrive, Melanie jumps out of the car enthusiastic, smiling from ear to ear. Shari says,

'It's so good to see you happy, makes my heart smile! See you when I pick you up – have a good time.'

As Shari drives back to the home she smiles when she thinks of the little girl who came into care two years ago. Melanie presented as the perfect child, the little girl who had buried her needs and feelings to try to please her mum. Now look at her! Beginning to think she might be deserving of being looked after, beginning even to feel that she might be likeable and lovable, growing in confidence, and even talking about what it was like to live with her mum.

Two hours later and Shari is waiting in the car for Melanie. Melanie comes out of the community centre with her head down, shoulders slumped, and joy gone.

Shari softly cuddles Melanie, who doesn't resist but doesn't respond. Shari says, 'Melanie, I don't know what's happened, but I can see that something really difficult has. Let's go home where it's safe, and we can talk about it, if you can and you want to. I'll put some music on, and we can listen as we drive. Is that okay?' There is no response, which Shari takes as being agreement.

Ten minutes later, they arrive at the home. Melanie has said nothing, and Shari judges that it's better to stay quiet; she wants to get her home and regulated. There are other children in the living room watching TV. Shari passes through, saying softly to another carer, 'Melanie's had a hard time at gymnastics; we're just going to get safe in her room.'

Shari gets Melanie's cuddle blanket, the one she leaves full of hugs for Melanie when she's not on shift. She guides Melanie to her bed and wraps the blanket around Melanie's shoulders. She tells Melanie, 'I think we could both do with some hot chocolate. I'll be back in a tick.' On the way to make the hot chocolate, she's wondering what on earth has happened. Also, she's aware it's bedtime soon for the other kids and is hoping that it's an easy settle night so she can get uninterrupted, quiet time with Melanie.

Shari returns to Melanie, hot chocolates in hand, and offers one to Melanie. Melanie shakes her head, and Shari is reassured by the non-verbal communication that Melanie is now emerging from being 'frozen inside' – Melanie's way of describing what happens when she gets scared. Shari sits down beside her, arm around her shoulders, and says, 'Melanie, something horrible has happened, and I can see that you went frozen inside. Can you tell me what happened?' Melanie shakes her head.

Shari continues. 'I wonder if someone has said or done something that's really, really upset you? You can tell me. I'm here and I'm staying here until you are completely unfrozen.' Then she adds, a little playfully, 'In fact, until you are melting, and the hot chocolate will help with that!'

Melanie smiles fleetingly. She says quietly, head going down, 'Lorna (another gymnast) said, "What have you done to your hair? It looks weird, you're weird, weirdo!"'

Shari: 'Oh, that's horrible for you! You're so pleased with your haircut. I love it and you were so keen to show it off. What a mean thing to say!'

Melanie: 'Lorna's always mean to me!'

Shari: 'She is? I didn't know that. I'm glad you've told me because we can think together what we're going to do about that because it's not okay. Tell me, though, if Lorna is always mean to you, then how have you coped with that before?'

Melanie: 'I ignore her and say to myself, "It's just Lorna being mean!"'

Shari: 'That's wise and brave – well done, you. I'm proud of you for being able to do that and proud of you for telling me what's been happening. How come you couldn't do the "it's just Lorna being mean today" I wonder?'

Melanie: 'I don't know, but as soon as she said it, I started to go frozen inside.'

Shari: 'So let's try and figure it out, shall we? We have chatted before about when you get big, scared feelings you go frozen inside. You remember when we went to the climbing wall? You were so excited to give it a go, and when we got there you just couldn't. You turned into a small block of ice. Is there something to do with being scared and that word "weird"?'

Melanie, whispering: 'My mum used to call me that when I couldn't do what she wanted me to do even though I tried. She would get angry and say she wished she hadn't had me as I embarrassed her, and everyone knew I was weird.'

Shari, cuddling Melanie: 'Oh my goodness, that's really awful for you. Ever since you were a little girl, your mum has told you, when you couldn't do what she wanted you to do, that you were weird and an embarrassment. I get why that word is so, so horrible for you and freezes you. Does that make sense to you?'

Melanie, falteringly: 'Sort of. Do you think I'm weird?'

Shari: 'Wow, that's a very brave question, Melanie. No, I don't. Do you believe me?'

Melanie: 'Not really.'

Shari: 'Thanks for being honest and not trying to please me. I'm going to have to work really hard to show you that I don't think you're weird. I'm really proud of you for figuring out what's happened. We can do some more chatting tomorrow about what to do about Lorna's comment, but I won't do anything without talking to you. So young lady, it's nearly time for bed,' adding playfully, 'now you've melted, you want to watch some TV with the other kids, or stay here in your room? We can talk some more tomorrow.'

- Notice how Shari supports Melanie to 'unfreeze' and then, when Melanie is ready, she starts to lead her into feeling and thinking together about how the present connects to the past, to co-create the meaning of being called weird.

> **Reflection**
> When seeing children in distress, it's tempting to try and make them feel better and/or immediately problem solve for them. What would have happened if Shari had just focused on what to do about Lorna?

- *A-R dialogue:* Affective-reflective conversations help the carer to move from fact finding to feeling finding. The story above with Melanie and Shari is an example of A-R dialogue, which goes hand in hand with the co-creation of meaning. Shari is much less interested in the facts of Lorna calling Melanie 'weird' than Melanie's experience of the event.

  This is different to how adults often talk to children. Although well intentioned, this can take the tone of an interrogation – what happened? The focus moves away from the child's experience towards facts and thinking about the others involved – why did you do that and how do you think they felt?

  Within DDP, we focus on the child's emotional experience and discover their story about the events we are exploring before expecting them to be able to think about others. Within an A-R dialogue, the adult attends to the emotional experience of the child expressed both verbally and non-verbally. The carer accepts and empathizes with this experience as the child relates it. In this way the child experiences their emotional world being validated – it is not right or wrong, it just is. Alongside this, the adult and child are figuring out what happened. This is the reflective part of the A-R dialogue. When affect and reflect are brought alongside each other, the story emerges in all its colours. The interaction moves from wise adult advising and instructing the child to one of collaborators joining together to build connection and trust.

- *Follow – lead – follow:* When children experience trust and safety, they often signal what they need. They lead and the carer can follow. They also need help and guidance to find new ways of understanding and new ways of being. They need us to lead so that they can follow. This is the process of follow – lead – follow, which can help them make sense of what they are experiencing. Children with a history of developmental trauma are poor at knowing what they think and feel. Their inner world can be closed to them, and they need help to discover its meaning. The caregiver needs to listen to the child's communications told through words and actions. This gives the adult clues about what the child is experiencing. This is very different from telling children what they think or feel, which can feel invalidating. Here is an example of how A-R dialogue and follow – lead – follow help the child and carer figure it out together.

Jenny, age 14, has had a difficult day at school. Jana, a care worker, has heard that she ripped up her book and that of another pupil, Alan. Her teacher tried to talk with her, but Jenny stormed out of class. She is now in her bedroom, banging things about and swearing. Jana decides to talk with her. Jenny is feisty and hot-tempered. Jana knows she has to assertively match affect and keep what she says to the point. She knocks on the door; no answer, so she assumes she can go in and does so.

Jenny, quietly through gritted teeth: 'Go away!'

Jana: 'I can hear and see that you're struggling just now, and I wanted to see if I can help. I know you've had a difficult day at school.'

Jenny stops banging about: 'How do you know? Is that because Mr Smartarse Smith (her teacher) ratted on me again?'

Jana, matching affect and following Jenny's lead: 'Yep, you're right. Mr Smith did phone me as he was concerned about you.'

Jenny: 'Concerned about me, oh yeah! And pigs can f****** fly. Do you think I'm stupid too?'

Jana: 'No, I don't think you're stupid, but it's hard if you think you are! And I know from when we've talked before that being smart is something you value, so being called stupid really presses your buttons. Is that what happened?'

Jenny: 'Alan called me "stupid" because I couldn't read the words in the play we were doing together. So I ripped up his book and I ripped mine up too and I don't care. What are you going to do about it, eh?'

Jana: 'Thanks for telling me what happened. I'm not going to do anything about it on my own. I need your help to know what to do.'

Jenny: 'I'm too stupid to help!'

Jana: 'You are helping me already because you told me what happened. I know why you got so angry that you ripped up books and stormed out of class.'

Jenny, feeling understood by Jana and now able to hear her offer of help, says, 'The damage is done, so Mr Smartarse Smith won't want me back in class, will he? I've blown it again.'

Jana: 'It's hard if you think you've blown it. I don't think you have, as Mr Smith did phone me out of concern, not because he wants you out of his class – far from it. I wonder if Mr Smith knows that being called "stupid" really makes you angry. You were called it so often by your mum, dad, and your brother that it flicks your rage switch. Is that what happened or maybe not?'

Jenny: 'Yes, I think so.'

Jana: 'I think it would help him to understand what happened and why. Can we tell him? I'll help you if you like or you can do it yourself.'

Jenny: 'And then what?'

Jana: 'I don't know, but we can figure it out with Mr Smith. We need to do some repair work, Jenny, as we both know that what you did was not okay for you or for Alan. Let's go and talk with Mr Smith tomorrow and then think about how to do the repair.'

- *Talking about (wondering) and talking for:* The conversations we have been describing allow the children to feel emotionally connected and understood. This, however, can be alarming for children who have learned not to trust others and have not had previous experiences of being known and understood at this level. Children we have known in residential care have variously told us that this feels patronizing, manipulative, or weird. We have been accused of being witches and of reading minds. The children need us to gently lead them into these connections, helping them to tolerate them without becoming overwhelmed.

One way of making this less overwhelming involves not talking directly to the child. The caregiver can wonder out loud, talk to another caregiver in the child's hearing, or even talk to a teddy or a poster on the wall. This 'talking about' is not critical of the child nor designed to give a lecture. Rather, it conveys interest in the child and their experience, helping them to feel understood but not overwhelmed. Here is an example of 'talking about'.

Edwina arrived at a children's home where she was a regular visitor and knew the adults and the children well. She was strolling towards the house when 14-year-old Jamie came bursting out of the front door clearly in an angry mood. Edwina knew that Jamie was having a challenging time figuring out his sexuality. Edwina called a greeting and was given the V sign in no uncertain terms. Jamie was picking up stones and throwing them around. Edwina could see he was contemplating breaking a window. Calum, one of the adults and openly gay, stepped outside, clearly following Jamie. Calum looked calm and relaxed. He called to Edwina.

Calum: 'Hi, Edwina. Good to see you. You visiting us today?'

Edwina: 'Hi, Calum, good to see you too and, yes, I'm visiting and looking forward to seeing you all. Oh my goodness, though, I can see Jamie is having a hard time right now. He looks angry.'

Jamie is still throwing stones around but is listening.

Calum: 'Yep, he's angry and he's doing a good job of showing us! I'm not sure why, though. He was angry as soon as he saw me this morning, so I think it might be something I've done or maybe not done.'

Edwina: 'Any idea what that might be?'

Calum: 'Hmm, Jamie and I have been having some really big conversations recently.'

Edwina knows Jamie has been talking a lot with Calum about his sexuality. Calum has appropriately shared some of the story about his being gay. However, this is not a conversation to have in a public space.

Edwina: 'Oh, I see, so do you think that Jamie might be angry with you because of the content of those big conversations?'

Jamie has now dropped the stones, although he is still looking disgruntled. He is listening.

Calum: 'I don't know, maybe. I wish I knew because then I could try to help. Right now, I don't know what to do. I wish he would tell me...'

Jamie, who can't resist joining in, shouts: 'You are never here to have conversations with, so I don't know what you are talking about, p****!'

Calum: 'Edwina, do you know what I'm thinking? But I might be wrong. I'm thinking that Jamie has shared a lot of feelings with me, and I've shared some of mine. I've not been at the house for a couple of days. I just came back this morning. I'm wondering if Jamie is angry with me because we'd been chatting a lot and then I wasn't there anymore. If that's what it is, then I get that. Horrible to feel you're left on your own with big feelings and lots of questions that you want to ask.'

Jamie, now more upset than angry: 'I thought you might not come back.'

Calum: 'Thanks for telling me, Jamie. I get that. Do you get that, Edwina?'

Edwina: 'I do. It's really hard being in care when adults you like and chat to are sometimes there and sometimes not. I guess you and Jamie need more of a private chat. If either of you fancy putting the kettle on for a cuppa, I'll leave you in peace.'

'Talking for' is another way of communicating that deepens the experience of being understood for the child. The adult gives them a voice by talking for them, allowing them to have words for their experience when they cannot find the words themselves. Although this can feel a little strange at first, with practice it can be a powerful way of helping the children to discover their experience. When talking for a child, it is important to give voice to the thoughts and feelings that the child has. This is not about trying to get the child to think and feel differently, however much a carer wants to protect them from the pain of their experience. A child needs to know that someone gets it and truly understands them. This reduces the pain far more effectively than trying to educate someone to be different.

Jamie and Calum go into the house together and find a private space to chat. Having gotten settled, Calum wants to let Jamie know that he really does want to understand just how difficult it is for Jamie to share his thoughts and confusion about his sexuality and then to feel left on his own.

Calum: 'If I was you, when I was not here for a couple of days, I'd have

been saying to myself, "See that Calum, I tell him all this really, really important, confusing stuff, and then he just disappears as if it doesn't matter and I
don't exist! Just wait until he comes back – if he comes back – I'm going to
tell him a thing or two." Is that what it's been like for you?'

> We must never forget how sensitive children who have experi-
> enced physical and/or emotional abandonment are to the regular
> comings and goings of adults who are trying to build a relation-
> ship with them, especially after children share their experiences
> and feelings.

Developing the children's capacity for conversations

With the DDP principles just described, conversations enhance the
children's verbal skills and communication abilities. Children living in
residential care have poorly developed abilities for reflection, making it
difficult for them to make sense of the day-to-day experiences impacting their inner emotional worlds. They can't make sense of what they
feel, why they feel it, what they did, and why they did it. If they can't
make sense of this, then they will not be able to communicate it through
words. Instead, it emerges in a range of behaviours, which can leave a
child dysregulated or shut down.

If carers focus on the behaviour at this point without attending to
the communication underneath the behaviour, they are missing opportunities to help the children to develop their reflective capacities and
to find their stories. In the process, this can confirm the child's sense of
self as bad and unlovable.

This gets more complex when we add in past trauma experiences
the child has had but cannot communicate. Some of this past trauma
can invade the present, triggering even more challenging behaviours.
Trauma has slashed their capacity to tell their story, and past and present get mixed up. Children like Rudra, Melanie, Jenny, and Jamie need
help to tell the story of their trauma. This allows them to process and
integrate this in order that the past stays in the past and the present
becomes less complicated.

We can't do all of this at once; this would be overwhelming for the
child. It might be helpful to think of this as a stepwise process, although
this needs to be done in a flexible manner. Carers can go backwards and

forwards in response to the child's needs when it comes to earlier steps and more difficult conversations (see Figure 4.1).

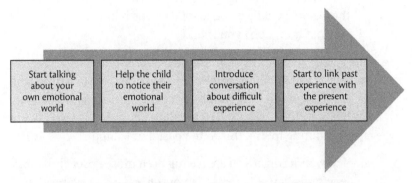

Figure 4.1: Helping Children to Discover and Tell Their Stories

1. *Start talking about your own emotional world.* Get the children used to hearing reflections about feelings so this becomes a normal way of being. This can be about the ordinary. For example:

   a. 'I'm feeling excited that my favourite rice pudding is for lunch today.'

   It can also be deeper. For example:

   b. 'I'm feeling so sad that Jack has left us.'

   The child is being introduced to emotional vocabulary.

2. *Help the child to notice their own emotional world.* For children to hear the emotional vocabulary being applied to themselves, the carers need to share their thoughts about the child. For example:

   a. 'I'm wondering if you're feeling excited that it is rice pudding for lunch.'

   b. 'Perhaps you are feeling extra sad today because Jack has left.'

   Over time the children start using this vocabulary themselves, noticing feelings of themselves and others.

3. *Introduce conversations about the more difficult current experience.* This builds on the emotional vocabulary the children are now becoming used to and extends into discovering stories of experience together. For example:

a. 'I think we are both feeling sad today because Jack has left us. Jack was such fun to be around, wasn't he? Do you remember when he got the hosepipe out and started spraying us all with the water? Luckily it was a hot day. The home feels a bit quiet without him, don't you think?'

4. *Start talking about past trauma and losses and linking past to present.* As the child becomes used to these conversations, the carer can begin to deepen the conversation further. This draws on the emotional vocabulary to think about the present while also beginning to link this to the past. For example:

a. 'I'm wondering if you are feeling even more upset about Jack leaving because it reminds you of leaving your brother. I know how much you've missed him since you came to live with us. It's so sad that you're not living with him anymore.'

Within the DDP model, there is a core belief that children who have been harmed by relationships are healed through relationships. This means that the residential worker's task is to foster healing relationships that have all the qualities needed to build secure attachments. These are authentic, unconditional, loving relationships that provide the children what they needed but didn't get enough of within their family of origin.

Responding to difficult conversations initiated by the child

There are a range of things that children can say to us that knock us off balance and we do not know how to respond. Here is an example of 'talking for'.

Edwina recalls a conversation with Mary. Her history was one of alcoholic parents who were violent with each other and her, the separation of her parents and separation from her brothers and sister, and a long string of foster care placements and children's homes. Mary, as is often the case with children who are in care, remained loyal to her parents despite their neglect and violence. On one of the very rare occasions that Mary allowed Edwina to comfort her, Mary asked, 'Does my mum love me?' Edwina was completely flummoxed by this question. What could she say? If she said, 'Yes, of course, your mum loves you,' then this potentially affirms to Mary that the neglect and violence she experienced were part and parcel of being loved by a mother. If Edwina said, 'No, your mum doesn't love you,' how potentially devastating that would be for Mary.

_____

Reflection
What would be a PACEful response to Mary?

There are a multitude of similar questions and statements that we and you may have been asked. For example:

- Why does my dad hate me?

- I'm just bad!

- Why did my parents hit me/sexually abuse me/abandon me?

We have all been told by various residential workers that having these conversations with children is difficult because of the fear of opening 'Pandora's box'. Often, there is a fear of hurting the child and that, once opened, the lid will not go back on. The child will be left with further distress. Sometimes, this triggers in us reminders of our own attachment stories, and sharing with the child activates this old pain.

The very fact the child has trusted an adult with the question or statement means that they are opening the door for the adult to have that conversation with them. These are such brave questions to ask, and the child is trusting that the adult is strong enough to cope with their difficult stories. We are not in danger of giving them more pain; they have this already. We are in danger of leaving them alone in their pain. Here is an opportunity, maybe for the first time, for the child to experience an adult who is able to hear and sit with the pain. Renowned American psychologist Diana Fosha (2021) notes the importance of undoing aloneness when helping people recover from trauma. In addition, if we don't respond, we are missing an opportunity to help the child transform their narratives about self, others, and events.

Let's think about some possible DDP-informed responses to the questions listed above, starting with PACE. Acceptance for the child's emotional experience is central, and it can be helpful with some children to express curiosity or playfulness.

Back to Mary asking Edwina if her mother loved her.

Dan Hughes gave Edwina a way of responding during level one training way back in 2003. The response both respects the depth of this question and also opens up the conversation: 'Mary, wow, that's a brave question with big feelings. Thank you for trusting me with that question. The answer is I don't know whether your mum loves you or not. I really want to help you figure it out, though, as it's so important to you to know.'

This would begin a curious conversation – possibly many conversations, all with acceptance and empathy – about how a child would know if a parent loved them or not.

Let's think about PACEful responses to some other questions or statements. Responses that focus on the child's experience of themselves and that could open up the conversation. For example:

Child: Why does my dad hate me?

Adult: That's a brave question! Oh my goodness, you took me by surprise. How hard for you if your experience of your dad is that he hates you. Are you OK to talk about things that your dad said or did that make you ask that question?

Child: I'm just bad!

Adult: That's some heavy weight to carry around. It must be really difficult for you if you feel that about yourself. I'm glad you shared that. Wait a minute, though – I wonder how you arrived at that conclusion. Is it something you've thought for a long time or just recently? If it's okay with you I'd like to chat more so I can understand what's going on for you.

Child: Why did my parents hit me/sexually abuse me/abandon me?

Adult: I don't know. I wish I could answer that question, but I can't. That's so hard for you and such a brave and big question. I'm so sad these things happened to you. It might sound strange, but I'm pleased you trusted me enough to ask me. If you want me to, I'll help you find out because it's really important for you to know.

In writing these examples, we have had the luxury of being able to sit and think about what these responses could be. This is much harder to do in the moment. A simple acceptance and empathy response is always a good placeholder to give yourself some time. For example:

- 'That sounds really hard.'
- 'I can see you are having some big feelings right now.'

At times, you will miss an opportunity for communication or respond in a less than helpful way. It is beneficial for children to know that we make mistakes, too, and to discover that your relationship with them is important enough for you to want to repair with them.

We hope in this section we have encouraged you to think about opening Pandora's box when the child invites this. Remember, in the original story of Pandora's box, hope always remained. In joining children in these conversations, we are also holding hope that their narratives are transformed in the process. As Hughes and colleagues tell us:

> Traumatic events strike against our minds and hearts and create a story that is fragmented, with gaps, and is distorted by strong emotions from which the child shrinks and hides. These stories are rigid, with meanings given to the child by the one abusing her. From these jagged stories of shame and terror that arose from relational trauma, DDP is creating stories of connection, strength and resilience. (Hughes *et al.*, 2019, p. 7)

Initiating conversations with children who don't want to talk

Kim remembers times she has offered psychological support to children in residential care. These children have needed to build the relationship slowly, to go at a pace led by them, and to offer therapy in less conventional ways. They are often reluctant to include their residential key worker in their sessions, and including this pivotal relationship in the work has to be done slowly and creatively.

To illustrate this, let's think about an imaginary child.

Cass is a young lady in her midteens still working out her sexuality. Emotionally young and with a troubled history, she has developed some challenging behaviours that have led to failed foster placements. Cass is very reluctant to talk to her therapist, and it is quickly apparent that she is not able to engage in therapy at the current time. Instead, the therapist offers a supportive relationship. This begins with sitting in silence, accepting Cass's discomfort with talking or listening, and instead just offering a time of being together. Cass then begins to share some interests with the therapist, still with little talking. They watch a TV programme together or engage in Cass's hobby centred around Pokémon cards.

Gradually, Cass allows some conversation, chatting about some of the things that have been happening in the home. Sometimes, they leave the home and go for a walk. As they walk side-by-side, Cass seems more relaxed and is able to be more open about her experiences. She shares her frustration with a particular staff member or her anger at a social worker who isn't giving her the answers she wants. The therapist listens and responds, always with an attitude of PACE and resisting the urge to offer advice, judging that this will just shut Cass down again. The therapist checks in with Cass about what she can share of their conversations with her key worker and encourages Cass to join her in this feeding back. Sometimes she will, and sometimes she won't.

It takes two or three months, but eventually Cass is able to talk about her past experiences of foster carers, touch on her birth family, and confide in the therapist about her worries about who she 'fancies' at school and her fears that others will reject her if they know that she is attracted to girls. She even allows some joint sessions with her key worker. It may not be a conventional therapy, but this relationship is therapeutic for Cass and provided at a pace and in a way that she can manage. Cass is ultimately able to have a successful relationship with another young woman and to move from the home into supported lodgings. She needs continuing support, and her experiences with the therapist, alongside the staff in the home, have given her the skills she needs to seek and use the support on offer.

As with Cass, talking to some children can feel like an uphill struggle at times. Patience and gentle persistence are needed while allowing the child to set the pace. The child needs regular and predictable time with the key worker who can provide this support. For a child not yet ready to talk, the primary purpose of key-work time is to build a relationship.

It can also provide the child with some fun, playful time away from the other children.

Individual time with a key worker also provides an opportunity to celebrate success and notice achievements. This gives the child an experience of sharing a positive story and having that story affirmed. Remember to notice the child's emotional responses as well as focusing on events in the child's life. This helps the child to discover their emotional world. Some children like loud affirmation and some children need this to be more muted and lower key. Some children can be resistant to feeling joy or to the experience of being likeable. We need to extend acceptance and empathy to them for their negative feelings about themselves while holding and speaking hope.

Another area in which children are likely to be resistant to talking is when there is a need for more difficult conversations stemming from the challenges that they have been presenting. Individual time with the child can offer a separate opportunity for a reflective space to think with the child more deeply. The key worker explores with the child the significance of the behaviour without pushing the child to talk and while expressing curiosity and empathy for the child's feelings underneath the behaviour. This can help the child reduce their sense of being mad or bad, better understand why they are doing what they are doing, and hopefully, in the future, adopt healthier ways to express emotion.

As with all these conversations, the starting point is PACE and demonstrating interest in and acceptance of the child's emotional experience and their story. The child is likely to be expecting a lecture on what they did wrong and what they should do now. Instead, the child gets an experience of an adult wanting to understand them. The child is then more likely to think about what went wrong and how to put it right. The consequences become collaborative rather than imposed by the adults (Golding, 2017a).

A child who initiates a conversation or is comfortable responding to the adult provides many signals, verbal and non-verbal, about what they feel comfortable talking about and when to draw back. For a child who is more shut down and less comfortable talking, these decisions are harder. Key work time is an opportunity for the carer to talk with the child about how their past is sometimes linked to present happenings. The adult understands the importance of this for helping the child to heal from past trauma. In fact, the key worker can feel under some pressure to do this even when the child is signalling 'no'. In these situations, monitoring the child's sense of safety and regulatory state becomes even more important. Allowing time to focus on this can potentially increase the child's comfort with more difficult conversations.

Noticing links between current experience, behaviour, and past experience may still be too difficult for the child. Introducing life story exploration more generally might be a gentler way to go. The child might feel able to chat about the past in response to something the adult and child are doing together. For example, the worker might know that the child had a positive relationship with an uncle and that they would often go fishing together. As they sit and watch a fishing programme on TV, the key worker can be curious about the child's experience, asking questions such as, what was the biggest fish you caught? What bait did you use when fishing with your uncle? Through these conversations, the child experiences an environment within which it is safe to talk about the past. These more casual chats about the past remove the pressure to go to the hardest part of the story, triggering current emotional experience and behaviour.

Some key workers might feel that life story exploration is the job of the social worker or a professional trained in this exploration, but this is an important part of the therapeutic package. Let's think about how children in healthy families acquire their life story. Chatting about the past arises very naturally in families who talk about a current event, a memory, or a question from the child. The child explores their life through these in-the-moment conversations and revisits this exploration with their developing curiosity as they mature.

This clearly is more complicated for children growing up in care where the people parenting them don't hold the memories of the past. As far as possible, children are helped by a process that parallels the healthy family. Children learn their stories from the people loving and caring for them, those that know them best, involving their parents when possible. If a decision is made that a more in-depth, focused life story work is needed for the child, we would still advocate involving the key worker who knows the child well. In addition to being there to help the child feel safe and supported, this adult can also extend the life story work into day-to-day exploration, as needed. There are some excellent resources for this work. For example, Richard Rose's training and books on therapeutic life story work fit well with DDP (Rose, 2012).

If the child is reluctant to engage in more informal life story exploration initiated by the key worker, it is important to acknowledge this. Let the child know that you understand that this is too much for the present while also providing the message that although this is hard now, you hope that at some point the child is able to come back to it. Relationship building continues with trust that, over time, provides the child with the safety and comfort to open up.

Responding when a child initiates a conversation at the wrong time

Children are adept at raising something important just as you need to get them out of the door to catch the school bus or when you have to attend to another child or visitor to the home. Sometimes, this is motivated by a need to test your reaction and how important they are to you. Alternatively, the child might be letting you know that they have something on their mind at a time when they won't have to engage further in the conversation. As always, a PACEful response is needed, which signals that the child is important to you even though there is not time to talk about what they have brought up in the moment. You can then suggest a time when you might talk about this further, being sure to make this time available for the child even if they choose not to take the opportunity when it occurs.

The importance of self-care, supervision, and support to help adults with their conversations with the children

Conversations with developmentally traumatized children can be emotionally draining. The children can respond in a way that triggers the adults' own emotional vulnerability, leading them to become defensive. It is important that the adults have regular professional supervision and support, personal support, such as friends, and time for self-care.

Time for reflection is an important part of working in a DDP-informed way. These reflective spaces are at risk when stress is high, such as times of crisis within the home. Yet these are the times when reflective spaces are most needed. Protecting time for reflection avoids the dangers of burnout, emotional overwhelm, and defensive responding.

Residential care involves caring for some of the most traumatized children in our society. These are the children who struggle most with the conversations that are needed. It is important that the adults don't feel alone in this work. With good support from colleagues, supervisors, and personal support, relationships are strengthened for all and nurtured by the stories we discover together.

Conclusion

We are all nurtured by being soothed, fed, watered, played with, hugged, and loved. Connections reduce loneliness and allows healing to occur. We can all find many things hard to talk about. When we have the courage to talk about our feelings, they can become less overwhelming, less upsetting, and less scary. The stories we discover, witness, share, and retell together nurture us. These stories of our life, experiences, joys, and day-to-day struggles are part of the sustenance we need. DDP-informed conversations help children harmed within relationships begin to heal within relationships.

CHAPTER 5

Co-Creating the Meaning of Love

The Connection to Shame, Guilt, Repair, and Consequences

In this chapter, we consider how children in healthy families discover the unique meaning of love through a hierarchical process of trust of adult care, trust of adult authority, and then trust of self. We also consider how this meaning of love and being cared for connects with the necessary socialization process of shame-to-guilt. In order to be emotionally healthy, we need, as children, to learn from Alexander Pope that 'To err is human' (1709, line 525). With good enough parenting, children learn to acknowledge mistakes, to accept responsibility, including consequences for their behaviour, and are motivated to value and repair relationships.

We go on to explore how the meaning of love for children who have experienced developmental trauma is often terrifying. In addition, although their humanness innately means that they need love and care, as we all do, they do not think they deserve it. These children have little investment in relationships. The socialization process of shame-to-guilt is significantly delayed and will not start to develop until trust of adult care is in place. Until then, adults who try to keep them safe with guidance and boundaries are viewed as mean and consequences viewed as punishment for being bad kids.

We discuss how the meaning of love can positively change through relationships with adults who understand the children's development age and stage, who offer the two hands of parenting with boundaries and empathy, and who model relationship repair.

We reflect on how our own experiences of love, shame, and consequences impact on the residential care we provide, and the importance of self-awareness and reflective practice.

The meaning of love

Let's think about the meaning of love. Each of us knows what the word means cognitively when applied to relationships; it's an intense feeling of deep affection. However, each of us has our own, quite unique, intersubjective experiences of love. The meaning of that word is initially created by the experiences of being parented as a baby and child. If the word and actions of a parent are, in the main, positive, warm, comforting, and joyful, then our felt sense of love is positive. It feels good to be loved, we learn to love others in that way. Growing up, we have positive expectations of love. On the other hand, if our experiences of parental love are hurtful and harmful, then this is what we expect of relational love.

Our experience and expectations of love as hurtful or harmful can change through a relationship that offers us comfort and joy. This is most likely if we are able to reflect on where the original meaning came from and we know that we deserve love, that we are lovable.

The story of love for each of us is different. The story of love for children who have been harmed needs to be told so that it can be co-created within another relationship that is positive. Edwina, George, and Kim love the film *Good Will Hunting* (Van Sant, 1997), which is about the co-creation of the meaning of love.

Edwina was working with Betsy and her foster carer, Mavis. Betsy was 15 years old with a history of emotional neglect, violent parenting from her mother and her mother's male partners, and many experiences of violence between her mother and her partners.

At eight years old, Betsy was accommodated in foster care, having disclosed to a teacher what was happening to her at home. Foster care was a positive, stable experience for her with a well-supported foster family. Indeed, her foster carers described Betsy as the 'perfect child', always smiling, always willing, and enjoying school. However, as adolescence arrived Betsy became violent to her foster family and unwilling to accept boundaries. She started mixing with a group of peers who were considerably older and on the fringes of offending.

Betsy, at 13 years old, was placed in residential care. For a short time, she again became the 'perfect child'. With the onset of puberty, her rage erupted over which she felt she had no control. Her foster family stayed connected with her. Supported by social services, they considered themselves to be her family for as long as she needed them to be.

Edwina had been working with Betsy and Mavis for a year. Edwina was also providing DDP training and consultancy for the residential team. Slowly, they began to talk in therapy about Betsy's 'perfect child' presentation being a way of numbing, hiding from relationships, and avoiding the terror of closeness.

Betsy began to genuinely smile, to allow herself to feel joy, to feel scared, to feel sad. Mavis was so proud of her. In one session she said to Betsy with an arm around her, 'I love you so much – you are so brave.' Edwina noticed Betsy's face at the words 'I love you'. It was full of alarm. She and Betsy had the following exchange:

Edwina: Betsy, I noticed something just then. When Mavis said she loved you, you looked alarmed. Has Mavis never said those words to you before?

Betsy: Yes, she's said those words, but she never meant it before!

Edwina: And now that you think that she means it, it doesn't feel like being loved is a good thing but a scary thing – I wonder what that's about. (Betsy shrugs 'don't know'.) Is it because you are beginning to feel that you might be lovable and that's scary because you've always felt like a bad kid and got used to it? (No response from Betsy.) I've got that wrong. What's the meaning of love for you I wonder?

Betsy: No, you don't get it! Mavis can't love me! If she did, she would do the things that my mum used to do to me when she said she loved me – ignore me, hit me, let those men hit me.

Edwina: Oh my goodness, Betsy, I completely get why you were scared when you heard those 'I love you' words. If Mavis really means it, she will start doing those things. If she doesn't do those things, then she doesn't love you. Now I understand the meaning of love for you – it's about abuse and pain and being ignored. It's a horrifying thing for you.

Now Betsy's story of the meaning of love has been told, we can start to co-create a different story. By the way, Betsy and Mavis also enjoyed the film *Good Will Hunting*!

Reflection
If you can be and stay safe, can you reflect on the meaning of love for you? How does this influence you in your caring or teaching role?

Shame and guilt

How does the meaning of love relate to shame, guilt, and consequences? In Chapter 2, we wrote about shame and the development of identity. Let's think a little about the experience of shame as part of the ordinary socialization process for all children.

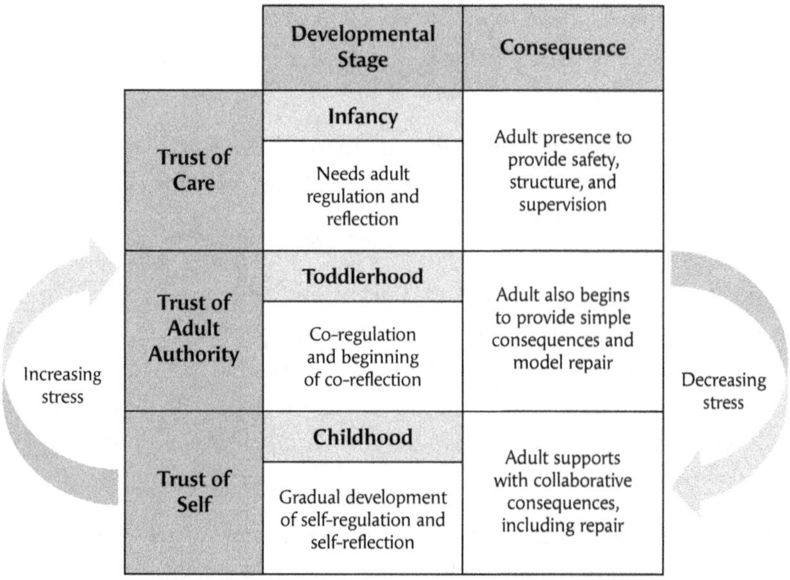

	Developmental Stage	Consequence
Trust of Care	**Infancy**	Adult presence to provide safety, structure, and supervision
	Needs adult regulation and reflection	
Trust of Adult Authority	**Toddlerhood**	Adult also begins to provide simple consequences and model repair
	Co-regulation and beginning of co-reflection	
Trust of Self	**Childhood**	Adult supports with collaborative consequences, including repair
	Gradual development of self-regulation and self-reflection	

Increasing stress (left arrow) / *Decreasing stress* (right arrow)

Figure 5.1: Trust of Care, Authority, and Self

Rikki is a toddler. He lives in a loving, attuned family. For the first year of his life, he has experienced great interest and joy from his parents in almost everything he does. His intersubjective experience of himself through his parents has been that he is lovable, likeable, smart, and delightful. He has developed *trust of adult care* (see Figure 5.1).

Rikki begins to be mobile – he's pretty good at crawling and beginning to get on his feet. He's curious about the world around about him but, of course, he has no sense of danger. He has trust of adult care and now he has to learn *trust of adult authority*, meaning that discipline and boundaries put in place by a parent are about his safety.

Rikki manages to grab the family cat, Casper, and starts to drag him across the floor. To him, Casper is a toy. His dad sees him and is alarmed; the cat can scratch! For the first time Rikki hears the word 'no' said firmly. Rikki is shocked by the word and his dad's tone of voice. He looks startled and starts to cry. His in-the-moment experience of being told 'no' is that he is being told he is a bad kid. His dad has broken the loving relationship he is familiar with. Rikki feels shame. He doesn't understand that his dad is saying 'no' to his behaviour, not to his self.

Rikki's dad separates Rikki from Casper (makes Rikki safe); he sees Rikki's upset (dysregulation), understands why Rikki is distressed, and moves to soothe him with a cuddle, to regulate him through co-regulation. Rikki sobs. With his dad's soothing he calms. Rikki's dad has started to repair the relationship. His dad says, 'I'm sorry Rikki, did I give you a fright when I said no like that? If you grab Casper like that, he could scratch you and hurt you or you could hurt him. That's not okay. Tell you what, let me show you how you can stroke Casper so that he likes it.'

Rikki's dad gets the (very tolerant) cat and shows Rikki how to stroke the cat safely. His dad says, 'Well done, Rikki, this is what Casper likes.' Rikki smiles and giggles. He no longer feels shame.

This relational process of safety, soothing, co-regulation, repair, storytelling, modelling the appropriate behaviour, and affirmation is the process that supports toddlers to move from feeling shame to feeling guilt (see Figure 2.1). They learn that they aren't a bad kid, it's their behaviour that is not okay, and they can change their behaviour. Relationships can be repaired. Centrally, unconditional love is not dependent on behaviour.

Of course, this shift from shame to guilt is not a one-off process. When Rikki's dad returned to what he was doing before the Casper incident, guess what Rikki was doing? Going back to grab the cat! Toddlers need eyes on them much of the time. In their eagerness to explore the world, they put themselves at risk. They have to learn that they cannot have what they want all the time, that others have needs and wants, too, and that relationships are reciprocal.

Toddlers have different ways of showing their shame. In addition to hiding or crying, toddlers can be overcome with rage – sometimes called 'toddler tantrums'.

In addition, it is important to recognize that different cultures have different views of toddler tantrums. As we wrote about in Chapter 2, shame is affected by culture. We commented on Inuit societies in which the whole community joins in the shaming of a young child who has stepped onto thin ice. Differentiating between thick and thin ice is a lesson learned early. Keller (2022), in her book on attachment and culture, views toddler tantrums as emerging predominantly in cultures which encourage autonomy. In cultures in which community is highly valued – for example, the Australian Aboriginal community – attachment is viewed as attachment to kin, community, and land. The Aboriginal word for their form of attachment is 'Kanyininpa', a Pintupi term. Kanyininpa incorporates a code for living socially, spiritually, physically, and morally. Toddler tantrums, an expression of negative affect, are seen as disrespectful to elders and as reducing social harmony. This does not mean that the shift from shame to guilt is not made, it is done differently.

Toddlers and young children require discipline from an emotionally regulated adult many times a day. The process of the shift from shame to guilt takes time and patience. The degree of shame a child experiences is determined by the way the parent, verbally and non-verbally, provides discipline. The bigger the response from the parent, a higher level of shame for the child. However, the bigger response from the parent is often a result of more risky behaviour from the toddler; it's life-saving and not necessarily an overreaction! Also, remember there is no such thing as the perfect parent. There are times when the most secure parenting figures over-react.

To quote from Chapter 2:

> As the child matures, the lessons from these experiences of shame are learned and the child internalizes the rules and values of the parents. Transgression of these rules leads to feelings of guilt instead of shame. In guilt, remorse is experienced and amends can be made.

It is important to remember that this is neuroscience. Toddlers can't regulate themselves well. They have baby brains that are still 'wiring up' through relational experiences. The process of a parent providing safety, soothing, repair, storytelling, modelling the required behaviour, and affirmation is supporting their brains to be able to regulate their emotions and to learn new behaviours. Shame – 'I'm a bad person' – is an awful feeling; guilt is prosocial. We need to feel guilt when we have done something wrong and know how to 'make good'. Often 'making good' involves apologizing and repairing the relationship. We learn from guilt but not from shame.

Reflection

All of us have experienced being shamed by an adult in our childhoods – a parent, a teacher. Do you remember how awful that felt? Do you recognize the difference between shame and guilt? Guilt is uncomfortable, but it motivates us to 'make good' and to change our behaviour.

Developmentally, following trust of care and trust of adult authority is *trust of self.* This is when children are able to have more autonomy, to make their own choices, some of which is positive and some of which will inevitably be mistakes. Children learn to acknowledge and take responsibility for their behaviours, to be able to repair relationships. This trust of self starts with, for example, choices about toys to play with, clothes to wear, food they like and don't like. It develops to making activity choices, subject preferences at school, and friendships. Of course, in teenage years, it can naturally develop into 'It's my life, I'll do what I want – don't tell me what to do!' This stage of growing autonomy is also influenced by culture, depending on whether the society values autonomy over the social group or vice-versa.

Let's return to toddlers and consider parents who do not respond to the toddler's unsafe behaviours with enough safety, soothing, co-regulation, repair, storytelling, modelling, and affirmation. Or where the parental response is actively threatening to the toddler. As we wrote in Chapter 2, this is when toxic shame develops (see Figure 2.2).

Toddlers can grow into children (and adults) who avoid connection. They cannot look at us and often they hide. In addition to physically hiding, they have learned to hide behind a shield (Golding & Hughes, 2012). This consists of characteristic behaviours developed to reduce the intense feelings associated with unregulated shame. The child lies, blames others, and minimizes their actions to defend themselves from an overwhelming sense of badness. When these fail, the children collapse into intense rages directed at others or themselves.

How does the meaning of love, shame, and guilt connect in residential care?

Many children in residential care have experienced overdoses of toxic shame, not only in their families of origin, but also as a result of having experienced changes of caregivers. Often, these changes occur because the caregivers have been unable to understand and/or cope with behaviours associated with the children's shields against shame, particularly in teenage years. The changes are experienced by the children as rejection because they experience themselves as unlovable. They do not have trust of adult care and don't trust adult authority. With reference to neuroscience, they have mistrusting brains, termed by Baylin and Hughes as 'blocked trust' (Hughes & Baylin, 2012).

In DDP-informed practice, the residential team understands that many of the young people have blocked trust and are stuck in the shield against shame with all the associated behaviours we have just described. The team know that the discipline needed for the young people to stay safe is experienced by them as the adults being mean and/or shaming them. The young people are highly reactive to boundaries, easily and quickly moving, often unconsciously, into fight/flight/freeze behaviours to protect and/or defend themselves. This is a challenge to the residential team who are trying to build a relationship with the young person. They want the young person to trust in their care. Unlike with infants, however, these young people are also displaying behaviours that cannot be ignored. The residential team have the challenging task of supporting the children to gain trust of care and trust of adult authority at the same time rather than sequentially. Neuroscientifically, this is the task of supporting a mistrusting brain to become a trusting brain. The co-creation of the meaning of a loving relationship is a mix of meeting young people's essential biological needs (such as food, warmth, health care), providing comfort and joy, and also setting boundaries intended to keep them safe.

Where do consequences fit?

In the authors' experience, consequences are a big deal in residential care! Indeed, they are one of the major causes of team disagreements. An understanding of blocked trust and the shield of shame are essential, and even if this understanding is in place there will still be disagreements.

Let's think more about this. What is the intention of consequences? In the authors' view consequences are needed to ensure emotional and physical safety, success, and positive, proactive adult supervision. Boundaries and structure appropriate to a child's emotional age need to be in place. Until the child is at a developmental stage where they are able to make choices for themselves, the adults decide what consequences are to be offered for appropriate and inappropriate behaviour. Children need consequences that they are equipped to handle.

For each child, there are some things – activities and interests – that, unless there is a safety issue, should not be withdrawn. Obviously, food, protection, care, affection, and respect should never be withdrawn. Other pointers for consequences include:

- always based on safety

- connection before correction

- the 'tighter' the boundaries around a child, the more empathy is required

- the meaning/expressed need behind the behaviour is taken into account

- consequences have a natural justice connection

- the intention is to teach (not to sanction, punish, or humiliate)

- individualized

- timely and reflective, not reactive

- delivered with the attitude of PACE, not a lecture (lectures are worthless)

- achievable

- followed-through

- opportunity for reparation and learning to say 'sorry'

- opportunity to practise new, more adaptive behaviours.

For discipline to be effective, the emotional connection with the child is important. This connection maintains the child's sense of safety and helps them to remain open to the relationship. Without this connection, the child is less likely to learn from the discipline (see Figure 5.2).

The combination of connection with correction is reflected in what is termed the 'two hands of parenting'.

Hand one provides warmth and structure, enabling the child appropriate autonomy matched to their developmental age. In other words, children are supported to make choices and to develop independence but only at a pace that they can cope with. This hand also contains the curiosity enabling the parent (or teacher) to wonder about and accept the child's internal experience.

Hand two complements PACE, providing structure and boundaries, the support that children need from a parent (or teacher) to be successful. This can include consequences but stemming from understanding and used collaboratively.

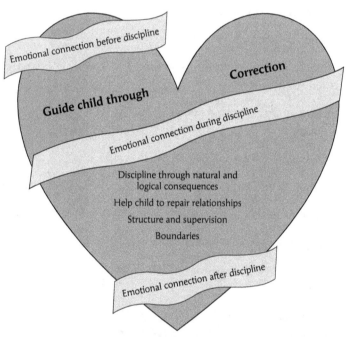

Figure 5.2: Connection and Correction (Discipline)

If we think about applying this to Figure 5.1 (trust of care, trust of adult authority, trust of self), then we need to consider consequences in the light of:

- what stage of development the child has reached

- how big their shield against shame is

- whether their misbehaviour was intentional or caused by the lack of capacity to regulate.

Let's reflect on the meaning of love that emerges in a conversation with a young person and her foster carer.

Aadesh is a ten-year-old child who was trafficked with his mum. His father is unknown. He was taken into foster care when he was two years old and had ten changes of carer before coming into residential care. His emotional and social development is that of a toddler. He has very little trust of adult care, no trust of adult authority and, inevitably, no trust of self. His inner world is chaotic. He can't make sense of what he or others feel or think. He is on the alert for perceived danger all the time.

To be safe, Aadesh needs constant positive, PACEful adult supervision. Left to his own devices, he hurts himself, hurts others, and damages anything that comes to hand. He is an excellent escapee and, given two minutes of an adult's back turned, he will be off and up to mischief. He is exhausting to be with, and the residential team respectfully share the responsibility of someone being with him at all times as it is too challenging for one person to be with him for a whole shift. He is not able to be at school.

From the moment Aadesh wakes up to the moment he goes to sleep, the care team provide tight structure, predictability, and routines to Aadesh's day. He is offered play and fun, but not too much as he is so easily dysregulated. He can't settle at night without an adult with him. He listens to bedtime stories but resists cuddles.

The adults understand that Aadesh is scared of adult care and adult authority. Frustrating though it is, the adults recognize that Aadesh can't regulate, can't reflect, and can't accept comfort. It's not a choice he is making – he can't, not won't. The consequences for Aadesh of his frequent 'misbehaviour' is PACEful adult supervision to keep him safe. There is little point in expecting reparation or remorse for misbehaviour until Aadesh has gained trust of care. Staff also notice and comment when he has success. For example, saying things like 'That's a great tower you've built with the lego' or 'Is that a smile I see on your face? I like to see you smiling.'

Six months on and Aadesh is beginning to have trust that he will be cared for no matter what he does. He asks questions like 'What's for tea?', 'Will you play lego with me?', 'Can you read me a story?', and 'Do you like the picture I drew?' He will accept an arm around the shoulders. The team start to give him short periods of unsupervised time when he's engaged in doing something and can self-regulate.

When Aadesh tries to hurt people or break things, staff start to comment that it's not safe for him and others. They chat with him about helping him to be safe so he can do the activities that the other children are doing and can have more independence. When he has broken something (not as frequently as he did), the adults ask him to clear it up with them. Sometimes he does and sometimes he doesn't. When he does the adult comments, 'Thanks for helping me, Aadesh. So much easier to tidy up when you help.' When he doesn't, the adult does not insist as this would potentially cause a slip back to the shield of shame. The adult comments, 'Today is obviously not a tidy-up day for you. Maybe tomorrow will be as I like it when you help.' Sometimes, Aadesh refuses, but he is starting to help even while saying he won't. Aadesh is beginning to accept adult authority.

Three years on, Aadesh is 13 years old, although emotionally he's more like a six-year-old with teenage hormones! He no longer needs constant adult supervision to be safe and regulated. The adults, as parents do, have taught him to play, share, and co-operate with them and with other children. He is invested in some of the adult relationships in the home, trusting their care and their authority. He is beginning to talk about his feelings rather than act them out. If he has become overwhelmed, hurt someone, or done damage he can, when calmed, sometimes accept responsibility, and sometimes take the initiative to repair the relationship. His shield of shame is reducing in size and his mistrusting brain is starting to trust.

Aadesh now attends the residential setting's school. He benefits from the small classes. His class has six pupils, a teacher, and a support worker. The children have a base in one class with pupils of similar developmental rather than chronological age. They have the same teacher and support worker teaching core subjects. Transitions are minimized. There is much learning through play, and many interesting activities available when the children are able to cope with the stimulation.

Aadesh has discovered a passion for horse riding and is taken by car by his education support worker, Josie, to weekly lessons as part of his school curriculum. He loves and has a talent for this. It's his thing and is good for him in so many ways, including his regulation, his relationships, taking instruction, having success, having a small taste of independence, and chats on the way there and on the way back. He and Josie have been going for a year. They usually go by themselves, but this week they will be joined by Peter who lives in the home with Aadesh but is in a different class. Josie knows that this is a big change for Aadesh, but it's necessary as the only way that Peter and Aadesh can get their horse riding this week is if they go together. Josie figures that Aadesh and Peter can manage this, although it's a stretch, particularly for Aadesh. She talks with Aadesh and with Peter, acknowledging the change and letting them know she is confident they can have a good time together.

All goes well until the drive home. Peter and Aadesh start to talk about who is the best horse rider, and the conversation quickly escalates until Aadesh, who is in the front seat, unbuckles his seatbelt and climbs into the back seat to punch Peter everywhere. Peter is trying to get out of the car. Mayhem ensues! Josie, alarmed by the danger their altercation presents, pulls onto the side of the road and stops the car. Peter gets out of the car and runs. Aadesh is shouting abuse after him and at Josie. Josie's adrenalin is pumping. She calls the school for support. Aadesh runs, too, but, fortunately, does not pursue Peter.

Both Aadesh and Peter are separately picked up. They have run themselves out of steam and get in cars willingly; some space between them is needed. Peter talks to the adult who has picked him up. He is more upset than angry. Staff soothe him, and when he is ready, he returns to his class.

It has been decided that Aadesh needs to go to the house rather than back to school. One of the care team has picked him up. He is clearly in shame. He won't talk but glowers. Back at the home, he goes to his bedroom, clearly saying that he does not want to talk about what's happened. The adults let him be, keeping an ear out for what he is doing in his room.

Meanwhile Josie has gone back to the school, had emotional support from colleagues, and is having a cup of tea. She is both angry and upset. All the 'what ifs?' are going through her mind. What if the car had gone off the road and crashed? What if she or one of the children had been hurt or even killed?

When Josie has calmed, she goes to speak to Peter who has settled back in class. She apologized for what has happened. She lets him know that Aadesh is at the house and that the care team know what's happened.

Josie feels too angry to speak with Aadesh just now, but knows she needs to repair the relationship with him today or he will simmer in shame. Their relationship is important to both of them. The relationship between Peter and Aadesh also needs to be repaired and there needs to be consequences for Aadesh's dangerous behaviour.

Josie lets the care team know she will be over before the end of the school day. She arrives at the house where Aadesh is in the garden, kicking a football about. He sees Josie.

Aadesh: 'What are you doing here? I don't want to talk to you!' (He carries on kicking the football, ignoring Josie.)

Josie: 'I'm here because I want to talk about what happened today. I'm thinking that you might think I won't care about you anymore because of what happened today, but I do still care, and I want us to sort it out.'

Aadesh (sulkily): 'Why do you care?'

Josie: 'Aadesh, I enjoy taking you to horse riding, watching how well you do and how much you love it. It makes me smile, too. I like chatting with you, too. I just want to figure out what happened today. You and I both know that was really dangerous behaviour in the car. It can't happen again, but it doesn't mean to say I don't like you and that I won't take you horse riding again.'

Aadesh: 'It was Peter's fault. He was boasting, thinks he's better than me. And besides, no one got hurt.'

Josie (playfully): 'Hey, I know you better than that! You might have got away with that a year ago when I first knew you, but not now! You know what you did was wrong and dangerous. I'm here to figure out why it happened and get back on track. Will you help me?'

Aadesh (bursting): 'Horse riding is our time! You like Peter better than me.'

Josie (with acceptance and empathy): 'Oh, now I get it! Thanks for helping me understand. That's hard if you think that I like Peter better than you. I'm not sure how you figure that one out? I do like Peter, but it doesn't mean I like you less. That's not how it works for me.'

Aadesh: 'Well you do!'

Josie: 'Do you know, Aadesh, I'm really sorry that you think that. I'm going to try harder to let you know that I really do like you. Also, when I think about it, I shouldn't have taken you and Peter together. I tried to explain to you both, but I sort of sprung it on you. You are used to you and I having our time together. I won't do that again, at least not until I absolutely know that what happened today won't happen again. I got a big fright. I was angry and upset, but now I just want to sort things out with you and with Peter. Any ideas?'

Aadesh: 'You could stop me horse riding!'

Josie: 'Goodness gracious, why would I do that! You love it so much; you are so good at it, and I enjoy it, too. (This response puzzles and surprises Aadesh, he was expecting to be "punished".) No, no, I think that's too harsh. Now, let me think what can be done…hmm…you were dangerous in the car, and you hurt Peter. So two things to think about. First things first – what about Peter?'

Aadesh: 'I could say I was sorry, but I don't really mean it. I *am* sorry I scared you.'

Josie: 'You are? Well thank you for that. (She gives Aadesh a hug and he doesn't resist.) That's honest about Peter, too. I'm going to be honest with you. Peter got a fright, too. You hurt him, and that's not okay no matter what he said. I think it would be good for you to say sorry to Peter. You and he have to live together, and that's not easy at times, I know. I'll help you say sorry if you like when he comes in from school. Saying sorry when you've done something wrong is the right thing to do. It's also the brave thing to do, and you can be brave. Look at you at horse riding – that's brave when you are jumping those jumps! Saying sorry is something you are still learning about. I think you might feel better if you do. It will help Peter and everyone else in the house to have a settled evening. Of course, he might not be ready to accept your sorry... shall we try?'

Aadesh (reluctantly): 'Okay, okay, I'll try.'

Josie: 'Great. Now what about being dangerous in the car? You need to be safe in the car to go to horse riding and other activities. So you and I are going to go out in the car together – just us. I'm going to pick you up for school and you're going to prove to me on the journey that you are safe – seatbelt on, hands and feet to yourself. I need to have confidence in your passenger skills as well as your horse riding skills!'

Aadesh does apologize, with Josie's help, and he shows Josie that he can be safe in the car. Josie lets Aadesh know she is proud of him.

Let's think about all the elements of this incident with respect to the shift from shame to guilt, something that usually occurs during toddlerhood. To facilitate this process, regulated parents make safe, soothe, co-regulate, repair, tell stories of experience, model, and affirm. Aadesh has received all of this from Josie and does, in the main, trust in her care. Aadesh is beginning to experience the meaning of a caring (loving) relationship. Now Josie can put in place consequences that, with high explanation (storytelling), he accepts, albeit reluctantly, for his dangerous behaviour. He is learning that no matter what his behaviour Josie still cares about him. Guilt about frightening Josie prompts him to want to repair the relationship and make reparation.

Move on three years and Aadesh is 16 years old. Emotionally and socially, he remains younger and can still 'fly off the handle', demonstrating a complex mix of adolescence and the continued impact of relational trauma. However, in the main, he can regulate, he can reflect, he is invested in adult and peer relationships, he can feel guilty and repair relationships, and he can accept consequences. He is at the stage of trust of self, able to have more independence and make good choices. At this stage, consequences for misbehaviour can become more collaborative with the adult seeking suggestions from the child for appropriate consequences. The adult continues to offer to help with repair when necessary.

Challenges of helping children shift from shame to guilt in residential care

The adults in residential teams have their own experiences of being parented and taught that is influenced by the culture and community they grew up in. In the main, consequences within families are given with good intention to teach their children how to live good lives. Some adults have experienced harsh parenting, including physical chastisement. Some have experienced the withdrawal of affection or the withdrawal of activities. Some have been shamed. Some have experienced parenting that was more akin to the two hands of parenting described above. Some may now be parents and have either maintained the way they were raised or consciously changed their ways of providing consequences.

It is, therefore, likely that all the adults have their own views about consequences, what was helpful to them growing up and what was not. It is helpful if these views and experiences are reflected upon both by individuals and within the team. This reflection is within the context of understanding the shift from shame to guilt, the meaning of love, and the model of trust of care, authority, and self. This includes regular review of where each of the children are developmentally. If reflection and discussion do not happen, there is a danger of team division.

Sometimes, adults, particularly in the heat of the moment, move into punishment mode rather than taking time to self-regulate and offering connection before correction. Of course, adults make mistakes and can be overly sanctioning at times. Self-awareness is required, and repair with the child is needed. Colleagues need to talk with the adult who has moved into sanctioning mode, accept and empathize with their feelings of anger and frustration, and also be clear that inappropriate sanctions need to be amended.

There is a danger that teams can collude with inappropriate consequences, carrying through the sanctions rather than having the conversation required to question the adult's decision. For example, in the case of Josie and Aadesh, Josie could have chosen to ban Aadesh from horse riding and from travelling in the car. This was what Aadesh was expecting. Having taken time to regulate and received colleague support, Josie was able to consider the incident as a learning experience that could strengthen Aadesh's sense of guilt (not shame), show him appropriate behaviour, strengthen their relationship, and offer Aadesh agency. Her hope was to leave him with a sense of 'Josie cares about me, she will help me learn to do the right thing when I have misbehaved. I can do this.' Far easier to teach natural consequences from success than misbehaviour.

Had Josie moved into punishment mode, taking away horse riding and travelling in the car, Aadesh would have learned nothing. He is a child who lived his first ten years having very little care or activities. He knows how to survive having nothing, and Josie's sanctions would only serve to reinforce his view that adults are mean. Josie could be helped if another adult, following the DDP way, PACEfully questioned her decision and helped her to reflect on what Aadesh needed.

Reflection
How were you disciplined as a child? Was it helpful or harmful? Have you changed the way you discipline?

Within residential care, all the adults know of incidents. This can lead to each arriving for their shift and commenting disapprovingly to the child, which increases their shame. It is far more helpful for the child to hear adults saying something like: 'Heard you had a difficult day yesterday, Aadesh, and I heard you handled it well. Well done you!'

There are occasions, particularly if adults have been physically hurt by a child or their personal property has been damaged or stolen, that they do not feel able to repair in a timely way, and understandably so. Team care and support is clearly needed for the adult as well as support for the child.

Offering support for the child can be challenging, particularly if violence is a regular feature of the child's behaviour. The child may well be in shame, denying, minimizing, threatening, and/or blaming the adult while being unable to show remorse. The adult team may be angry on behalf of the adult who has been hurt. Some of the adults may be feeling unsafe, either anxious or scared. How safety is restored and how repairs happen need delicate handling.

If the child is feeling guilty and wants to repair, the adult involved, still hurting, may struggle to accept the apology in whatever form it takes. In this situation, the adult needs to know that the child wants to repair, and the child needs to know that the adult needs time to be ready to accept this because they are angry and hurt. A mediator in the form of another team member (maybe the team manager) can help to communicate between adult and child and to support the repair. In these situations, the team can use a reflective debrief to express their feelings, consider what happened, why it happened, and what to do, all with safety uppermost in mind.

When the child is at a developmental stage where they can be curious about what happened and why, this also needs to be supported. Consequences can then be put in place, collaborative when possible.

The balance of boundaries and empathy

In the authors' experience, adults working with children in whatever capacity need to be able to offer a balance of boundaries – based on keeping the child safe – and empathy for how difficult accepting boundaries can be for the child. The tighter the boundaries, the more empathy is required.

In residential care, both the individuals in the team and the team as a whole offer this balance alongside the two hands of parenting. It is easier for some adults to offer empathy and for others to offer boundaries. Getting the balance right is challenging, and, as always, mistakes will be made. To complicate the issue further, it is necessary to know the particular child's stage of development, their temperament, and how best to offer boundaries and empathy that connect with and have meaning for the particular child. As we have been exploring, children who have been relationally traumatized can be very reactive to boundaries, even though they need them. Also, children who have experienced very little empathy in the past can experience it with suspicion, anxiety, and even fear. The right prescription of boundaries and empathy is required for each child.

Edwina's experience in residential care is that she tended to lean towards empathy. She reflects that this is based on her own experiences of being parented, which tended to be over-boundaried with high expectations. Rather than repeat this parenting in residential care, she could be over-lenient, often called overly 'soft' by other team members! Edwina needed colleagues to give her a nudge to put boundaries in place for safety reasons. Likewise, Edwina worked with colleagues who were over-tight in their boundaries without offering sufficient empathy, and she would nudge them for more empathy!

Achieving a balance in individuals and in the team takes time, confidence in the adult role, practice, trust in colleagues, supervision, and reflection. Holding an awareness that some adults are better at delivering boundaries and others at offering empathy must also ensure that this is not used to set some adults up as authority figures and others as fun figures, an unhelpful dynamic for the adults and the children.

Saying sorry

As we have written, repairing relationships by apologizing in words and deeds is of primary importance. This relates both to adults taking responsibility for repair with the children and to modelling apology and repair with each other for the children to see and to experience.

Let's think about how children develop the capacity for repair. This starts to develop in toddler stage during the socialization shift from shame to guilt. Remember Rikki who was dragging the cat? His dad went through the process of safety, soothing, co-regulation, repair, storytelling, modelling, and affirmation. Over time, Rikki becomes motivated to repair the relationship with his dad and other significant adults. He wants to please them, he enjoys the affirmation, and he is learning to have empathy for others and be reciprocal.

A toddler's 'sorry' is often not a heartfelt apology but rather a way of pleasing the adult and being able to move on with playing. It's practising repair. A heartfelt 'sorry' that has empathy for others is just developing. The current thinking is that children are five or six years old before they can fully understand they have caused pain, feel empathy for the other, and feel guilt.

Reflection

When you said 'sorry' as a child to an adult and meant it, what was the adult response? Was the response accepting and affirmative or was the response something more disparaging? For example, 'Say it like you mean it!' or 'What are you sorry for?' or 'Sorry's only a word!' Maybe there was a mixture of affirmation and disparagement.

Remember, children in residential care are developmentally young. When they first feel motivated to say 'sorry', it's likely to be a toddler sorry and not heartfelt. It's a way of getting the adult 'off their back' and getting on with what they are doing. It can be tempting to say what was said to you as a child. If this was affirmative – 'Thank you for saying sorry' – then this is a positive response, recognizing that the child is practising and starting to develop the motivation to repair. If your experience was somewhat disparaging and you respond with the same to the child, then you have missed a golden opportunity to affirm real progress.

Apologizing, whether we are adults or children, can make us feel vulnerable. What if our repair is rejected? We want children in residential care to be able to show vulnerability, it's part of developing trust of adult care and authority, something to be celebrated. It means we are making relational progress. It feeds the child's growing positivity about self and the meaning of love.

Conclusion

In this chapter, we have informed the reader of the DDP way to support both the children and adults and their relationships in the positive, co-creation of the meaning of love and care. We have written about how shame, guilt, and the hierarchy of trust intersect with the meaning of love. All these elements are affected by the culture, identity, and experience of both the children and the adults. We have written about the central importance of children being shown, motivated, and supported to repair relationships. This is learning for life and equips the children to have healthier relationships in their adult lives. As always in the DDP model, supporting the adults as well as the children is essential, complex, challenging, and, of course, possible.

CHAPTER 6

The Pot Noodle Story

Team Working and Establishing Structure the DDP Way

It is important that we don't just think of a DDP approach as being something for the children only. In Chapter 1, we described the Dyadic Developmental Practice model (see Figure 1.1). DDP therapy may or may not be available in the residential setting. Whether present or not, this model illustrates how DDP supports the children alongside all those involved in their care, education, and health. In turn, the practitioners and parents can be supported by the systems in which they are embedded.

Let's turn our attention to the adults. We explore team working within residential care and education and how this can be supported by managers and leadership. This support acknowledges the complexity of caring for children within residential settings and the challenges that this can present to teams working together to provide a therapeutic, healing environment for the children.

We also explore the positives and challenges of multiple practitioners and parenting figures being involved with the children, each having their own stories with respect to their culture, identity, and experience. Their attachment histories and values have been influenced by the context in which they grew up in and in which they live now. This influence impacts on the way they provide residential care.

Working with complexity
A philosophy of practice needs to support the complex relational environment featured within residential care. All families consist of multiple relationships, which itself can be complex. In residential care complexity is added to complexity. Multiple parenting figures with

multiple attachment histories, some traumatic, care for and educate multiple children. The adults, whatever their role, have opted to work in the residential environment with a variety of experience of what this means. The care staff live and work at the home in shifts, returning to their own homes and families when the shifts end.

The children have not chosen and sometimes do not want to be living in the home. They had no say in what residential home they were moved to and are unsure what to expect. They don't have a family to go home to each night. In fact, they often feel abandoned by their family. Many of the children have been through multiple families before entering residential care, including failed adoption, foster care, and/or kinship care. It is hard to make sense of these multiple moves which have so often been in response to challenging behaviours presented by the children. Many children conclude that they are to blame for these transitions, and, unfortunately, this can be reinforced by families at the end of their limits. Intersubjectively, they have absorbed all this prior experience of relationships, informing their sense of who they are. They bring this into the residential home. Often the children arrive feeling not lovable, not likeable, that they are stupid, 'bad', or wrong in some way. Additionally, the children are often having ongoing contact with their birth family, and this can add to the difficulty of adjusting to residential life. Moving between very different environments, receiving messages from birth family members which are different from what they are being told elsewhere, and experiencing feelings of loyalty to birth family can all make settling into the residential home difficult.

The task of residential care and education is to give the children an experience of themselves within which they discover that they are likeable and lovable and that they are not bad kids, even though life can feel difficult at times. This can be very discombobulating, and it is not uncommon for children to cling to their established sense of self and the certainty of this, rather than embracing a new sense of who they are and can be. Understanding this about the children and working with various levels of resistance to care becomes the task of the adults in the team.

Complexity extends to how teams work together. Staff dynamics and conflict resolution can be challenging in an organization that is caring for traumatized children. It is easy for the trauma to end up organizing the environment unhelpfully rather than being a source of information to help provide a healing environment. To understand more about trauma-informed and trauma-organized models of practice, we highly recommend the work of Sandra Bloom (Bloom, 2013, 2017; Bloom & Farragher, 2013), Karen Treisman (Treisman, 2016; Treisman *et al.*, 2021), and Ruth Emond (Emond & Burns, 2022; Emond *et al.*, 2016).

Each adult brings the rhythms, routines, and rituals experienced within their own families into the residential environment. Parenting children who are developmentally traumatized is a big stretch from ordinary parenting, and it is likely that the parenting the adults received, although perfectly fit for purpose in healthy family environments, is not sufficient as a model for the new parenting challenges that residential care brings. In addition, the adults are caring for and supporting children who have often experienced very different rhythms, routines, and rituals (or the absence of these) within the families they have lived in. The chances of conflict are high when such varied experience is being brought together.

For example, some caregivers have grown up in families in which conflict is dealt with by sweeping it under the carpet, and strong feelings are not acknowledged or talked about. Other families might be more volatile in expressing conflict and strong feelings. Some adults might have grown up in cultures in which respect for elders is paramount or in which eye contact is considered disrespectful. The expectations, rhythm, and routines in these different families work for the individual families, and all family members feel safe in this way of being. In a team, adults with a mix of different experiences are coming together. This is part and parcel of working together with many opportunities for conflict or at least differences of opinion.

Reflection
How was conflict dealt with in your culture and in your family, and how has this affected the way you deal with conflict now?

Recognizing and resolving conflicts and differences of opinion is central to safe and healthy practice. The DDP model encourages courageous conversations during which people are able to say 'let's talk about this'. Practice that is reflective is an important part of residential care. Understanding ourselves and others and challenging our assumptions is central within these reflections. Within DDP, we encourage all adults to have awareness of their own histories and ways of being so that when these conversations happen, they feel safe and able to stay curious. This means purposefully having sessions with staff to explore their own experiences, how these are displayed in their current roles, and how these may differ from others. Through these reflections, ways forward often emerge.

Here is an example of reflective practice in residential care.

Edwina was on her weekly visit to a care and education service where she provided DDP training and consultancy. She was crossing the courtyard between the children's houses and the education block when she saw one of the care managers, Chris, coming the other way. She knew him and his team well. Chris was shaking his head and looking frustrated. There was no one else in eye or earshot.

Edwina: 'Hi Chris, what's up?'

Chris: 'F****** Pot Noodles!'

(Pot Noodles are a UK snack food consisting of noodles, dried vegetables and/or meat, and a whole lot of flavouring, to which boiling water is added so they can be eaten out of the tub they are bought in. Not exactly health food, in the authors' opinion, of course!)

Edwina: (confused but getting Chris's angst) 'I can see you're frustrated. What's the story with the pot noodles?'

Chris: 'My head's exploding! We've just had a team meeting and we spent 45 minutes talking about Pot Noodles! Some of the adults think the kids should never have Pot Noodles, some think they should have the occasional Pot Noodles, and some think they should have free rein to Pot Noodles – no way is that happening! After 45 minutes we still haven't agreed!'

Edwina: 'So a waste of time?'

Chris: 'Oh no, far from it! I just get frustrated that there is never enough time. I'm proud of myself, I stayed PACEful, despite my inside voice muttering "Get a move on, we've got a lot to get through!" Sounds a bizarre thing to say, but I stayed curious about Pot Noodles, and what emerged was each of the adults sharing a little of their own story of their relationship with food. Who grew up in a family where you ate what was put in front of you; who grew up in a family where you chose what you wanted to eat; who ate lots of 'rubbish' food; who didn't; who sat at the table and who ate in front of the TV. No judgement, just folks' experiences. It really helped me, and I hope everyone, to get that however much we might want to, we can't have a strict

Pot Noodle rule. Just like us, the kids all have different experiences of food and eating. If they've only ever had Pot Noodles – or tinned food, packet soup, sweets, or whatever – then we are going to have to, whether we like it or not, give them these foods with a smile on our faces, at least to begin with. Next stop, we need to talk more about each of the kid's experiences of food as far as we know it and ask them too!'

In making sense of differences and potential points of conflict, it is also important to consider attachment histories. Everyone has their own cultural, identity, and relational history which is impacting on their current way of being. This can be very different from what developmentally traumatized children need, especially when the parenting has had a higher level of focus on behaviour and not enough attention paid to emotional security. An adult saying 'Well, I was parented like that (e.g. smacked, time-outed, withdrawal of affection) and it didn't do me any harm!' is a cue for a reflective conversation!

As human beings it is important for our well-being that we have some degree of self-interest when it comes to choosing relationships. This helps us to get what we need alongside any altruistic motivations we might have. When we apply this to choosing a caring job, it is likely that residential care workers and educators have a cultural, attachment, and relational history which has led them to this choice. The need to care for others is in some way also taking care of themselves. This can be complicated when the response from the children they are trying to care for and teach is not to be taken care of or taught. The adults need to have or to develop an awareness of why they want to do the job and to understand how painful it can be when the children reject this care. Once again, this highlights the importance of reflective practice, providing adults the support that they need with many opportunities and space for reflection, both about the children and the impact of parenting them that they are experiencing.

Building a DDP-informed approach to residential care needs to be mindful of all the complexity we have been discussing. Staff teams come together to provide an environment within which the caregivers and teaching staff feel sufficient safety to join together to find a common DDP-informed way of parenting and teaching the children. This has different levels of familiarity to them given their own histories and parenting and teaching styles. For some, a DDP way of being feels familiar and comfortable, while for others it is more of a stretch. Support of each other with high levels of acceptance and empathy is important if the team is to stay curious and working together to provide a cohesive approach. A liberal dose of playfulness is also important in bringing the team together. In this way the DDP approach is accepted and implemented from top down and bottom up.

A manager's perspective:[1] Emond and Burns (2022) quote a senior residential manager as an example of the relational culture in a DDP-informed residential setting:

> What I witness is, people invest a lot of themselves. Absolutely. And I think that does make it a lot more difficult, because I think there's not a switch off in the same way. Yeah, because I think it goes both ways. I think because of the intensity of time spent with the children, it can be really loving, beautiful relationships, or it can be incredibly challenging. So pushing you to your absolute limit [in] relationships in the same way that, you know, a parent who's got a child who's not coping particularly well and going through a lot, you know, when it affects them to the core. And I think the way in which relationships develop, it's the same thing. So I think that's why the support was so important is because you can't be here and not invest part of yourself [...] there is a bit where these children become part of your life, because the reality is, the adults here spend as much time with these kids as they are [with] any other person in their lives (Interview, Quin, 13/9/21). (pp. 28–29)

A DDP-informed team

As a staff team, we check in with each other to make sure we are as well as we can be. We were talking about how the children's distressing behaviours can have an impact on us. If we are not

---

1   This quote is taken from a research project and report about a residential school with DDP as its philosophy of care and operational practice.

taking care of ourselves and each other, this can impact on the way that we interact.

(Woodier, 2019, p. 2)

In this section, we explore how to develop a team within residential care that is DDP-informed. This emphasizes the importance of taking care of the adults and the parallels this support has with the care and support that the adults are giving to the children. The care of the children is mirrored by the care of the adults. This values the way of being which is seen as central to building relationships. The doing, that is, the day-to-day tasks that need to be attended to, although important, is secondary to these relationships.

> To highlight that staff-staff relationships are an important part of residential care, Emond and Burns (2022) provide this quotation from a staff interview as an example:
>
> > I think the most important thing when you're working in a team is everybody's working in unison with each other. In the past, I've worked with teams where they don't work in unison, and it becomes cliquey. And it becomes an environment where the kids start struggling because they can see they can pick these things up very, very quickly [...] So, I think it's just about realising that we're here to, all here for the children. But we're also here for each other as well. Yeah. And we've got to support each other no matter what. I think it's important as well, [to] be constructive, criticism-wise with each other. I don't think there's enough of that in care, right [...] it's just about being able to talk to each other openly and honestly. I think it's important that we're able to get people that if, we're able to take constructive criticism from folk as well, because that allows us to reflect on our practice, but I think we've got quite a bit of that here that we can actually speak to each other. (p. 25)

DDP practice and therapy places primary importance on the support for the adults as the vehicle for the relationship that heals the children. Therefore, we need a range of supports and interventions for the adults no matter what their role is within the team. The whole team, from top down and bottom up, is impacted by what the children bring, and therefore everyone within the setting needs access to support.

Staff need to be cared for, nurtured, and provided with a structured working environment within which boundaries are clear. This also provides them with a model for providing the same level of care and structure for the children. If adults are managed in a way that focuses more on 'doing' (outcomes, recording, and reporting) than 'being', it is likely that they are the same with the children. They focus on doing to the child rather than placing importance on being with them. Of course, there are always things that need to be attended to, like assessing the child's progress, recording, and reporting. Residential care is not one big therapy session; rooms have to be tidied. However, once there is focus on relationship, then these more doing tasks are achieved in a more relational way.

Support and supervision for the adults need to model the attitude of PACE that the adults are adopting with the children.

Leadership to build capacity within the team for attachment-focused relationships

When the staff team, including the leadership team and managers, are well cared for, their capacity for offering attachment-focused relationships is strengthened. There are key features that need to be in place for this to happen, including leadership, safety, clear structure, support and supervision, and reflective practice. These features are explored below.

Leadership

The leadership team also need to feel safe and supported with appropriate supervision and time for reflection. This team is responsible for articulating and supporting clear management values and practices in collaboration with the whole team. This provides the team with a philosophy of practice that they can all sign up to. Within DDP, we would see the attitude of PACE being core within this philosophy. PACE guides the leadership team in a way of being that offers staff appropriate autonomy alongside accountability.

Dan Hughes has built into the DDP model three assumptions to hold when working with parents (Hughes *et al.*, 2019):

- They are good people.

- They are doing the best they can.

- They have a genuine desire to love their child.

In leadership terms, this translates into the adults in the team are all good people with a genuine desire to do the best they can; they care for (indeed can come to love) the children that they are supporting. Our experience is that a fourth assumption is also helpful:

- All parents need support, with some needing more support than others.

Holding onto these four assumptions supports the leadership team to remain open and engaged to each other and also to the adults they are supervising, even when there are differences of opinion. Differences of opinion are valued, and discussing them leads to a better understanding of each other.

Even when practice falters and poor decisions are made, these assumptions are important to support a PACEful attitude so that the team member can reflect and revise their practice. When we hold these assumptions, we are naturally more curious about the other. We become less judgemental and more open to accepting the experience of the other. With this understanding, we experience empathy for them and the place they have arrived at, even if it is a place that needs to change. This in turn helps the other to know that they are understood and valued, and, as a consequence, they are more open to considering the issue at hand.

Woodier emphasized that '[a] *no blame* culture helps adults stay open and engaged', and quoted a residential child care worker from Aberdeen, Scotland, to illustrate the point:

My supervisor and I reflect a lot on things that have happened; we are curious about things. We will look at how I have handled things, and we talk about how I am feeling. We had a situation last weekend where one of our young people...had been doing a lot of alcohol and this affected his behaviour. He had gone out saying he was going to hurt himself, and I had to hold him to stop him from hurting himself. It was quite a traumatic event, but my supervisor talked through how I was feeling and how I was going to go forward with this young person. There's never any blame and that helps me stay more open and engaged with a young person. (Woodier, 2019, pp. 3–4)

The DDP model advocates a relational approach at all levels, and this includes the way the leadership team works with the staff team. This does not devalue the importance of accountability. Within healthy relationships, accountability is easier to promote and accept. The leadership team find a balance between relationship and accountability.

Leading a team parallels the DDP approach to parenting. The reader will remember that in parenting the DDP way, two hands of parenting are needed. The first hand provides the attitude of PACE. This includes the support, nurture, warmth, and curiosity about the child's experience that helps them to trust in the relationship. The second hand provides boundaries and discipline while supporting appropriate autonomy. This helps children to feel safe. In our view, managers and leaders also need two hands. Boundaries and discipline are an important part of a manager's job. When these are provided in an atmosphere of respect for the relationship, the adults feel understood and supported and, therefore, able to stay open and engaged to the manager's perspective on why the boundary is needed. This is PACEful management and supervision.

A strong leadership team ensures that the home runs according to the philosophy of care that has been envisaged. When this model is informed by the DDP approach, it is one which values:

- *Safety:* As for the children, everyone in the staff team needs to feel physically and emotionally safe. This means the team working together in a way that fosters safety for all. A safe environment allows the creation of a positive and playful emotional atmosphere. Children only feel safe, thrive, and engage in this environment if the adults are feeling safe. The nature of the challenges that traumatized children bring into the residential home inevitably leads to loss of safety at times. Violence, dysregulation, running away, and the impact of unhelpful peer groups can all compromise the safety that has been created. These are the times when supportive team working is most needed. The DDP model, as with good practice generally, always prioritizes re-establishing safety. Communication, reflection, and clear leadership is an important part of this.

- *Clear structure:* Staff teams work best when there are clear tasks, roles, and responsibilities. We all, children and adults alike, need predictability. We think of this as the home being supported by two pillars. Relationships are one central pillar in residential care. The balancing pillar is structure (see Figure 6.1). This is modelled in the way that the staff team works together, providing each other with relational experiences alongside structure. This same experience is then offered to the children.

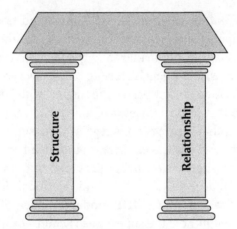

Figure 6.1: The Pillars of Residential Care

The schedule of meetings provides this structure. This includes team and individual meetings, providing opportunities for supervision, shift co-ordination, debriefings, reflection, and planning. The structure of meetings provides staff with an opportunity to feel that they are part of the decision-making. The management team still hold the boundaries concerning what is negotiable and what is not. The structure of meetings provides vehicles for communication, allowing staff voices to be heard and managers to hold the lines when necessary. In this way, staff feel supported and valued, their views and frustrations are listened to, and the team get a sense of working together.

At times of increased stress and crisis, it is often the structure that is first to go. However, holding on to this structure at these times is essential. When structure slips, team members tend to start to work as individuals rather than part of a team. For example, they might move back to default ways of parenting, stemming from their own history of being parented, and the unified approach that the team is working to slips. It is also not uncommon at times of stress for the parent figures to become more punitive in their parenting. The lack of safety the stress creates leads to more defensive responding. Structure provides time and space for team members to pause, breathe, and notice what is happening. It allows team members to get back to the ethos and approach that all have signed up to. PACE becomes central again.

- *Support and supervision:* A DDP-informed home is one in which support is everywhere for everyone. A culture of support informs supervision, management, reflection, teamwork, peer relationships, and a general feeling of 'we have got your back'.

    Supervision is a key part of the support within the residential home and an important part of any social care practice. It is important that supervision is regular alongside more informal mentoring and guidance. There is an element of accountability within the supervision being provided but always managed in a way that feels supportive and relational. It is this focus on the relational that a DDP model provides. The supervisor is interested in how the supervisee is and in exploring current experience. This is the time for focusing on how caring for this child is impacting on the supervisee. The focus can then move onto the supervisee's practice, finding some joint understanding of the issues being raised, including understanding the child. Only when these have been fully explored will supervisor and supervisee move on to consider how to deal with any issues that have arisen.

    This is a great deal to cover, and it can feel frustrating when there is much to discuss with what can be limited time. However, we believe this slowing down ultimately builds greater success. Within DDP, we talk about 'slowing down to get there quicker', and our experience is that taking this time is ultimately more successful. By taking the time to understand the experience of the supervisee and reflect on this experience, the way forward becomes clearer. This moves from supervision being directive to supervision in which supervisor and supervisee figure things out together.

Here is an example of a DDP-informed supervision conversation between a residential worker and his manager.

The reader will remember Bill from Chapter 3. Bill has moved into residential care and his primary key worker is Ralph. Ralph is in his first year of residential work and loves the job. Bill is his first key child, and Ralph is keen to do the best he can. Bill, as we know, has blocked trust, which Ralph is aware of from training; however, this is his first experience of being consistently rejected by a child he is working hard to connect with. He has supervision with the Team Manager.

Team Manager: 'Hi Ralph. We have tasks to chat about today, but first things first, how are you doing?'

Ralph (a little defensively): 'I'm fine. What tasks are we going to talk about? I know I still have a lot to learn about recording the day's events. I'm finding it hard to get used to this writing to the child that we do here. I do like it as it's far more child-friendly than writing about them, but it's hard. Never done it before!'

Team Manager (who has picked up Ralph's defensiveness in his facial expression and tone of voice): 'Hey, can we slow down a bit? That's great that you want to talk about recording, and that you recognize it's hard to do it the way we do it here. However, when I asked how you are doing, the words said 'I'm fine', but the face and tone of voice said 'maybe not so fine'. Can we talk about this, because my first priority is finding out what's going on for you.'

Ralph: 'I love this job, but I'm sick to death of being pushed away by Bill. No matter what I do, I'm being told to f*** off. Anytime I ask him to do anything he says no! He constantly says he wants a change of key worker as he hates me. He does things for other people and smirks at me while he does it. I don't think I'm the right person for Bill.'

Team Manager: 'That's really hard for you, being pushed away when you're trying so hard to connect. I've seen you keep on trying. Respect, that takes courage and perseverance. Thanks for telling me how you are really feeling – that takes guts too.'

Ralph: 'Bill's my first key child and I want to do a good job. He's making me feel like I'm useless!'

Team Manager: 'Yep, I get that. Bill's really good at that, isn't he? I wonder why he's doing that?'

Ralph: 'Because I am useless!'

Team Manager: 'Hmm...I get why you feel that way. It's not my experience of you when I see you on shift. Do you believe me?'

Ralph: 'I want to. What do you see?'

Team Manager: 'I see someone who comes into the home with a smile on their face, greeting the kids and the adults, good to go, a team player. Bill may be really resistant to you, but the other kids like being with you. Sure, you've got things to learn, like recording! (Team Manager says this playfully) Do you agree that the other kids like being with you?'

Ralph (feeling a little more buoyant): 'I suppose so, but what about Bill?'

The Team Manager goes on to remind Ralph of Bill's history, the impact of developmental trauma, and of Bill's changes of parenting figures. Blocked trust means that Bill is really resistant to adult care and authority, particularly with someone like Ralph who is trying hard to connect. There are ways in which Bill feels, like Ralph, useless, but he is a long way off being able to realize or talk about this. Bill needs an adult who perseveres and does not give up on him. The Team Manager will support Ralph to stick with Bill for the long haul. They agree that Ralph will tell the team how he is feeling so they can support him too. Ralph and the Team Manager then go on to talk about writing to the child.

If the Team Manager had accepted Ralph's 'I'm fine', then the opportunity for emotional support from him and from the team would have been lost. This would make it harder for Ralph to persevere with Bill. Slowing down also provided an opportunity for a psychoeducation reminder about the impact of developmental trauma and blocked trust. The supervision would have focused on recording, and Ralph would have potentially left supervision feeling as useless as he did when he went in. There was a real danger that, without the acceptance, empathy, and curiosity of the Team Manager, Ralph would eventually experience blocked care.

DDP-informed supervision reminds us to focus on the well-being of the supervisee rather than a too-quick focus on the tasks at hand. We are reminded of John Adair's (1983) leadership model which focuses on individual, team, and task (see Figure 6.2).

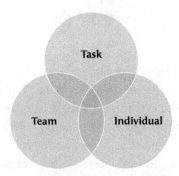

Figure 6.2: Action-Centred Leadership Model
© JOHN ADAIR, 1983. USED WITH PERMISSION.

Adair's concept asserts that effective leadership means having an overview of the task, the team, the individual, and their intersection. People expect their leaders to help them achieve the common task, build the synergy of teamwork, and respond to individuals' needs.

The supervisor's role is to facilitate reflective discussion, in line with DDP principles and practices, with the supervisee. This explores how they are thinking, feeling, and behaving with respect to themselves (the individual circle), the team (the team circle inclusive of their own team, the close team, and the wider team), and their job (the task circle). The DDP way prioritizes checking in with the individual, and the individual in relation to the team, so that supervisor and supervisee can focus together on the children, issues, and tasks. PACE is central to this process. Critical to this is an understanding of acceptance: the emotional experience of the supervisee is not right, nor wrong, it just is. Once the supervisee experiences this, they feel validated, less judged, and, therefore, more able to focus on the evaluative parts of the supervision.

Let's consider another supervision conversation between Ralph and his manager.

In the Team Manager's view, Ralph has been intervening too quickly when Bill and the other kids in the home have been challenging to the female staff. The female staff have commented on this to Ralph and asked him not to intervene unless he is asked to do so. Ralph appears to think that it is his job to defend the female staff. The Team Manager has started supervision, as always, with checking in with how Ralph is doing. This time Ralph says he is fine, and he genuinely is.

Team Manager: 'It's really great that you are feeling all is fine at the moment, feeling useful not useless. I want to chat with you about something I'm curious about. I've noticed, and the female staff have noticed, that you tend to intervene when the kids are challenging towards them. I think a couple of them have tried to talk with you about this.'

Ralph (a little defensive): 'Have they? I don't remember. Why did they tell you?'

Team Manager: 'Good question and I get you're feeling a bit defensive. I wonder if you're thinking, "Are folk talking about me behind my back?" Their view would be that they have tried to talk with you and your view is that intervening is part of your job. They asked me to talk with you and then maybe we can chat together. Do you remember the other evening? I was there, too. Bill was shouting, calling the female staff whores, threatening to physically harm them. You stepped in telling Bill to stop it. He said no and turned his anger on you. All credit to you, you stayed regulated and the situation calmed.'

Ralph (quizzically): 'So what's the problem? Everything calmed.'

Team Manager: 'It did. I am wondering, though, is it because you're a man and you think you need to protect the women?'

Ralph: 'Of course. I don't want them to get hurt.'

Team Manager: 'That's honest. I wonder how the women feel about your view that they need protection and how Bill experienced you intervening? I think that's what they've tried to talk with you about. Our view is that they want to show the kids that women have the same authority as men. Bill, with his past experiences of couple relationships, needs to see a way of relating that demonstrates that both men and women can be authoritative and keep him safe. Do you agree?'

Ralph: 'I'm not sure. My dad always had, and still has, the last word in our house. I mean he wasn't violent or anything, but he laid the law down when I was a kid. That felt safe for me. Mum was one of those "wait until your father gets home" mums. Mind you, he never did anything apart from tell me off.'

Team Manager: 'Okay, so I see in your house growing up the man, your dad, had the final word. That was okay for you. It was safe, you knew where you stood. So you try to do "a dad" – keep the women and the kids safe?'

Ralph: 'Yes, I guess so.'

Team Manager: 'Can you see that although that was okay for you it's not okay for the kids or the women here? You're going to have to work to change that behaviour because it's reinforcing that men have authority and women don't.'

Ralph: 'Phew, I've just never thought about that before. This job, it challenges everything!'

Team Manager: 'It sure does, but you are up for it, I know you are. Now, let's go and sort out a time to meet with the women and chat about how they're going to help you not poke your nose in!' (Said playfully.)

Notice that supervision within complex environments needs to provide a culture in which difficulties and challenges for the individual, within the team and with the children, are talked about. Remember the phrase 'the elephant in the room'? The elephant takes up space but is never noticed or mentioned. Within DDP, we always advocate that the elephant is named! If not, the conflicts and difficulties are likely to escalate. Alternatively, the supervisor might try to sort the problem out in a more simplistic way that doesn't actually deal with the issue.

- *Reflective practice:* The structure of meetings fosters an atmosphere of reflective practice. This includes regular team meetings as well as individual planned or requested meetings. These do not just attend to the business at hand but allow everyone to step back from the immediacy of the business and reflect on what they are doing, why they are doing it, and where they want to get to. This is a time to notice impacts the individual is experiencing and to make sense of them. A staff member, for example, has an opportunity to reflect on the way a particular young person is triggering them, leading to a defensive response. With this understanding they are better prepared next time and more able to stay open and engaged to the young person. Reflective practice also provides opportunities for team dynamics to be explored. A culture of open and engaged reflection on points of strength and tension allows conflicts to be managed as patterns within the team become better understood.

Woodier illustrates that '[r]eawakening compassion begins with understanding trauma' (2019, p. 2) by quoting another residential child care worker from Aberdeen, Scotland:

> We have one young person who displays a really high level of emotional need and that's incredibly draining on the whole staff team. We check in with each other and make sure we have regular discussions. In order to reawaken compassion, we have taken the timeline to team meetings. We go through it and look where a young person has come from and the trauma that they have experienced. We remind ourselves that the young person isn't doing something because they won't do it but because they can't do it. We think about the unmet need within a young person's developmental trajectory. (2019, p. 2)

When working in the DDP way, the authors are of the opinion that the availability, use, and valuing of both external therapeutic support and facilitation of reflective practice are absolutely essential. Supervision and reflective practice are therapeutic; however, neither are therapy. Working relationally is personally and professionally challenging and undoubtedly triggers all of the adults' attachment histories whether for better or worse. The adults need to know that they can access therapeutic support for themselves that is provided by the organization, is confidential, and is relationally informed.

With regard to reflective practice, a DDP practitioner, consultant, or trainer, knowledgeable about the joys and challenges of residential care, can provide regular opportunities for teams, whether care or education, to come together. The primary focus is adult well-being. How are individuals in the team? How is the team? The involvement of an external DDP professional means that the whole team, including the manager and leaders, can be reflective together, sharing experiences, sharing understanding, and developing a shared language.

A care worker from Kinbrae, a residential setting in Scotland, described the meaning of shared experiences, understanding, and language for their work (Emond & Burns, 2022):

> [Y]ou have more empathy, you have, obviously, there's not a single person in this world that hasn't got a backstory; everyone's got a story. And you come to work sometimes, and you leave your story at the door. And sometimes you have these groups, and you end up sharing your stories and you, you will get shared somebody else's stories. And it does mean you have a better relationship to each other. Whenever we do like our sessions with [the consultant] and that and we do it as confidential and as within the room, only share what you want to share, but sometimes it's good to, to understand the reason why it might be a person got into this role when, you know, why they work maybe that wee bit different from you because we're not all going to work the same way (Interview, Pru, 27/8/21). (p. 32)

Within this consultancy, there is also opportunity to revisit DDP training, relating DDP principles to the adults' experiences with each other and with the children.

Team working that builds attachment-focused relationships

When a leadership team is steering a DDP-informed philosophy of practice, it facilitates team working that promotes key attributes among the staff team:

- *PACE as the guiding attitude:* Human relationships are messy. We are all prone to becoming defensive at times and it is at these times when working together is at its most difficult. This tension in the team is both inevitable and necessary. From tension can arise creativity and change. A culture of noticing and talking about this can help manage the tensions that inevitably arise. The adults then have a better understanding of each other and why they are doing or thinking as they are; with this understanding comes an improved working together based on mutual respect.

This is when a culture of being PACEful can be so helpful. The attitude of PACE allows all within the team to be open and engaged with each other and helps the team to move on from moments when defensiveness has arisen.

- *Modelling:* PACE also facilitates positive role modelling between staff. The children watch how staff relate to each other. They notice how everyone relates to everyone else, including the way that race, gender, sexuality, and disability intersects with this. For example, noticing how the men treat the women, how the gay member of staff is respected, how those with obvious differences are included, and how racist attitudes are avoided. This is a huge responsibility to model to children who have come from a variety of home environments with levels of disrespect, violence, and negative attitudes to each other. Staff teams have an opportunity to model respect for each other, including at points of conflict and disagreement. This is an important corrective experience for young people who are going to grow up and take their place in the world. This is the core of helping children to have successful relationships in the future.

  Following on from this is the importance of modelling relational repair: noticing when the relationship has potentially been harmed by the interaction and acknowledging it. The essence of this repair is letting the other know that the relationship is valued and more important than the issue that has led to the tension. As the children live in a culture in which the importance of relationship is being modelled, they in turn start to value relationships more and learn to offer their own repairs when they experience tension and conflict with both adults and peers.

- *Affirmations:* Within the staff structure are opportunities to notice, affirm, and celebrate the good work that is happening within the home. It is these positive things that allow the home to offer a supportive, safe environment. This might be a specific handling of an incident with a child. Equally, however, it could be acknowledging the structure that the administrator has successfully put into place, the revised menus that the cook has put together, or the new approach to supervision that one of the managers has just introduced. This is something that often feels uncomfortable for those of us who have grown up in a culture in which affirmation is low. Affirmation is different from praise. We tend to use praise as a form of evaluation, often with a motivation to increase the behaviour of the other person. While there is nothing wrong with praise, for people who are already feeling insecure, it can lead to defensiveness. While it is nice to be approved of, it also leads to worries about maintaining this approval. The focus is on the behaviour – am I good enough? – rather than the person – am I valued by you? Affirmation offers a relational experience of noticing and enjoying together something that has gone well. Shifting from praise to affirmation for both staff and children can shift the culture of the home from one of feeling judged to one of mutual celebration.

This creates an atmosphere of safety within which people can also talk about points of disagreement. It allows the team to come together with those mutual assumptions of 'we are all good people, doing the best we can'; when this is understood, it becomes easier to reflect on times when we have not felt we have done our best. We all know we are good people and that we can sometimes make mistakes. Notice that this shift moves from an attitude of 'you are wrong', to noticing a behavioural choice that went wrong.

According to Emond and Burns (2022), reflecting during ongoing supervision builds staff members' confidence that they were doing things correctly, as demonstrated in this interview quotation:

Annie: Yeah, I think it was confirming, it's what we were already doing. But having, you know, [the consultant] then always keeping on top, and having these talks with [the consultant] you know, just reminds you and keeps you – 'yeah, I am doing the right thing' – and it makes a big difference that you've got somebody that's, although, putting into words what you were doing before, we were doing all this but there's not a…a name for it. You know? And it's always nice to have that refreshing talk of why we're doing it, you know the reasons, and I like having the DDP, you know, getting that every so often. It's good (Interview, Education Team 3, 17/6/21). (p. 35)

- *Storytelling:* This is a way of communicating without lecturing. Communication within teams is critical to the good functioning of a residential organization. DDP encourages a focus on sharing stories rather than giving lectures within this communication. This involves holding curiosity about self and others and a focus on finding meaning together. Sharing stories is more collaborative and allows each person's experience to be appreciated. Through the sharing of these stories, a way forward can be discovered. The team are finding ways to figure out together what is happening and what to do about it, whether this is a team conflict, a challenge a child is presenting, or a frustration because of external constraints. This storytelling approach is then mirrored with the children.

  Storytelling involves both a sharing of experience and the conveying of this with a tone of voice that is not critical or lecturing but conveys deep interest in the other. In validating the experience of the other, this also gives space to allow healthy venting. It is okay to share experience which can be hard to talk about (e.g. 'I hate him just now', 'PACE is a load of rubbish'). These are experiences that can feel uncomfortable to share, but in the sharing of it the experiences themselves can be reduced.

- *Playfulness:* A good sense of humour is essential when working in a challenging environment. A team that laughs together works well together. The 'P' of PACE is an anchor for good team working and to help children feel comfortable in relationships. When people feel safe and supported, playfulness naturally follows. A DDP-informed approach pays attention to this. We focus on having fun together, even among the seriousness of the care being provided, and notice when fun is getting lost. At these moments the team can think together about how to bring fun back in. Making sure that playfulness is valuing of others is also important; there is no room for sarcasm, sneaky lectures, or evaluation when being playful.

  Playfulness enables the team to take their foot off the pedal at times. This can be helpful when tensions are high and frustrations are being experienced with the children or each other. Notice when a lot of 'shoulds' are creeping into people's expectations. This highlights that the staff are holding unrealistic expectations that the children or other adults can't meet at this moment. Moving back from this place and focusing on fun and well-being can return the team to a place of balance where they hold expectations that are realistic and provides an environment that is fun and supportive.

Notice, too, that playfulness is the opposite of shame. A home which has good structures, supports, rhythms, and routines alongside a healthy dose of playfulness and fun is a home where shame is low.

Team working that notices and supports blocked care

When caring for children in states of blocked trust, the adults can develop blocked care. This is a biological response to managing the pain of frustrated relationships. The carer is offering reciprocity, and the child remains firmly in control; the carer offers connection, and the child rejects it; the carer offers support, and the child holds onto self-reliance. When caring for a child who can't enter into reciprocal relationships with us, we are not getting the relationship we need and there is a higher risk that our caregiving circuits will shut down just as children's care-eliciting circuits have. Neither child nor carer can engage in intersubjective relationships, and the carer experiences no joy in parenting. It becomes a job to do, and a sense of fulfilment is low. The risk of blocked care increases with the level of stress the caregiver is experiencing; this includes external stressors, such as a bereavement, illness, or money worries. Social isolation and a lack of support also increase this risk.

Team members can support each other, offering protection from blocked care and noticing when a colleague is moving into this state. Increasing self-care, social support, and opportunities for reflection with trusted colleagues and managers can all make a significant difference.

How supported adults within a cohesive team can care and support the children

A good, functioning team, underpinned by a consistent philosophy of care, is well supported and taken care of so that attention can focus on the care and support that the children need. This involves good working together to facilitate the individual support for the child.

Emond and Burns (2022) say that when staff study DDP principles, their approach becomes more consistent and aligned, as affirmed by the following staff quotation:

> And I definitely think DDP as a philosophy has given Kinbrae the foundations they need for kids to offer that consistency in our value base and what we do, what we stand for, how we work with kids, and it's given kids that added security and safety of adults, that all adults are on the same page, all adults do the same thing. They all help us reflect and repair in the same way. And they all help us talk about and sit within the difficult (Interview, Casey, 26/10/21). (p. 33)

Conclusion

Residential care is a complex environment within which we care for children who have struggled to live in family homes. The range and experiences of the children and adults provides a dynamic environment with potential for tension and conflict as well as opportunities for joy, growth, and healing for everyone.

Within this chapter we have explored how the DDP model can inform the setting up of the residential environment, providing a philosophy of practice which cares for and supports the adults, enabling the adults to support and care for the children. There is a congruence of support that moves through the organization from top down and bottom up.

CHAPTER 7

Managing the Pain of What Happens

Emotional pain is part and parcel of the experience of residential interventions. Children come to residential homes because their emotional pain causes them to act out in dangerous ways. The separations involved in leaving home to go to a residential setting can add to the burden of emotional suffering. The intervention itself involves revisiting painful events. Often to be successful, residential care needs to awaken the urge to be cared for and to be in relationships, a longing that caused the child substantial pain in the past. Upsets naturally happen when children with significant emotional and behavioural issues are brought together under one roof. Then there's the pain of success. When residential care is helpful, it results in taking risks, such as being vulnerable and trusting. Even when success means a joyful reunion with loved ones at discharge, the child likely leaves behind people who have understood, supported, and cared for them.

It is essential to acknowledge pain as an integral part of residential care and to have an explicit and sensible approach to dealing with those upsets. It is important to recognize that pain is not to be avoided – it's part of life. As James Baldwin put it, '[n]ot everything that is faced can be changed; but nothing can be changed until it is faced' (1962, p. 38). In fact, by dealing effectively with traumatic events and the pain they cause, some people experience post-traumatic growth (Tedeschi & Calhoun, 1995). Our experience is that when a child successfully deals with trauma, they end up feeling bigger than whatever happened to them. They are on a journey that starts with feeling beaten down and diminished by trauma and ends up with feeling expanded by the way they have dealt with it.

At the same time, staff give their all to help, and sometimes the kids don't get better. It is wise to have an approach to pain that is both therapeutic and preserves the well-being of the staff. This is addressed in this chapter.

The pain of children in residential programmes

In some ways, residential care provides asylum from suffering (Bloom, 2017). The child may have been removed from an abusive situation or a situation of neglect. They may have had multiple placements and separations. They may have been out of control in ways that caused suffering to others as well as themselves. Residential care promises the child will be safe, have their basic needs met, and be treated with kindness, compassion, and understanding. The placement will be stable for the time they are there because the facility knows how to handle the dysregulations that led to admission. Any intervention will address the behaviours that cause the child to suffer. They will learn impulse control, appropriate expression of emotion, and how to get along with others.

It's important to recognize that children carry their trauma with them. Many have experienced themselves as having failed, in the home, in school, and in life. A number have been the target of abuse by their caregivers because of a disability, such as autism, cerebral palsy, or stuttering. Others have been attacked by peers because they belong to a non-dominant racial or ethnic group, or because of their gender identity or sexual orientation.

Children experience pain inherent with living in a residential setting. There can be the pain of separation from whatever family admitted them there, along with the pain of feeling they were unacceptable and sent away. There are the daily pains of hurt feelings, restricted freedoms, school failures, and receiving bad news, like finding out that their parents' parental rights have been terminated. There is pain from how children treat each other. When you put children together who all have emotional dysregulation, it's inevitable that they will treat each other badly, at least at times.

There is also unexpressed or unacknowledged pain, such as frightening experiences children have told no one about and worries that these will happen again in this place. They may worry that they will be forced to talk about what happened to them. They may worry that no one will care what happened to them. As they feel safer and begin to trust more, they may experience the fear that the people they are becoming close to will be taken away or that they gave up their protective isolation too soon.

Finally, there is the pain of saying goodbye at discharge. It may be the closest they have gotten to other people, adults, and children alike. Will they find companionship like that again? For some, they leave at a time that makes sense, when they have made gains they feel good about and that have prepared them for their next step. They are going back to a familiar place with decent people who are prepared to welcome and care for them. Yet even in these best-case scenarios, they may find themselves anxious about how it will go. Have things really changed? Will they fail again? Then there are those children whose discharge is filled with uncertainty. They are leaving sooner than would be best due to funding issues or other external demands. They are going somewhere they haven't visited before, and they don't know who they will be with or what's in store for them. For some older adolescents, their discharge may be to a level of independent living before they are ready to care for themselves.

The suffering of these three time frames – what happened in the past, what's happening now, and what might happen in the future – can interact with each other. What is happening now may be intensified because it is reminiscent of past hurts. Uncertainty about the future may make what they are experiencing now feel worse. Understanding how past, present, and future interact can help us better comprehend the child's experience.

Handling pain in a non-traumatic childhood

All children experience painful events, no matter how good their childhood may be. Their bike is stolen, they don't make the team, or other kids laugh at them when they give a talk in front of the class. The painful experience may be bigger, like when a pet or a grandparent dies, their best friend moves away, or they have to repeat a grade in school.

As we read about in previous chapters, when a child has attuned and consistent parenting, they develop a sense of security that gets internalized. When they experience shame, their parent can regulate emotional distress and repair the relationship. These breaks in connection are short-lived, and the repair deepens the stability and intimacy of a child's connection with their parent. They develop the neural circuitry that allows for emotional regulation, giving them capacity to reflect on what has happened and to put this experience into words. The story they tell themselves about what happened makes sense to them, and it fits coherently into an integrated whole. The child's sense of self and their experiences are integrated and cohesive.

All this happens within the context of continued support of parents, who co-regulate the child's emotions, sharing in the big feelings that their child is experiencing. Feelings that are shared become more manageable and less intense. Parent and child talk about what happened, including the child's emotional reaction to it. As feelings are put into words, they become more understandable and less scary. Naming feelings causes changes in the amygdala's reactivity to negative emotional images (Lieberman *et al.*, 2007). As the parent enters the child's experience, there is a sense that the child and parent are 'in it together'. The presence of the parent decreases the intensity of their experience, a process known as social buffering, the observation that stress levels decrease when people are together (Kikusui *et al.*, 2006).

When our children are suffering, that can feel threatening to us as caregivers. Something is hurting our child, and we feel called to take action. If there's nothing we can do to arrest the cause of their anguish, we can become defensive to avoid feeling our children's pain. Nevertheless, as caregivers, we must stay open and engaged in order to enter our beloved child's experience, even when the child tells us how bad they feel. It can be tempting to solve the child's problem in those moments, rather than being present to what the child is feeling. Hughes and colleagues instruct us on how to embody an open and engaged manner. To be open, they say, the caregiver must allow themselves to be in contact with their own experience and that of their child (Hughes *et al.*, 2019). To be engaged, caregivers must allow themselves to be moved by their child's experience as well as their own. This sort of open engagement supports the child to feel the attuned presence of the adult, which in turn lessens the child's sense of being alone. The intensity of the suffering subsides as the child's affect is co-regulated by the parent's regulated state and by their reassuring presence.

As this process happens repeatedly over time, the child develops confidence that their parent will be responsive to their distress and the parent's comfort will be consistently available and reliably calming. Approaching the child's upsets, instead of avoiding them, builds the child's internalized sense of security, capacity for emotional regulation, and ability to reach out for help when challenges are greater than the child can handle alone. Each upset is an opportunity to reinforce these qualities. A similar process is required to handle the upsets of a child who has experienced developmental trauma, but there are some important differences.

Approaching a child's pain in the residential setting

Approaching a child's pain is a key element in developing a secure relationship that supports the child's growth. As with children who haven't experienced significant trauma, it's crucial for the parents and other caregivers of a child with early trauma to approach the child from an open and engaged stance. This open and engaged attitude conveys that the adult is interested in what the child is experiencing, no matter how painful. The adult wants to know about the child's hurts and lets themselves be touched by the child's suffering. The child senses that their relationship with their parent is important and sturdy enough to tolerate the parent's awareness of the child's distress.

Avoidance of the child's pain, in contrast to approaching it, communicates to the child that what they are experiencing is not acceptable. They may assume that their experience is not important enough to merit their parent's interest. They may conclude that their suffering is unmanageable for their parent. When adults avoid the child's heartache, the child may conclude that their suffering can't be shared without causing others' harm, and they continue to be alone in their anguish. Therefore, it is essential that the pain of a child in residential care is not ignored or avoided, but approached with compassion, care, and skill.

As mentioned in Chapter 2, children who have experienced early trauma and have an insecure pattern of attachment often hide their needs from others (Dozier, 2003). Therefore, it is possible for a parent or carer to inadvertently overlook a child's needs because the needs have been concealed. In our work in residential centres, we have observed some of the following reasons that children hide their painful experiences and need to be comforted:

- They are afraid of distressing their carers with their shame, grief, or terror. This can be an altruistic motive to keep from harming an adult they care about.

- They worry that if they burden their parent with their troubles, it will overwhelm their parent's ability to provide for their basic needs.

- Their blocked trust keeps them from believing that any adult would want to help, even if they could.

- They have shut down their awareness of their needs to avoid the pain of knowing their needs have not been met.

- They want to prevent feeling rejected if their caregiver does not meet their need for comfort.

Because children in residential care hide their distress, staff need to understand the various ways that a traumatized child's distress can show up. Again, children in residential programmes often have intense feelings of shame, terror, and grief. They develop behaviours that camouflage and deflect these feelings and hide their need for co-regulation of the corrosive effect. As depicted in the shield against shame (see Figure 2.3), they lie about their actions, shift the blame to others, and minimize the harm they cause in order to turn down the intensity of their shame (Golding & Hughes, 2012). When confronted, cornered, and forced into accepting responsibility for what they have done, they often have a rageful meltdown, directing their hatred and disgust at themselves or at the person who they consider made them feel so bad.

As an example:

Robert was a 12-year-old boy who was regularly frustrated with small inconveniences and setbacks. It would often escalate into a full meltdown, in which he got really angry and would lash out at anyone who got too close. He had lived in his residential placement for eight months, and this frustration had not gotten much better. In one session, his therapist commented on his irritability and anger, but wanted to focus on what was happening right before the big upset. She homed in on those few seconds when Robert felt something wasn't going right, and Robert kept saying, 'It just makes me so mad.' The therapist slowed things down, asking, 'Right in that second, when you found out they ran out of pizza, what were you feeling in that second?' Eventually, Robert began to get teary and then immediately got angry, saying, 'I hate feeling sad. I hate this feeling! I'm not a baby. I shouldn't be crying.' As the therapist empathized with how bad the sadness made Robert feel, he got quieter and calmer. The therapist took a deep breath and then let it out.

Robert did the same. She said, 'Sadness is so upsetting for you. You'd rather feel anything rather than sad.' Robert agreed, and said quietly, 'I hate feeling sad.' The therapist asked, 'What is it about the sadness that you hate so badly?' Robert thought for a moment and said, 'What's the point of feeling sad? These things keep happening. It doesn't do anything to feel sad.'

Some children are unable to deflect or decrease the intensity of their shame, terror, or grief and are left to deal with unbearable affect alone. In those circumstances, they often develop an ability to shut down emotionally and even become unaware of their anguish. Dissociation, one way to shut down the pain, is an automatic, unconscious process of disconnecting from emotions or awareness of what is happening. It is an instinctive and protective measure that allows the child to make it through their suffering.

Children in residential care often dissociate when they are feeling frightened, overwhelmed, rageful, or in despair. When a person dissociates, they disconnect their awareness from their surroundings, sometimes by focusing on a 'happy place', a welcome scene or memory. Sometimes, they simply disconnect their awareness from their surroundings and aren't aware of anything, which one person we know refers to as 'being on screensaver'. Some traumatized children start dissociating in the face of stress early on, and then they disconnect more and more as protection from being overwhelmed by the pain that surrounds them.

As an example:

One girl, who had lost her parents in a tragic accident that she survived, reviewed a movie in her head for most of the day. Disconnecting from present-time reality, which was unbearably sad for her, and concentrating on an imaginary and pleasant reality, allowed her to cope with her life situation. For the first few weeks of residential treatment, staff were not aware that she was engaging her imagination in this way. A curious staff member discovered this fact when she wasn't very responsive to her questions. In asking 'Where are you just now?' she discovered what the child was doing.

Each child living in a residential home has their own unique patterns of distress – what causes it, how they handle it, how it looks, and what helps them manage it. This is one reason that it is important for a child to have one or two key staff members who connect with them and really get to know them. As discussed in previous chapters, these key staff members' role is to build trust with the child and learn what stirs them up, causes them shame, signals their distress, and how the staff can best help the child calm down. They can communicate what they learn to the rest of the team so everyone can be on the lookout for signs of distress.

What to handle when

By now, we know that the goal of residential care is not the avoidance of pain but creating a way to approach the child's pain with compassion and sensitivity. When we observe or suspect a child is in distress, we want them to feel our presence and to help them tell us what they are feeling. Sometimes, it is possible to talk with the child about their distress right then and there, and sometimes it's better to wait. We need the right environment and circumstances to contain the emotion. If it is a smaller upset, it can be handled where we find ourselves, whether on the playground, when lining up for school, or in the dining area. If it is a bigger upset, it needs a quiet place without interruptions. Sometimes, you don't know how big the upset is until you start the conversation. One way to manage is to say something like this:

> 'I can tell that something big is happening for you right now. Can you hold on until we get back to our cottage, or does it feel like it's going to leak out everywhere now? Okay, let's walk back to the cottage together. You walk beside me and help me guide the rest of the kids the right way back. We've got a few new kids right now, and I am not sure they have learned the way.'

If the child says that the issue is really big, they may be hesitant to tell you about it. You can say:

> 'Sounds really important to get this right. Who do you think the best person to talk with is? You know, you could talk to more than one person. I am happy to come talk with your therapist if that helps. I can either sit there quietly or talk if you want.'

When a staff member talks with a child about their big feelings, they need to alert the right people about the conversation. Sharing information among the team members ensures that the care is integrated. Depending on the setting, others to inform may include the programme manager, case coordinator, nurse, or therapist.

PACE makes every interaction therapeutic (without being a therapy)

Residential caregivers who want to help their children take responsibility for their behaviour would do well to follow Dan Hughes's advice to connect with the child before correcting them. As we have seen, shame, the sense that one is defective or unlovable, occurs earlier in development than guilt, which is remorse for how we have harmed another. Until a person has learned to handle shame, they cannot experience guilt (Tangney & Dearing, 2002). Being told they have done something wrong (or becoming aware of it themselves) only increases the sense that there is something wrong with them. Their attention is totally fixed on how bad they are, and it is too excruciating to consider that they may have caused another to suffer. But when we connect with a child who is experiencing a toxic level of shame, when we use a PACE attitude and co-regulate their affect, and when we follow them away from the topic temporarily to help decrease the intensity of what they are feeling, we make their shame tolerable.

As an aside, we have noticed that well-meaning professionals who do not appear to be aware of the shame dynamics of children who have suffered developmental trauma take the traumatized child's lack of remorse as a sign that they have a conduct disorder, meaning their 'bad' behaviour is wilful and deliberate. As is described in Chapter 11, they may even write in their official evaluations and reports that the child is a budding sociopath, meaning that they will never develop a healthy concern for others. The evaluating professional predicts that the child's future is destined to be one filled with law enforcement contact and time spent behind bars. We have worked with a number of children who have received such reports, and it is often clear that they *do* care about the harm they cause; they simply can't bear the shame that awareness of that harm inflicts upon them. When their shame is co-regulated, they develop the capacity to feel guilt and remorse, and their reaction to harming others shifts from feeling like a bad person to feeling bad for harming another.

Here is an example of this shift from a child feeling shame, which emerged as rage, to guilt about her behaviour.

Mila was a nine-year-old girl who was sexually abused by her grandfather for four years. Her rage, which took the form of doing things to harm the family's cat, Rosebud, led to a residential admission. After 14 months in the facility, her therapist revisited how she had treated the cat. 'I remember when you arrived here, and we talked about how you hurt Rosebud,' said her therapist. 'You told me that you didn't care that your family loved Rosebud and that they were upset that you had hurt her. I'm wondering if you still feel the same way.' Mila told her, 'I do care,' and looked sad as she said it. Her therapist said, 'Sometimes, hurting someone makes us feel terrible about ourselves. We can't even stand to think we did it.' Mila replied, 'I just felt so bad about what I did that I didn't know what to do.'

The more cycles of moving through pain with PACE the child experiences, the more they become confident in their ability to manage painful emotions, thoughts, and events. When the carer is able to use a PACE attitude to address shame, terror, or grief in one of their children, it demonstrates that the pain is not overwhelming to the carer. Demonstration is more powerful than words alone. The child can see with their own eyes that the caregiver is able to stay regulated and to accept that the child has had quite a difficult experience. The child sees that the caregiver still has their wits about them enough to be curious about the child's experience. The caregiver can even put themselves in the shoes of the child, empathizing with how frightening or sad the experience was for them. As the affect is co-regulated and the mood lightens, the caregiver's playfulness shows that the carer has tolerated the child's pain. The playfulness the caregiver and child can feel in each other demonstrates to them both that they made it through the experience together.

It can be heartbreaking to see a child suffer. Here's the advice we give staff who are approaching a child in deep distress: Remember that we're talking to the child who has survived, not the child who wasn't sure they would survive. A child in agony may feel they won't survive what they are feeling, but we know that they can. When we hold the perspective 'this child is a survivor', we have a sense that things will turn out alright. We can protect ourselves from the contagion of the danger the child is experiencing. We can remind ourselves that going back through the experience is not the same as the child going through the events themselves. If a parent held a gun to a child's head, as happened to one of our patients, and now the child is telling you about it, the event is not happening now. Even if the child is fully reliving the experience and their nervous system has shifted to an absolute state of fight-or-flight hyperarousal, no one is going to shoot the child with a gun at that moment.

A reason that thinking about things in this way is helpful is that when the child comes out of the deep end of the experience, they are more open to experiencing themselves as the one who survived, maybe for the first time. They have just relived the experience in a real way, and they made it through. Their present-time experience of making it through is a bridge to their sense of survival. Since they can connect with the feeling that the past situation was difficult, and here they are now, they can distinguish that past moment from the present moment. A PACE attitude comes into play again here with the caregiver saying:

> 'Wow, you were such a brave girl to make it through those big feelings you just had. You weren't sure you could do it at first, but [with a huge smile on the caregiver's face] you did it! And you know what? You also made it through all those hard things back then. What a brave, brave girl you are!'

You know that you are making progress when she lets out a deep sigh, matches the caregiver's huge smile with one of her own, wiggles around a bit, and says, 'That's right. I'm a brave, brave girl!'

When children have experienced unimaginable horror, we may feel wholly inadequate to be of any help to them. At these times, we can consider that their aloneness in their experience is now the biggest issue. If we can *accompany* the child through their experience, walking alongside as they tell us what it was or is like, then the experience can change. When they recall that experience in the future, they have the opportunity to feel our presence with them, and that sense of being accompanied is an encouragement that has healing powers.

While this chapter reviews how to work with the pain that the children in our care have experienced, we also need to remember that joy and delight are crucial parts of the human experience, too. If we focus only on the pain that a child feels, then the child comes to identify with the trauma, as in 'that's all I am – a traumatized child'. But the child is more than the traumatic things that have happened to them. In non-traumatic development, a child and parent repeatedly experience positive moments together. They look at each other, examine bugs together, laugh, and enjoy sharing the delight of being with one another. Joining together in enjoyment builds the child's capacity to experience joy. In the tender closeness of sharing pleasant feelings, the child learns that it's safe and wonderful to be connected, that relationships are a source of joy, and that they themselves are a delight.

We can offer a traumatized child opportunities to play, to be silly, and to have fun. Sharing pleasurable moments can be challenging for them. First of all, the child's shame is a barrier to allowing joy. As Dan Hughes puts it, '[s]hame etches its message into [their] muscles, [their] heart, and [their] mind: You are flawed. You bring no joy to others. You are bad and without merit' (2017, p. 34). In addition, it can be difficult for the traumatized child to stay emotionally regulated when excited or gleeful. The strong affect of these states can be overwhelming in the same way that strong negative feelings can be. Just as a PACEful attitude regulates negative affect, so too does PACEfulness help children manage their potentially destabilizing pleasurable feelings as well. Supported by this co-regulation, the child learns little by little to tolerate sharing enjoyment with their caregivers until they can relax into moments of mutual delight.

PACE widens the window of tolerance

Dan Siegel introduced the idea of a 'window of tolerance' to indicate the range of emotional intensity a person can handle and still function well (see Figure 7.1) (1999, p. 253). Within the tolerable range of intensity, the person is able to think logically and abstractly, to reflect upon themselves and their environment, and to develop flexible and adaptive responses to the situation in which they find themselves. If a person experiences something that is more intense than that tolerable range, or less intense, it interferes with their usual ability to think, feel, or act, and we say they are emotionally dysregulated.

Simply stated, within the window of tolerance, we feel open to experiencing life as it happens. Outside the window of tolerance, we are destabilized and feel a need to defend ourselves from what life presents us.

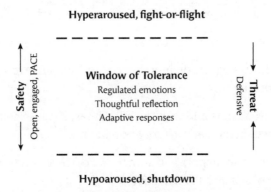

When an experience falls within the window of tolerance, a person maintains good functioning, meaning that they're able to regulate emotions, reflect thoughtfully, and respond adaptively. Relating to a person with an open, engaged, and PACEful attitude conveys a sense of safety, widens their window of tolerance, and allows them a greater range of experience while maintaining functioning. Defensive postures convey a sense of threat, which narrows their window of tolerance, meaning that the person is only able to function well within a narrow range of experience.

Figure 7.1: The Window of Tolerance
ADAPTED FROM SIEGEL, 1999.

Children who have experienced developmental trauma often respond to many things around them as if they represented a major threat. The range of experiences within which they can function is smaller, and we say they have a narrowed window of tolerance. In addition, as we have discussed in this chapter, traumatized children have been subjected to more frequent and painful experiences, so the burden of what they have been asked to tolerate is greater. Both their narrowed capacity and their increased exposure to painful circumstances cause them to live much of their lives outside their window of tolerance in hyperaroused, fight-or-flight states or in a state of hypoaroused shutdown. Children who are hyperaroused are impulsively reactive rather than thoughtfully reflective, and their reactivity continues to provoke conflictual inter-actions in a vicious cycle, increasing the likelihood that the child will experience hostile social relations.

The functions that support a child to heal from early trauma are available within the window of tolerance. Therefore, a child with a constricted range of manageable experience can't access these abilities. Among other things, a contracted window of tolerance is associated with the following conditions:

- physical sensations, emotions, thoughts, and events are inter-preted as dangerous, even when they are benign

- traumatic triggers cause repeated emotional dysregulation

- inability to curb intense emotions and physiological arousal

- chronic dysregulation inhibits access to cognitive resources, such as reflection

- can't learn new and adaptive responses, because a child who is focused on danger can't focus on learning

- unable to incorporate traumatic experiences into a coherent sense of self and life narrative.

How can we widen a traumatized child's window of tolerance, giving them access to brain functions necessary for their healing? As we have learned, PACEful interaction is one of the main strategies used within a residential facility to co-regulate a child's too-intense emotions. The PACE attitude provides social buffering that dampens the intensity of the child's affects, and the lowered intensity may fit better within that child's ability to tolerate. As we repeatedly support a child's emotional regulation through PACEful, intersubjective interactions, the child is desensitized to those levels of intensity, meaning that they are not as frightening and the child doesn't feel as out of control. In other words, a PACEful attitude helps make the intolerable tolerable (Sanders & Thompson, 2022). This widens the window of tolerance.

During some moments of residential treatment, the child doesn't start out with too-intense emotions, but rather our interactions with the child evoke emotional intensity. We need to set limits or ask a difficult question that we know might trigger a reaction. It could be a moment in a session when the therapist needs to ask about something that happened and knows that the child is likely to feel shame. In both cases, we know we are bound to stretch the child beyond what is comfortable. Porges calls this stretching beyond what is comfortable 'neural exercise' and says that it also can widen the window of tolerance (2017, pp. 23–24). While we don't set out to cause these sorts of reactions, we know that they can be a collateral consequence of what we need to do. So, we support the child using the two hands of parenting – delivering the message about the limit on the one hand and supporting emotional regulation with PACEful relations on the other. Because extreme reactivity to limits and being told 'no' is a common reason for admission to residential homes or treatment, assisting the child to increase their tolerance for these occurrences can have important therapeutic benefits.

The pain of awakening love

Another major goal of residential treatment, as the subtitle of Dan Hughes's book *Building the Bonds of Attachment* proclaims, is '[a]wakening love in deeply traumatized children' (2017). As we have seen, they have shut down their attachment longings because these needs have been unmet, mishandled, or exploited. The child desperately wanted to be seen, nurtured, and cherished, but they experienced the wrenching pain of rejection instead. Now, they have concluded that it is better not to need people than to experience continued rejection. So, they do their best to push people away, even good people who have their best interests at heart, good people like the staff of residential settings.

The problem with this defence against rejection is that the child's attempt to survive without relationships leaves them struggling alone in the world. Their suffering doesn't get better from their solo efforts. If they are to heal, they need help from other people. But because they see people as dangerous, they see their attachment longings as threatening too. The beauty of the PACEful attitude is that it accepts the child's experience just as it is; even the child's rejection of attempts to connect are acceptable. A PACEful attitude then moves inside the child's experience with empathy and curiosity. Thus, the residential caregiver becomes a gentle but relentless relationship builder, one PACEful encounter at a time. Over time, the child lets down their guard and allows the caregiver to know more about them and to enter their world more fully. They are learning about emotionally safe relationships. In essence, the staff have assisted the child in widening their window of tolerance for feelings of closeness and connection, and this serves as the basis for establishing stable supportive relationships.

Managing transitions in residential care: The good ending

A wider window of tolerance and an awakened desire for and enjoyment of relationships is key to establishing a child's felt sense of security. We know that love, security, and permanence are important to a child's well-being and healthy development. Yet residential homes and interventions are often designed to be temporary arrangements, so one of the paradoxes of a residential setting is that we intend to awaken the child's attachment longings, encourage them to form a bond to at least one or two of the residential caregivers, then discharge them to another setting or family or maybe to an independent living setting. How do we keep these contradictory intentions from becoming just another cruel trick in the life of a child who has already known far too many?

Because residential care is often time-limited, transitions are built into the experience of living in a residential home. Children who live there come and go. Staff who work there come and go. For children who have had many changes not of their choosing, these transitions can be agonizing. If we don't help children manage the pain of these transitions, we know that they will attempt to shut down their attachment longings once again. As before, our goal is to support a widening window of tolerance for the pain inherent in human relationships, this time related to comings and goings, for greetings and goodbyes. A DDP-informed approach does not avoid the pain of endings. Instead, it understands that transitions, temporary and permanent, need to be proactively co-created.

One way to widen a child's or an adult's window of tolerance for the feelings associated with transitions is to highlight smaller endings. We can prepare the child for bigger transitions by increasing a child's awareness of the conclusion of easier-to-manage events and happenings. When an activity that a child enjoys is winding down, staff can alert them that the activity will come to an end soon. We can provide these alerts when it's the end of playtime, a meal, a class, a therapy session, or a visit from parents or loved ones. This is a common practice in working with children with a developmental trauma history because even 'easy' transitions can be difficult for these children. An additional step that can be added to these preparations for transition is to focus on the experience of the transition itself.

Here are some ideas as to how this can be achieved.

Kelsie, the teacher of 11- and 12-year-olds in the therapeutic classroom for a residential treatment centre in the US, was aware that the centre really wanted to help children learn to manage transitions. After discussion and planning with the larger team, Kelsie informed the students that they would have a new activity at the end of each class period. They would 'push pause' several minutes before the end of each class and do some breathing exercises together. Then Kelsie would invite them to think about something they had enjoyed about the class. When they had that in mind, Kelsie would set a timer and ask them to savour the thing they had enjoyed.

Kelsie had led the children through savouring exercises before and the children knew that savouring meant to take pleasure in tasting and enjoying food thoroughly or to appreciate an experience completely, especially by taking great delight in it. Kelsie started the savouring activity at ten seconds and now they had worked up to 30 seconds. After savouring, Kelsie asked the children to imagine saying goodbye to the experience, and saying, 'I'll see you again soon!' Then the children would write in their daily journal three words to say how they felt leaving that enjoyable experience. Some of the words that the children wrote included 'sad', 'bad', 'upset', 'lonely', 'confused', 'mad', 'happy', 'tricked', 'sorry', and 'nice'. The team on the residential unit started doing the same thing at the end of the day. The children would tell their enjoyable experience, 'Good night, friend. I'll see you tomorrow.'

Reflection

Imagine doing something you enjoy. Then imagine someone tells you that you need to stop doing that thing. Stop. Now. Notice how you feel. What sensations are you aware of in your body? What's your emotional reaction? What happens to your relationship with the person?

Take a few breaths until you return to a neutral state. Again, in your mind's eye, enjoy doing that thing again. Now imagine the person telling you to 'push pause' with what you are doing. Once more notice your physical sensations and your emotional reaction. What happens to your relationship with the person this time? What considerations do you have as a result of this reflection?

Among the changes we have seen in the US in the last 10 to 20 years is that the amount of time that a child stays in a residential treatment centre has decreased, and the way decisions are made has changed. When George arrived at KidsTLC[1] in 2008, children would stay in treatment for 9 to 18 months, with the residential staff, the child's family or foster care worker, and the child's local mental health centre working together

---

1   KidsTLC is a DDP-certified psychiatric residential treatment facility in Kansas in the US.

to decide how long the child needed to stay. Then, because the state switched to a managed care insurance model, lengths of stay decreased to around three months.

The changes in residential decision-making had repercussions beyond the change in the length of stay. Before the change, everyone felt there would be enough time to meet the treatment goals. After the change, they were never sure how long a child would get to stay. Children, families, and mental health centre and residential staff had trouble relaxing enough to focus on treatment. They all experienced these threatened transitions as assaults on their felt sense of security and permanence, which had a significantly negative impact on treatment.

A good ending to treatment, from a DDP perspective, acknowledges and preserves the relationships the child has developed, when possible. In addition, it is important to create a narrative with the child about the meaning of their time in the residential home, the nature of the relationships, and the work that was done. The narrative is captured in a form that the child can take with them and look back on for months and years after their stay has ended. Sometimes, it is a therapeutic letter, or an audio or video recording. Sometimes, the team sends a photo album along with the child. The therapeutic communication, whatever its form, can include the following elements:

- The team documents their relationships with the child. It may include statements like:

  - 'I really enjoyed getting to know you. I'll always remember that you were the boy who loved finding frogs.'

  - 'These are the things that we learned about each other...'

  - 'I remember when we repaired that old bicycle together.'

  There will be comments from as many of the people as possible at the home with whom the child interacted.

- The team help the child develop a catalogue of the therapeutic lessons learned while living in the home. One way to create this list is for different staff members to ask the child what they have learned and for the staff member to offer their ideas as well. The list could include statements like:

  - 'You learned that asking for help with your laundry wasn't such a bad thing after all. In fact, you kind of started to enjoy it when we washed your clothes together.'

- Another message to convey in this therapeutic communication is how the child knows their key people are still holding them in their hearts and minds. It may be a statement such as:

  - 'I'll always think of you when I eat Brussels sprouts, because you are the only kid I ever met who loved Brussels sprouts.'

If it is appropriate for the key person to stay in touch with the child, they may say something like:

  - 'I'll always be there for you. Here's how you can get in touch with me (or how I will contact you).'

If the child may be going to a less-than-desirable placement, the key person who is planning to maintain contact can say:

  - 'I'll always remember you as the girl with the biggest heart. While you have been here with us, you have realized how big your heart is. If you ever have trouble remembering that you have a big heart, or the people you are with don't seem to see it, just give me a call and I can tell you that I remember. You do have a big heart!'

- If the child is leaving the home before people feel they are ready, the therapeutic communication can acknowledge that too. It can say:

  - 'Well, no one is ready for you to be leaving us, but here we are. Sometimes, chapters end in the middle. Every ending is also a beginning. You are going to start a new chapter. Here are some questions left from the chapter with us: "What's all this nervousness around grown-ups about? How can I learn to feel comfortable in my body? What's the best way for me to get better at maths?" When you get answers to these questions, please give us a call to tell us what you discovered.'

Another aspect of a good ending to a residential stay is the rituals surrounding the child's departure. Some residential places arrange times for the child to meet with all the people who were important to them while they were there. Perhaps their key staff person goes with them to all of these goodbye chats. Often there is a celebration of the child's success, which may be a graduation of sorts, with cake, ice cream, and decorations.

At KidsTLC, the custom is for the children to sit in a circle. Each child tells the departing child something they admire about them, and the departing child tells each of their residential companions something they appreciate about them. Another facility we know of has a large tree painted on a wall. Each leaf represents one of the children who has stayed with them. Each time a child departs, another leaf with that child's initials is added to the tree. If and when the child returns to the facility for a visit, they can still find their leaf and initials on that tree. Another facility keeps the exiting children's photos in a photo album.

Supported discharge to maintain gains

At a certain point, KidsTLC began to accept referrals from other states in the US, sometimes across one or more time zones. Early in the process, there were children who made great gains in their residential treatment, but they were not able to maintain their gains once they got back home, or the plans made for community treatment fell through. The team met and reviewed the situation. To assure a successful transition home, they needed to make sure their process for accepting, treating, and discharging these children was robust.

KidsTLC increased its preadmission review process to assure that they had the means to address the child's issues in the programme and that there was a good plan to return the child home when treatment was complete.

KidsTLC asked the parents to stay in the area for three days at admission, to provide information about the child and to get oriented to the programme and DDP treatment approach. Parents met with various team members, including the therapist, care coordinator, unit programme manager, physician, and nurse. They returned every month or so for 2–3 days for more meetings, therapy, and education. When it was time for discharge, one or two staff members would accompany the child home and would stay for 2–3 days to assure that everything was going smoothly. The therapist continued family therapy sessions via televideo, often in conjunction with a local therapist, and even made two or three in-person visits following discharge at 4–6 week intervals. During these visits, plans would be revised and updated to address any unanticipated challenges. When it was clear that the child was stably established back at home, therapy was transferred to the local therapist.

This strategy accomplished the goals KidsTLC set out to accomplish. Children returned home successfully and were able to sustain the growth they experienced while in the centre.

Continued contact after discharge

It is often beneficial for residential staff to maintain contact with the child following their discharge. This contact may continue for weeks or months and sometimes much longer. As described above, one purpose of continuing the relationship is to support the child's successful return to the community and to help the child maintain the gains they made. Another intention is to provide a relational thread in the child's life. Contact with the staff member reminds the child that there is someone who knows who they are and what they have been through, especially when the child is discharged to a new placement. Furthermore, continued contact provides a parallel to how things happen in ordinary life. A child may see some of the people who are important to them, like aunts, uncles, and grandparents, on an infrequent schedule. Nevertheless, these relatives can fill a critical function for the child as additional caring adults who know the child and their life story.

From a practical standpoint, postdischarge conversations with the child are usually scheduled and may be via phone calls or televideo meetings. If the child lives nearby, they may visit the staff member directly at the facility. Conversations range from the child's daily activities, what they have been enjoying, who they have met, and any interesting events in the family. The conversation, especially when conducted in the lively form of affective-reflective dialogue with lots of PACE thrown in, invites the child back into this form of relating. Stories can emerge about the child's life, and the child is reminded that their experiences are worth knowing. Their sense of being valued and valuable gets a boost. When the child has returned to a difficult situation, as sometimes is the case, the staff member can remind the child that they know they are a good person, they have seen their good heart, and even if no one else is seeing it now, the staff member knows it is still in there (Dan Hughes, 2018, personal communication).

On occasion, the staff member may talk with the child about how they have been doing emotionally, how they have handled difficult situations, or any upcoming challenges. These topics should be planned for in advance to account for a child who becomes dysregulated. Usually, the staff member speaks first with the child's caregiver and finds out if there have been any big events in the child's life, how the child has been doing during the prior few days, and how they are at the moment. They also plan for how the caregiver will handle a situation in which the child gets upset or is likely to get upset on the call.

Many facilities in Canada, the US, and Europe prohibit staff contact with the child outside of the facility and after discharge. However, there are also countries where the continuation of relationships is valued. Edwina notes that, in Scotland, the importance of enabling loving relationships and the importance of the continuity of these beyond residential care is recognized and supported (The Promise Scotland Ltd., 2023).

KidsTLC recognizes the importance of such contact and has established a clear structure to provide ongoing connection while protecting the child from inappropriate contact. The structure starts with discharge planning, when teams at that facility discuss whether ongoing communication could be beneficial. Reasons that it might be helpful include the child is going to a new placement where they do not know anyone; the child has made only tenuous gains that need to be supported; or there is a good working relationship with the family and they would like to continue the contact. If the team recommends continued contact, they review the plan with their director, who needs to approve it. The plan includes the names of the staff member(s) who will stay in contact, how often, by what means, and how long into the future the contacts will continue. The plan specifies what communication looks like, meaning to whom does the staff member talk ahead of time, to whom do they report concerns, and whether there is continued review by the team. Last, the staff member documents the contacts in the same way they write other notes about a client.

A residential setting can have 'alumni weekends' where children who have graduated, along with their parents, come to reconnect, brush up on skills, and reflect on how they have learned and grown. Parents can also reconnect, receive support, and get a refresher in things like the PACE attitude and the two hands of parenting.

Conclusion

In this chapter, we have confronted the reality that children who come to residential placements bring emotional pain with them. These children have developed coping strategies that are maladaptive: they either create additional problems for the child and people around them, or they keep the child stuck in reactive patterns that perpetuate the experience of living in a hostile world. Residential staff are most helpful when they approach the child's pain with a PACEful attitude that co-regulates the child's emotional intensity, widens their window of tolerance, and co-creates new narratives about survivorship and success. When a child has learned to manage the pain of rejection by shutting down their attachment longings, the residential staff hold an intention to reawaken the child's desire to love and be loved. They interact PACEfully and repeatedly with a relentless aim to build a relationship with the child.

When a child is leaving the residential home, the staff take measures to create a good ending for the child, which acknowledges the relationships built and the gains accomplished and makes plans for continued contact when appropriate. A farewell celebration ritualizes the recognition that the child has grown, and they have developed new skills and awareness to prepare them for life in the community.

PART 3

HOW WE EMBED AND EMBODY DDP PRINCIPLES IN RESIDENTIAL SETTINGS

Building a Congruent Culture
of Hope and Healing

CHAPTER 8

Finding Hope in the Midst of Trauma

Moving from Compassion Fatigue to Compassion Satisfaction

At this point in the book, we hope our stories have shown you how using a DDP model provides a path to a better future for the children we work with. We, the authors, have each had our own sense of hope restored, first in encountering Dan Hughes's model, and then in seeing its miraculous effects at times over the past decades. This chapter journeys through the darkness of despair into which this work can bring as well as into navigational guides for finding your way toward the light of hope.

People are drawn to work with children who have experienced early trauma for a variety of reasons. In general, we want to make a significant difference in the life of a youngster who has faced substantial adversity. We may have encountered traumatized children as our friends when we were growing up. We may have been inspired by a mentor to study the treatment of child trauma. We residential workers may have experienced our own tough childhoods.

In each of these cases, we arrive hopeful that, using what we learned from our own early experiences and education, we can assist children to heal and recover from their traumatic experiences. We may have identified this work as part of our life purpose, a way of making meaning from our own suffering, or from what we witnessed of others' suffering. If our pain can be the catalyst for someone else's healing, we tell ourselves, then maybe it can be made to count for something. Therefore, there can be a lot riding on the residential caregiver's hope for success in treating the child's trauma; the hope for a different outcome is invested with a great deal of personal meaning. Our hope is a precious resource that will face numerous challenges as we move into this career, but, if managed with knowledge, skill, and compassionate understanding, it can be preserved and enhanced to the benefit of both the staff member and the people we work with alike.

This work, the success of which is so important to the child, the family, and the staff, is often emotionally tough or worse. It is not unusual for staff members to get a taste of the emotional state of the children we work with. We may feel an echo of the hopelessness, terror, confusion, and despair that the child felt during the abuse. We may feel the desperation, anger, and rage at the injustices perpetrated on the child. We may experience the emotional numbness and emptiness that a child is left feeling in the wake of abuse. To compound matters, we may be unprepared for the onslaught of these feelings. We may have arrived expecting to be filled with the satisfaction, joy, and hopefulness of serving in a significant role in turning around the life of a child. It can be a rude shock to discover that the work can leave a person emotionally drained and beaten down.

Mercifully, research and theory now clarify the ways that residential caregivers may be impacted in their work with a traumatized child. We list these specific complications and meet them head on because we recognize the importance of making all our experiences discussable. We also know that naming difficult emotions may even help to reduce their intensity (Kircanski *et al.*, 2012). In this process, we discover that a residential caregiver is at risk of blocked care, secondary trauma, and moral injury. At times, our own psychological issues may get stirred up, and we may feel temporarily destabilized by the work itself. We may come to know that our hope can be repeatedly threatened because the healing and recovery of the children we work with is by no means guaranteed. Children don't always get better. When they do get better, the child may leave the residential setting, and the staff member is faced with a loss. Sometimes, we are troubled because the child discharges to a situation that the staff deem inappropriate or less than optimal. No matter how robust the staff member's induction, onboarding, and training, working in residential care can feel overwhelming, with the adults often reaching a point where they wonder if this is the job for them. We examine the challenges of residential work, not to dampen our hope, but to secure it in reality.

We understand that a challenge can be both a hindrance as well as a call to show up in one's courage, strength, and idealism. This work is not easy, but neither is it hopeless. The late oncologist, author, and Harvard medical school professor Jerome Groopman (2004) provides us with wise counsel regarding the intersection of hope, clarity, and courage:

> Hope is the elevating feeling we experience when we see – in the mind's eye – a path to a better future. Hope acknowledges the significant obstacles and deep pitfalls along that path. True hope has no room for delusion... Clear eyed, hope gives us the courage to confront our circumstances and the capacity to surmount them. (p. xiv)

Our hope depends on seeing Groopman's path to a better future. That path includes ways to protect, nurture, and support our hope. Your caregiving presence is a therapeutic elixir for those young people whose symptoms of relational trauma are so severe that they require residential placement. How do we nurture and protect the hope on which this caregiving attitude depends? We look at ways the residential setting's management and leadership can support the staff. We also look at the structure of the facility, including the routines and rituals that provide support as well. In general, there are other adults available to support the staff. Then there are ways that staff can engage in self-care and self-development that boost their resilience in the face of stressful or even threatening circumstances. The goal of residential care, and our goal in writing this book, is to demonstrate that there is a path for a child to heal from even the worst trauma, and there is a path for us to do the work that affirms our intentions, our abilities, and our aspirations. When DDP-informed work is successful, it affirms life itself and elevates human dignity above all degradations that man's inhumanity to man has attempted to perpetrate. This work is truly a noble calling.

The neurobiology of caregiving

In *Brain-Based Parenting* (2012), Dan Hughes and Jon Baylin examine the neurobiological dynamics of caregiving in both animal models and human studies. They start by describing how early, healthy experiences with our own caregivers prepare our brains to manage stress, regulate emotions, and feel secure in our relationships. These are some of the capacities that comprise what Hughes and Baylin call 'the parental state of mind' (p. 45). The caregiving brain, therefore, has its origins in our first months and years of life, and is transmitted from one generation to the next through these earliest influences. Caregiving, when looked at from this perspective, originates from a set of neural circuits pro-grammed through the care we received from our caregivers.

As we recall from Chapter 3, Bill's first parents, Elijah and Adina, did not receive attuned and nurturing care from *their* parents. Elijah and Adina's neural circuits, therefore, were not prepared to handle stress or strong emotions well, and they did not develop a secure pattern of attachment. The arrival of Bill and Olivia presented them with chal-lenges they were not equipped to deal with or even tolerate. Elijah and Adina in turn failed to provide their children with attuned and nur-turing care, and Bill and Olivia were left without the ability to manage stress and emotions or to experience security in their relationships. In this way, the non-caregiving brain is also passed generation to gener-ation as well. Fortunately for Bill, his biological father, José, received good-enough care from his mother and aunt, and José's caregiving circuits were relatively intact. He was at least somewhat prepared to provide the corrective care that Bill needed so desperately.

For those of us wondering if our own childhood experiences have left us with the caregiving circuits needed to do this work, we can take comfort in knowing that we can develop what's called 'an earned secure attachment pattern' by identifying unresolved memories and integrat-ing them (Golding *et al.*, 2021). As we identify past experiences that are associated with increased present-time reactivity, we start to understand ourselves better. Through self-reflection and reappraisal, we make sense of our present-time reactions, opening the door to taking self-corrective action. As Golding and colleagues explain, '[f]or example, developing your need for connection if you tend to distance yourself emotionally; developing your capacity to soothe yourself when others make you anxious' (2021, p. 204).

Hughes and Baylin (2012) also review remarkable factors that prime us for caregiving when we become parents. They say, '[i]n some species, including humans, both mothers and fathers undergo powerful brain changes that shift the brains of both from other preoccupations to a keen interest in protecting and nurturing the young' (p. 30). The arrival of a child stimulates the release of neuropeptides, like oxytocin and vaso-pressin, which promote bonding in couples and between parents and children along with parental nurturing. Furthermore, oxytocin calms the amygdala's warning functions, making it easier for the parent to move into the social engagement system, the autonomic nervous system state associated with safety and connection. Additionally, a combination of oxytocin and dopamine intensifies the pleasure that comes from parenting. Finally, when a certain part of the hypothalamus in female mammals is primed by oxytocin, oestrogen, and progesterone, the body is prepared to nurse the newborn, and a number of other parenting behaviours emerge. If residential care workers who don't have children of their own are worried about their caregiving brains, Hughes and Baylin reassure us that 'non-biological parents can develop a nurturing brain; just being exposed to children can activate the caregiving system' (p. 31). George experienced a flood of paternal feelings the moment he first met and held his adopted daughter. With a sense of awe, he realized the moment felt just as miraculous as the birth of his biological son.

Blocked care and other challenges to caregivers

We find it helpful to review this neurobiology of caregiving because it highlights impersonal factors that are at play in working in a residential setting. Our early experiences prepare our neural circuits for caregiving, and being around children primes our parental behaviours, just as occurs in other mammals. However, under certain conditions, our motivation to care for our young residential charges wanes, a condition that Hughes and Baylin call 'blocked care' (2012). They say that the lovely parental behaviours we have just discussed can be blocked when raising children who push us away, threaten our safety, or counter our self-image as good-hearted, well-meaning people. We go into defensive states to protect ourselves from these dangers, but a chronically defensive state turns off parental behaviours. Therefore, blocked care can represent an impersonal neurobiological reaction as well.

To fully describe blocked care, Hughes and Baylin point out that there are five brain systems that we use to provide the care that all children need (2012). These brain systems are approach, reward, child reading, meaning-making, and the executive system. The first four systems have an interesting characteristic – they are reciprocally reinforced by activation of the corresponding system in the child. For instance, when we approach a child, if the child is comfortable with our approach and maintains the proximity, it strengthens our approach system. The same is true for the reward system, which is responsible for the pleasure we feel. If we have a pleasurable response to the child, and the child in turn responds to us with pleasure, our reward system is boosted. As caregivers operating from a parental state of mind, we approach our children and enjoy them simply because they delight us, not to get something for ourselves. Nevertheless, we receive a benefit from this reciprocal reinforcement: when our child delights in the delight we are feeling toward them, our approach and reward systems are strengthened and primed to stay in good working order.

When the child doesn't respond reciprocally, as is often the case in children who have experienced developmental trauma, our approach, reward, child reading, and parental meaning-making systems are not reciprocally reinforced, causing these brain systems to wind down. Lack of reciprocal reinforcement is another major cause of blocked care in parents of traumatized children as well as in residential workers. This winding down means that the wind goes out of our sails, our heart is no longer in the work. Our executive system allows us to continue to provide care to the children, but we are now just going through the motions. If we are not able to use the willpower of the executive system to act parental, the child's rejection causes us to retaliate in anger or to quit this work. Fortunately, our caregiving systems can be bolstered and sustained by reciprocal relationships with our friends, coworkers, and our other loved ones.

Once again, the neurobiological dynamics of these systems give us insight into the impersonal nature of blocked care, though it is often extremely distressing to a parent or residential worker. We may experience shame that our lack of caring feelings is a personal failing. This change in our functioning may represent a significant loss of identity for us – we are no longer the caring person we once experienced ourselves to be. We may feel we have turned into the opposite: an angry caregiver who blames the child for how we feel. When residential caregivers experience blocked care, which Hughes and Baylin also call 'stressed out parenting' (2012, p. 92), it can cause the following:

- feeling like things are threats when they actually aren't

- struggling to put things into proper perspective

- unable to stay emotionally regulated and to use our thinking brains

- feeling like our main job is to survive our current circumstances

- unreliable self-observation and self-assessment as well as inaccurate observation and assessment of the child

- difficulty resolving problems and conflicts

- overreacting to a child's negative attitude

- being overly critical of the child and oneself.

This dive into the neurobiology of caregiving also gives us insight into why we sometimes take things so personally when working with traumatized children. First, our caring brain circuits and hormonal responses to the presence of children ready us to devote ourselves to the children in our care. We feel they are 'our' children. For our work with children to be effective, it can't be academic or coldly clinical. We have to put ourselves into the work and be invested.

What's more, when we become emotionally dysregulated, neurobiological changes amplify our tendency to take things personally. Top-down cortical brain circuits help to contain emotions that come from bottom-up limbic circuits. When we become emotionally dysregulated, as we might if a child rejects our efforts to help them, the bottom-up circuits surge while top-down circuits diminish. When bottom-up, emotional, limbic-system neural circuits predominate, we tend to take things personally. This happens because top-down cortical circuits are offline and don't provide the reflective and reappraisal capacities that give us distance and perspective from our experiences. In these circumstances, our colleagues and mentors can supply external and auxiliary reflective capacity. We talk more about the role of external support later in the chapter.

Our experience is that a significant percentage of residential care workers are drawn to this work because their own early experiences make them aware of the pain of a traumatic childhood and the value of an understanding ear. The significance of their understanding can't be underestimated. It creates a wellspring of compassion and provides them with the confidence that the unbearable can be borne. The children they work with can borrow this conviction to bolster their own faith in the possibility that they can live a different reality.

At the same time, residential caregivers may still 'have unresolved memories of painful, frightening, or shaming experiences [which make them] prone to being triggered by their interactions with their children into unparental states of mind, during which they lose touch with what is really happening in the parent–child relationship in the moment' (Hughes & Baylin, 2012, p. 94). These episodes of emotional hijacking can be profoundly dispiriting to staff members for several reasons. The staff member may experience shame at a sense of loss of control, especially a loss of control that injures the relationship with a child. They may feel that they have switched into the role of perpetrator, a self-betrayal of their purpose in life to heal the pain caused by perpetrators of trauma. They may have a sense that their healing hasn't come as far as they thought and be left with a sense that they have been deceiving themselves.

Trauma and compassion fatigue in the residential setting

While it can be discouraging to consider the potentially negative repercussions of working with traumatized children, we can't maintain the hope needed to succeed in the work if we turn our heads away from these effects and pretend they don't exist. If we can see the challenges of this work plainly, we can develop plans for how to manage them. Therefore, we move forward resolutely to consider the literature on the psychological and emotional hazards of working with traumatized people, then later discuss how to manage them. These perils have been variously termed vicarious or secondary trauma, compassion fatigue, and burnout (Geoffrion *et al.*, 2016; Osofsky *et al.*, 2008; Pirelli *et al.*, 2020).

Charles Figley, who coined the term 'compassion fatigue' (1995), distinguished between primary and secondary trauma. In primary trauma, a person is the direct victim of a traumatic stressor, that is, the person was seriously threatened or directly witnessed a traumatic event. In secondary trauma, the person learns about a serious threat to someone significant in their life. Workers in a residential home may experience both primary and secondary trauma. They may be traumatized directly. For example, if they are assaulted by a child, or they may witness one child attacking another. They may experience secondary trauma by empathically listening to a child's stories of traumatic events, like the stories that Bill tells his therapist, Kiran, which we describe in Chapter 11. Secondary trauma may also be known as vicarious trauma, compassion stress, or compassion fatigue.

From this framework, we can conclude that blocked care often arises from a form of direct or primary trauma. Here's how it works: when a traumatized child deliberately rebuffs the care offered by a well-meaning adult, it can trigger a hurtful experience of rejection. As Hughes and Baylin point out, experiences of both physical and emotional pain result in similar patterns of brain activation (2012). As a result, the adult's brain processes emotional rejection in the same painful way that it would process a physical injury (Zhang *et al.*, 2019). Emotional injury is just as traumatic as physical injury. This can feel true even though another part of us knows that the child is rejecting our care to feel safe and in control.

Geoffrion and colleagues describe the symptoms of compassion fatigue that arise from secondary, vicarious traumatization (2016, p. 272):

- preoccupation with the recounted traumatic events

- avoidance and numbing

- an increase in negative arousal

- lowered frustration and tolerance

- intrusive thoughts of client's material

- dread of working with certain clients

- a decrease in the subjective feeling of safety

- a sense of therapeutic impotence

- a diminished sense of purpose

- a decreased level of functioning in a number of areas.

Yet, Geoffrion and his collaborators do not feel like compassion fatigue is an inevitable sentence for those working with traumatized youth. Rather, they say it is more likely to occur when workers are unprepared to accurately measure the effectiveness of their efforts, or they take their results as a reflection of their value. Furthermore, residential caregivers who aren't prepared to ask for and receive care themselves are at higher risk of compassion fatigue. One additional factor that increases a residential worker's stress is the weight that assuming responsibility for making important decisions can add to an already difficult job. We discuss that next.

Accountability stress and moral injury[1]

Geoffrion and colleagues (2016) describe how stressful it can be to make decisions about the lives of children who are at risk of harming themselves and others. In their article on compassion fatigue in child protection workers, they point out that the compassion fatigue model doesn't take into consideration the 'accountability stress' that child protection workers face. Additionally, they reflect on how intensely emotional it is for a child protection worker when there is a bad outcome for a child. In their examples, they contemplate situations in which a child commits suicide or is assaulted after the worker gives the okay for them to have a weekend away from foster care. These situations are the worst nightmares of people who dedicate their careers to caring for traumatized children. On the other hand, given the severity of the difficulties these children face and the dearth of resources often available to address them, it is no wonder that sometimes bad things happen.

Nevertheless, when there is a bad outcome, the worker is at high risk for self-blame and self-criticism (Geoffrion *et al.*, 2016). Similar to a traumatized child who blames their abuse on their own actions, the worker may find it less painful to criticize themselves than to experience the helplessness that comes from acknowledging that something horrific occurred despite doing one's best. To compound matters, there are likely to be evaluations or investigations of the circumstances of the unfortunate occurrence that review the worker's decision-making process in those events. In addition, there are times that we do make mistakes – we are careless, miss something, or make an error in judgement.

If we widen our perspective and consider the larger context in which bad outcomes occur, we can gain some additional insights. Widening our perspective requires that we regulate the affective intensity stirred up by unfortunate events so that cognitive reappraisal may take place. We can then ask questions such as 'Would the child have been suicidal if they hadn't been sexually abused?' 'If there had been adequate resources to treat the child when the abuse was first reported, would their despair have gotten to the level of severity it had reached?', or 'If the child's family had received the support they needed when they first came to the attention of social services…?'

---

1   In this section, we refer to several articles that address either child protection workers or other groups of people. We extrapolate from this experience to the residential setting because (1) we know of no similar research in these settings; and (2) we observe residential care workers to face similar issues and have similar experiences.

Asking these broader questions naturally leads us to consider larger issues of social adversity and social injustice that people face. These hardships are often not random occurrences but the result of systemic oppression (Hatzenbuehler & Link, 2014). Racial oppression impacts where an affected person can live, go to school, and work; shapes policies that have a negative impact on their economic and physical well-being; and exposes them to stressors that put them at higher risk for health problems (Williams & Mohammed, 2013). Furthermore, Berry and colleagues (2021) describe how different patterns and levels of racism disrupt the socioemotional development of very young children, with the negative effects reverberating into adolescence and adulthood. Hatzenbuehler and Link (2014) list people with mental illness, sexual minorities, and people living with HIV/AIDS as also subject to structural stigma, which has a negative impact on health. In our experience, the children who come to residential settings are vulnerable to structural as well as individual discrimination.

Consideration of social injustice leads us to explore an additional area of inquiry known as moral injury. According to Haight and colleagues, '[m]oral injury refers to the lasting psychological, spiritual and social harm caused by one's own or another's actions in high-stakes situations that transgress deeply held moral beliefs and expectations' (2017, p. 27). In their integrative review of moral injury, Griffin and colleagues point out that the conceptualization and study of moral injury has largely come from military circumstances, and 'might include injuring or killing enemy combatants, failing to prevent the suffering of fellow service members or civilians, or being betrayed by a leader or fellow service member in a position of power' (Griffin *et al.*, 2019, p. 351). They say that these events can have a wide range of adverse effects on biological, psychological, social, and spiritual well-being. Therefore, moral injury is hypothesized to involve both an exposure to an adverse event and a subsequent set of symptoms, just like PTSD and developmental trauma. Although not much discussed in the context of residential care, in our experience, residential workers are also at risk of harm from moral injury.

In expanding from a focus on military situations, Haight and colleagues (2017) began to examine the ways in which child protection professionals might be subject to moral injury as a result of their work, first reviewing research involving moral injury in healthcare and education. Phenomena consistent with moral injury were observed when physicians made mistakes or when nurses felt they were prevented from doing what they considered was in the patient's best interest. Teachers experienced moral injury in administering standardized tests that they didn't believe in. Teachers also encountered moral injury when required to suspend students who had been aggressive, when they knew that suspending the student was not in their best interest.

Haight and colleagues (2017) interviewed child protection professionals. Their findings indicate that these professionals had experienced potentially morally injurious events in their work with child protective services, and their responses were similar to those of military personnel. We believe that residential caregivers are likely to have experiences of moral injury similar to the child protection professionals. A partial list of what the child protection professionals reported, and we have heard residential caregivers report, includes:

- witnessing events they considered morally wrong

- breaking their own moral code through things they did or failed to do

- feeling that people they considered trustworthy had betrayed them

- concluding that systems intended to help had caused harm instead

- access to services was hindered by a lack of resources

- systemic discrimination, including racial, gender, and class discrimination, resulted in events causing moral injury

- contact with child welfare services actually harmed the children they were supposed to help.

Responses to these potentially morally injurious events included:

- prolonged distress that interfered with functioning

- emotional suffering (angry, sad, frustrated, betrayed, ashamed, lack of joy)

- doubting their own professional competence or even the beneficence of humanity

- leaving a position that had once held hope and promise.

We have heard residential caregivers discuss the distress they feel when a child arrives in their care, and it is clear from the history provided that they were not protected from harm, they didn't receive adequate care for the trauma they experienced, and supposedly trustworthy professionals had let them down. Similarly, we are aware of the sorrow and anger that residential workers experience when a child has been subject to systemic discrimination on account of their race, gender, class, or other identity. We also know the anguish that residential caregivers experience when a child must be discharged to a setting where the worker fears for the child's well-being. We believe these experiences and the psychological distress and dysfunction they may cause the worker all fit within the conceptualization of moral injury.

Sandra Bloom (2017) describes in detail how a system itself can become organized by the trauma of working with children who have experienced moral injury and whose staff members are experiencing moral distress. She points out that a trauma-organized system develops the following characteristics:

- authoritarian leadership
- inalterable social dominance structure
- demand for obedience, from both children and staff members
- denial of conflict and troublesome issues
- culture of secrecy and control.

In fact, this is one of the most serious risks to the well-being of a DDP-informed residential home: that cumulative traumas may put the organization on the defensive and shift leadership from an open, engaged, empathic stance to one that is protective and disengaged. For an in-depth exploration of moral injury, moral safety, and moral repair in organizations, we refer the reader to Bloom's excellent chapter (Bloom, 2017).

Summary of the challenges that residential caregivers face

We have seen in the first half of this chapter that the caregiver's brain is prepped in their early months of life and primed by hormonal influences when they come to work with children (or have children of their own). Working with traumatized children carries a number of risks to the residential worker's hope, emotional well-being, and ability to function. Blocked care is a specific kind of primary trauma that creates a chronic state of defensiveness that shuts down caregiving functions and causes us shame and loss. We can understand the neurobiology of taking things personally when we realize that, in times of intense emotional distress, our top-down cortical brain circuits go offline rather than providing us with the reflective functioning that lets us put things into perspective. Likewise, our top-down circuits go offline when our unresolved painful memories are triggered by the work and our actions become 'unparental'.

We may be affected by secondary trauma, vicarious trauma, and compassion fatigue, as our systems are overwhelmed by the quantity of traumatic stories that we hear. We may be demoralized by actions we witness or engage in that violate our own personal code of what is right and wrong. The social injustices we become aware of in working with traumatized children are disheartening as well. All of this can leave us distressed, emotionally overwhelmed, and unable to function at our best. If left unaddressed, we may feel that the work is not possible, that there is no point in continuing, and that we need to seek a different line of work. In short, we have lost hope.

A neurobiologically based model of hope in residential care

The neurobiological model we have put forward in the book and this chapter emphasizes the crucial role that co-regulation, intersubjectivity, and competent companionship play in creating healthy brains, minds, and relationships. It is no wonder that our answer to the despair-inducing challenges presented so far rely on activating and supporting the residential worker's caregiving brain and protecting it from primary and vicarious traumas. Geoffrion and colleagues (2016) point out, and our experience confirms, that not all child protection workers experience compassion fatigue. They propose that there are a number of factors that stem the tide of hopelessness which can overwhelm our work, including a strong professional identity and the way identity influences the meaning we assign to events. They say compassion fatigue is not an inevitable result of exposure to trauma. Another possible outcome of providing children with supportive caregiving is 'compassion satisfaction, which refers to the pleasure one derives from helping others' (p. 271). Tedeschi and colleagues (2015) describe a complementary concept that they have termed post-traumatic growth, defined as the benefits that arise when one engages with challenging stressors. These benefits include 'improved relationships, new possibilities for one's life, a greater appreciation for life, a greater sense of personal strength, and spiritual development' (2015, p. 504).

How do we address moral injury? Jonathan Haidt (2003) points out that, while we can be brought down by moral injury, we can also be uplifted by witnessing acts of virtue, which he refers to as moral beauty. In the last chapter, we discussed how seeing a child as a *brave survivor* helps ease the impact of the trauma on both the child and on us. The moral beauty of the child's courage and overcoming of terrible hardship produces a response that Haidt calls 'elevation', 'an emotion triggered by people behaving in a virtuous, pure, or superhuman way' (2003, p. 281). Elevation produces a warm, expansive feeling in the chest that naturally directs our attention to the well-being of others and how we might improve it. As Dacher Keltner summarizes, '[w]itnessing acts of moral beauty prompts us more generally to be ready to share and lend a helping hand' (2023, p. 81), producing feelings of inspiration, optimism, and integration into the community. Other positive moral emotions include gratitude, admiration, and awe (Haidt, 2003). In fact, when people experienced awe in their daily lives, 95 per cent of the time it was elicited by moral beauty (Keltner, 2023). In addition to producing positive moral emotions, there is evidence that discussing and writing about moral beauty increases a person's degree of hopefulness as well (Diessner *et al.*, 2006).

Seeking moral beauty in a residential setting caring for children who have experienced developmental trauma may seem paradoxical at first. But acts of bravery, kindness, and faith stand out when circumstances are toughest. In his books, Dan Hughes regularly describes the therapeutic value of naming and appreciating the courage that a child has demonstrated in facing the horrors of abuse. In addition, Baylin and Hughes (2016) emphasize that parents must persevere through multiple challenges when raising a child with blocked trust. By the same token, they outline the commitment needed from the child's therapist, and by extension the other members of the residential team, who need to be 'a real presence and engage with children and caregivers in ways that are immediate, unambiguous, emotional, sensory, affective' (2016, p. 204).

Putting the heroic and virtuous actions of children and caregivers into words uplifts and inspires us all, supplying the elevation and inspiration that a residential home especially needs.

Reflection

Think back over the past day or several days. What act(s) of courage, kindness, or overcoming have you observed? What happens if you say to yourself that person was really courageous (or kind or heroic)? How do you feel? What do you feel like doing?

Or, think of something someone did that you witnessed or heard about that made a lasting impression on you at some point in your life. Why did it stick with you? How do you feel recalling that?

Consider adding as an agenda item to your meetings a brief reflection on moral beauty, along with an acknowledgement of the impact of moral beauty on your emotional or physiological state.

Just as we maintain hope for the child by a clearly envisioned pathway to positive change as delineated in this book, so, too, do we maintain hope for ourselves as residential care workers by a clearly envisioned pathway to our success and well-being. We now have the elements necessary to detail the path that leads from stressful exposures to compassion satisfaction and post-traumatic growth.

Our neurobiological model states that when bottom-up emotions are regulated, then top-down cognitive reflective and reappraisal processes provide context to experiences, which can remain within the window of tolerance (see Figure 7.1). Within that window, our thinking and problem-solving remain flexible, and we handle whatever life throws at us. Because our top-down circuits are intact, we are able to shift from an 'it's about me' perspective to a 'let's see what we can do here' attitude. We are not overly threatened by the challenges we face, and our felt sense of safety keeps us in the social engagement system, able to connect with others, communicate effectively, collaborate with colleagues, and access our curiosity and creativity. Though this may sound like an ungrounded fantasy after the litany of trauma effects we just reviewed, there are residential workers who function in this way most days in a number of countries we know of.

How does this magic good functioning come into being? By using the same strategies that we have described as therapeutic for the children we aim to help. We embed the residential worker in a supportive environment that provides them with the same emotional regulation, intersubjectivity, and meaning-making that a child needs for their development. We provide the caregiver with needed skills to make them effective, supervision to guide and point out their efficacy, realistic expectations for their work, and a sense that, though the system may be broken at times, their efforts will make a difference. We help foster a professional identity that allows them pride in their values, and the awareness that their values align with their colleagues' values and with the larger purpose of the facility for which they work. They hear stories of success that demonstrate that healing is possible, even in the most dire of circumstances. Last, but probably most importantly, we create an environment of support, in which difficult experiences can be put into words, listened to, heard, empathized with, and understood.

This model, depicted in Figure 8.1, helps us to understand why some people suffer from compassion fatigue while others enjoy compassion satisfaction, even under similarly stressful conditions. An individual's ability to meet stress head on depends upon their inner resources: their ability to stay emotionally regulated, reflect on experience, reappraise it, connect with, make use of support, and make meaning of suffering through the lens of a strong professional identity. The individual's ability to manage stress also depends upon the social buffering capacity of the support they receive from their relationships and the organization in which they are embedded. Under optimal conditions, the residential worker's inner resources plus the support they receive will be greater than the primary and secondary traumas and potentially morally injurious events they are exposed to. They will be able to manage the stress of the work and experience compassion satisfaction.

This model also informs our efforts to maintain staff hopefulness in the face of stressful work. We need to regularly monitor how well they are managing the stressors of working with traumatized children. We need to assure that staff members have the interpersonal and organizational support required to sufficiently buffer those stresses. We need to support the development of their abilities to work effectively with traumatized children. Training staff members in a PACEful attitude, co-regulation of affect, intersubjective sharing of experiences, and in using the two hands of parenting are all critical to both their professional success and their aptitude for personal stress management. Staff members need to develop and practise their reflective capacity in a culture that values reflection. Their identity as child mental health or social care practitioners needs to be defined and nurtured. The rest of this chapter describes how staff in a residential setting might engage in these efforts through supervision, routines and rituals, support efforts, and self-development practices.

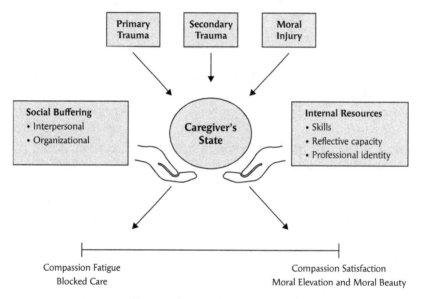

Residential work with youth who have experienced developmental trauma can subject caregivers to the stresses of primary and secondary trauma as well as moral injury. But sufficient social buffering and internal resources will support caregivers to remain in an open, socially engaged state and to experience compassion satisfaction, moral elevation, and moral beauty. If the caregiver's social buffering and internal resources are overwhelmed by stress, then they will move into fight-or-flight or shutdown, states that lead to compassion fatigue and blocked care.

Figure 8.1: Trauma, Resilience, and State in Residential Work
ADAPTED FROM GEOFFRION *ET AL*., 2016.

Supervision and additional staff support

Supervision, which was discussed in depth in Chapter 6, is an important part of a DDP-informed residential setting and is an important part of the support needed to move toward compassion satisfaction. Staff members often meet with their supervisor for 60 to 90 minutes, one to four times a month. In the meeting, the supervisor asks the staff member how they are doing to get a sense of their well-being. How well are they managing the stresses of the work? Do they have signs of blocked care, secondary trauma, moral injury? Have any personal traumatic memories been triggered? If there is an area in which the staff member feels stirred up, the supervisor listens PACEfully and helps them put the experience into words. The staff member can use their supervisor's reflections as a temporary external source of reflective capacity to gain perspective on the situation. The supervisor's PACEful attitude co-regulates escalated emotions and can begin to attend to any blocked care the staff member may be experiencing. For instance, if the supervisor enjoys the staff member, it stimulates the staff member's reward system. If the supervisor can approach the staff member, it stimulates the staff member's approach system. The goal is for the staff member to feel heard and understood, to not feel alone in their experience. The supervisor knows that it is important to address their relationship with the staff member, before providing solutions or guidance. This is a corollary to the 'connection before correction' guideline that is utilized with the children. Once the connection is made, then problem-solving, planning, and coaching can occur.

The coaching portion of a supervision session focuses on the most salient issues. Sometimes, the staff member needs support developing a skill related to their work. Maybe they don't understand the two hands of parenting and need clarification. Maybe they have been inappropriately playful and need a better understanding of PACEful playfulness. The supervisor may use role play to improve the caregiver's ability to manage a situation that didn't go well recently. Supervision can also take up inaccuracies in the caregiver's self-assessment of their skills or performance. The supervisor can discuss a supervisee's overestimate of their ability to handle certain situations, by providing clear feedback grounded in observation of the consequences of the staff member's actions. It can take the form 'I noticed when you did _____, the child responded by _____. Because we are looking for a different response from the child, let's consider what you might do to make it more likely they will respond that way.' On the other hand, staff members sometimes underestimate the helpfulness of their actions. In this case, the supervisor can give feedback using the same formula. Here's a story to illustrate this point.

An issue similar to underestimating one's effectiveness is unfamiliarity with the signs that indicate a child is making progress. Eight-year-old Remy, who had blocked trust and a controlling disorganized attachment pattern, had been fiercely independent for the first four months at the residential home. One evening, he asked his key person to read them a story before bedtime. Because eight-year-olds often like for their caregiver to read them bedtime stories, it is possible to miss the significance of this request. For Remy, this is a major step forward as it represents an awakening of the child's longing for connection and trusting the support that the key person provides. If these gains are missed, it can leave the staff member feeling like their actions do make a difference for the child. If the gains are highlighted and celebrated, it provides staff members with real evidence that what they do matters. They see signs of their success.

Other issues that can be brought up for consideration in supervision include staff members who are too self-critical of their performance or who perceive the child's reactivity as representing a poor reflection of the staff member's self-worth. In order to ground staff members in the realities of treating developmental trauma, they can be educated about signs, sequence, and timing of the children's positive response to care, which is often slower than anticipated. If they are eager for progress, they may find themselves discouraged quickly after starting their jobs. Their supervisor may encourage them to pace themselves, look for small signs of progress, and to recognize the cumulative effect of moments of connection they share with the children in their care.

There are other opportunities to supplement the support provided to staff members. A DDP consultant, hired by the residential home, can provide support to groups of residential caregivers and in one-on-one meetings. In addition, agency board members, advisors, and retired staff are motivated to comfort, encourage, and be a source of strength for staff members who face tough circumstances. Sanders and Thompson (2022) point out that often small groups of people come together in mutual support organically. They say, '[i]deally, secondary traumatic stress can be prevented or at least mitigated by developing a microculture of individuals who support each other through both encouragement and accountability' (p. 141). In each of these situations, it is helpful if the supportive person has some knowledge of DDP and the ability to engage with a struggling staff member PACEfully.

Overall, supervision provides a need for companionship as we engage in this difficult but significant work. The supervisor's support of the staff member forms a model for the staff member's work with the children. We explore this congruence between core values and principles across organizational levels in Chapter 10, which also answers the question, 'Who supports the supervisor?'

Structure, rituals, and routines

In Chapter 6, we discussed the importance of structure within the DDP approach. There are regular activities in a residential setting that provide structure and support to the life of the people who live and work there. While many of the activities are geared toward increasing a stabilizing sense of predictability for the children, these activities provide a familiar routine that is settling to the staff members as well. We can think of these regular activities as rituals and routines, which are predictable patterns of responding in specific situations. For example, there is a regular routine to welcome a new child to the home, and a routine to say goodbye when they leave. The children have a regular schedule of their activities through the week that can include play, study, cleaning, therapy groups, and the like.

Here are some other rituals and routines to consider:

- Report on remarkable occurrences within the residential care settings. KidsTLC calls these 'Miracle Moment Reports'. Another facility calls them 'PACE Bragging'.

- Celebrate a child's birthday or when they reach a significant milestone in residential care, like when they have been there for one year, two years, and so forth.

- Chronicle the children who have been in the programme. One facility has children write their initials on a leaf of a big tree mural so that all the children who have been there are noted. Another facility puts pictures of the children who have been there in a book that can be looked through.

- Host visits from former clients who may speak to children

currently in the residential home about what their time there was like and how they are doing now.

- Celebrate various cultural or religious rituals that the children or staff members might celebrate. These are opportunities to honour the diversity of people who have come together and develop cross-cultural respect and understanding.

Staff members follow a set of routine activities as well. When they arrive at work, they may receive a report from the caregivers going off duty. At the end of their shift, they give a report to the next arriving shift. There are regular team meetings for staff members who work together. The agenda for the meeting can include a check in to take the emotional temperature of the team. Are they managing the stresses of their work or have events overwhelmed their capacity to respond? What are the stress points that the team faces? For example, a situation with a particular child, a concern about staff relationships, an event that was disturbing to the team. There may be areas that the team leader would like to address. There should be time allocated for organization-wide announcements to facilitate communication.

There may be special meetings as well. For example, KidsTLC has 'wraparound meetings' to include a child in the team discussion. They also bring several staff members to meet with a parent or other interested party when the stakes and emotions are high. The extra staff members provide additional social buffering and auxiliary reflective function for that discussion. Special meetings can address relational issues within the team, organizational changes, or distressing news for the residential home. There are also discharge planning meetings that address, among other things, the ways in which the child will stay in contact with people from residential care.

As Baylin and Hughes helpfully point out, 'knowing what's happening and what to do about it' provides us with a sense of safety (2016, p. 226). Structure, rituals, and routines are our answer to what's happening and what to do. When our residential home has upsets that are out of the ordinary, we can check whether we are following our planned structures or whether new plans might be needed. We know we are on the right track when rituals and routines cause us to relax. They give us the feeling 'oh, I know where we are', and a certainty about what will happen next. Ahhh…

Self-care, self-development, and resilience

While it is in the interest of an organization that works with traumatized children to support their staff members' ability to stay in an open and engaged state as much as possible (Sanders & Thompson, 2022), it is also in everyone's interest if their staff members assume a degree of responsibility for their own self-care, self-development, and resilience as well. Jon Baylin and Dan Hughes devote a chapter of *The Neurobiology of Attachment-Focused Therapy* (2016) to discussing 'brain-based approaches to staying open and engaged' (p. 223). They lay out a challenging requirement for working with children who have experienced developmental trauma: therapists 'must have the capacity to sustain a compassionate and reflective state of mind toward the caregivers, children, and themselves to evoke a similar state of mind within the caregivers and children they are treating' (p. 224). If we discover that we are no longer in a therapeutic state of mind, Baylin and Hughes recommend considering that something in our attachment history has gotten stirred up. Using self-reflection to uncover unquestioned assumptions increases our self-awareness and our success with children and families. When we integrate unresolved attachment events and memories, we earn a more secure attachment pattern (Golding *et al.*, 2021).

Baylin and Hughes (2016) advise that the therapist must maintain a felt sense of safety, have a good understanding of the meaning of both the child's and parent's behaviour, be aware of their own trauma triggers, and have good supervision and the support of a well-functioning team. Having good skills helps to promote a sense of self-efficacy that avoids defensive states of helplessness. In addition, we can take moments when we aren't as open and engaged as would be helpful as opportunities to examine with curiosity whether issues from our attachment histories are getting stirred up. Finally, they point out the importance of acknowledging to the child or parent when we become defensive, and then openly working to repair the relationship.

Baylin and Hughes (2016, pp. 239–242) offer self-care recommendations for therapists, including paying attention to diet, exercise, and getting the emotional support one needs. It is wise to also ask staff members to generate their own lists of what nurtures and nourishes them. Activities like yoga and massage provide care to the body. Sensory measures like essential oils with various scents can be restorative as well. As simple as it sounds, staff members have found that learning to make small adjustments to the position in which they are sitting or standing may help them feel more comfortable, and the action of making these adjustments can be experienced as empowering. In addition, we can't overemphasize the value of play as a means to regulate our emotions, put things in perspective, and reinforce the bonds that buffer the events that stress us out. When staff play together, with each other and with the children, it sends a powerful message that, despite everything that is happening, things are okay. Finally, we should point out that as stressful events increase, we need to increase our self-care correspondingly. Our well-being is an important part of our effectiveness in helping children heal.

Conclusion

In this chapter, we have examined the potentially traumatizing and demoralizing experiences that a residential care worker may be exposed to. While it is important to acknowledge that these experiences can have serious impacts on residential staff well-being, it is important to note that these impacts aren't preordained. It is possible to navigate difficult events and situations and maintain our sense of well-being. We have the opportunity to feel a sense of compassion satisfaction or even post-traumatic growth. Focusing on the heroic aspect of the work provides moral elevation to sustain our efforts. The same things that help children who have experienced developmental trauma help protect residential caregivers from vicarious traumatization and compassion fatigue.

Compassionate companionship provides emotional co-regulation, new meanings for events, and the sense that one is not alone. It provides a social buffer that protects from the effects of trauma. When the residential worker's inner resources and external supports are sufficient, then their experiences do not overwhelm them. They can use their connection and skills to make a positive difference in the lives of the children at the facility. They learn the truth that there is nothing more rewarding than helping a child learn their worth, discover their capacity and competence, and enjoy the satisfactions that trustworthy relationships bring.

CHAPTER 9

Behind the Walls

Balancing Physical Safety with Relational Safety for
Young People in a Secure Children's Home

RACHEL SWANN

Dyadic Developmental Practice, I believe, offers the best hope of connection with those young people who need this most, and who are also most likely to reject it – no small challenge! It is a gentle yet dynamic, respectful, and genuine approach based on transparency and openness that seeks to support young people to move from mistrust to trust in their relationship with us and in the context of which we can offer them an alternative way to view themselves, their relationships, their choices, and their future.

I am a consultant clinical psychologist employed as the lead for an integrated health team embedded in a social care secure residential setting for complex young people in England. In this chapter, I would like to offer my experience of applying DDP principles to practice in this setting. Use of the term 'secure' describes the restrictions of liberty that are placed on the young people (10 to 17 years old) who, because of significant concerns for their safety, live temporarily in a locked environment. They are subject to a series of rules and routines that limit what belongings they have access to, where they can go, who they can have contact with, and what they can do.

Although written from an English perspective, I hope that much of the discussion generalizes to similar services elsewhere in the world. The setting described in this chapter is a secure welfare setting. There are other secure settings in England. For example, young people detained for justice reasons, youth offending institutions, and secure children and adolescent mental health settings.

The legislation

Precipitating the deprivation of liberty for young people accommodated under 'welfare' legislation in England and Wales are significant concerns about their safety. The criteria for this are set out in Section 25 of the United Kingdom's Children Act 1989 (available at www.legislation. gov.uk). The welfare criteria that must be met before a looked after child may be placed in secure accommodation are that:

- the child has a history of absconding and is likely to abscond from any other type of accommodation

- if the child absconds, they are likely to suffer significant harm, or

- if the child is kept in any other type of accommodation, they are likely to injure themselves or others.

The aim of the secure accommodation order, which should be for the minimum period necessary, is to:

- keep the young person safe

- explore, understand, and contribute to a reduction in the risks that precipitated their admission

- support a return to a community setting at the earliest opportunity.

It is an intervention utilized at the end of an extended period of escalating concerns for the young person in the community. The high level of risk, vulnerability, and unmet need that underlie the concerns for the young person are usually complex, requiring a co-ordinated, multi-agency approach, in collaboration with the young person, to support a reduction in risk on return to a community setting. The average length of an admission in the setting I work in over the last two years (to January 2023) is 177 days, with the shortest admission being 20 hours and the longest admission 629 days.

The framework – SECURE STAIRS

In England and Wales, The Integrated Framework for Children and Young People in the Secure Estate, also known as SECURE STAIRS, has been in operation since 2018 (Taylor *et al.*, 2018).

It is underpinned by the principles of trauma and attachment with a focus on understanding the issues the young people bring. Relationships with staff are paramount. In addition, it states that '[a]ll interventions will be driven by a "formulation" approach, which takes into account the child or young person's life experience, rather than concentrating on labels, categories or diagnoses, settings, and the quality of health services delivered to children and young people in this environment' (NHS England, 2018, p. 5).

Our setting

The secure children's home where I work is a modern, clean, spacious, high ceilinged building compartmentalized into a series of smaller areas and accessed by a series of closed doors that are operated by keys and fingerprint recognition. There is a high staff-to-young-person ratio providing supervision and support to the young people, who are encouraged to access the communal areas throughout the daytime. They are then locked in their individual rooms at night-time. The internal spaces are punctuated by a series of external spaces designed for sport and leisure.

The young people

Similar to the other young people described in this book, the cohort of young people accommodated for welfare reasons usually have extensive histories of disrupted care, with early lives characterized by abuse and neglect. As a consequence of their experiences, they are, understandably, inherently mistrustful of the systems that are supporting them and the intentions of the adults that are caring for them. Very rarely do they agree with the concerns of others that have precipitated their admission. Alongside the persistent absconding are serious social, emotional, and behavioural difficulties, such as aggression and destructive acts, and/or extensive histories of self-harm, and suicidal ideation and behaviour. They are a cohort of young people who have often missed out on key developmental opportunities – for example, education – and who present with a range of physical health, mental health, and neurodevelopmental vulnerabilities and needs. The young people who spend time with us have not been 'locked up' for committing a crime, although some will be involved with the youth offending system. The experience of being deprived of their liberty can feel like imprisonment, reinforcing any pre-existing internal sense of the self as being bad and of others as coercive and punishing.

Let's reflect on a young person's experience of being admitted to secure care.

Clayton was a 13-year-old, dual heritage, looked after child for whom there were significant concerns about violence involving a weapon and exploitation, notably his involvement with 'county lines', that is, moving drugs around the country. Late on the previous evening, he had returned to his residential care home after having been 'missing' for 12 days. This was not unusual for him. He was awoken abruptly in his bedroom by a staff member and three stocky males who instructed him to get dressed and to leave with them. Clayton was told that they were taking him to a new children's home where he would be 'looked after and kept safe' – neither of which were needs Clayton identified for himself at that moment! The escorts supervised him continuously while he gathered a few key belongings and was then handcuffed while they escorted him to their car. He and they both knew he would run if he could.

His first impression of the new 'home', after a five-hour journey, was his reception into a high-walled courtyard where shutters closed down behind the car. He was greeted by three staff – two males and a female. He appeared to share some cultural similarity with two of them, and they appeared friendly enough, but he was suspicious of their smiles. There was a solitary door from the courtyard into a building, which they encouraged him to enter. They sought to reassure him that it was not a prison and explained what a secure children's home was and what would happen next. Clayton surveyed the perimeter of the courtyard for some indication of where he was and how he was going to get out. He heard parts of what they told him but was distracted by a preoccupation about what he had on his possession and what he was going to do with it.

In the admissions suite, he was asked to empty his pockets and informed that the staff would need to conduct a pat down search and 'wand' him to pick up any hidden metal objects. As the staff demonstrated what this would look like, the gravitas of Clayton's situation began to dawn on him. He questioned every request, rejected their authority to do what they asked, and tried to find a way to bargain with them, agreeing to a 'wand' if they did not touch him or his clothing.

The care team supporting his admission gave him time, time to resist, time to question, time to challenge, time to engage. They interspersed requests about what needed to happen before he could move on with information about the setting, the legal status of him being there, and the plan for the next few hours and days ahead. They understood that, behind his bravado, he was likely to be feeling frightened. They sought to make him feel welcomed while accepting his rejection and acknowledging that he didn't want to be there.

Aware that there was no alternative ending to the situation, Clayton began to empty his pockets. He handed in his mobile and cigarettes and hoped that when he handed over his coat, they wouldn't notice the broken seams inside in which his drugs were stashed. They did. There was no judgement or evaluation of Clayton from the staff, who maintained an attitude of acceptance and empathy for the situation Clayton found himself in. Clayton began to worry about what he had lost, what he owed, and what was going to happen to him. He was deliberately cautious about what information he shared, as the context of where he was, and why, remained confusing. He was anxious that he might incriminate himself or others.

The task

In the secure setting, we want to establish a sense of safety and trust as we know this is the platform for healing and change. However, there are dynamics that work against this:

- A young person accommodated under a secure welfare order has no definitive sense of how long their liberty is being deprived.

- Their care plan is the responsibility of their placing local authority, who must seek the authority of the courts. An independent secure accommodation review panel regularly review whether the criteria for secure accommodation continue to be met and advise a judge accordingly.

- Although the young people don't know how long they will be in secure accommodation, they do know that this period in their life will end. It is hard for a young person to invest in a relationship which they know is not going to last, especially when they have already had so much experience of disrupted relationships.

- The hierarchy of power is always present. Within the building, there are those with keys/liberty (the staff) and those without (the young people). Additionally, these staff are asked to monitor/evaluate the young person's behaviour and contribute to the regular reviews of risk informing the decision-making process about whether or not their liberty should continue to be deprived.

- Although diversity is well represented in the social care team who provide 24/7 care, in the education and health teams this is not the case. They are predominantly, as I am, white British, cisgender, heterosexual, middle class, middle aged, neurotypical women without disability. This imbalance of power in the staff team members can reflect disparities in social and economic opportunities. For some young people, the differences between 'them and us' may exacerbate experiences of discrimination and prompt them to feel judged, shamed, misunderstood, or alienated.

- The secure setting can have an intense and emotionally charged atmosphere.

DDP as an approach to the challenges of the secure setting

The security provided by a locked unit provides some immediate physical safety for the young person and some containment of the behavioural concerns. The DDP approach builds on this. DDP's focus on establishing safety in relationships is a way of being that is congruent with the values and principles of a trauma-informed approach. It's also a model which recognizes the need to balance emotional support and nurture with physical structure. At the centre are genuine, authentic, and compassionate relationships in which the following principles are core: safety and trust, developmentally appropriate choice and control, compassion, and collaboration.

It is our duty to ensure that, in supporting the young person to stabilize and thrive, we honour all voices when trying to make sense of the complexity of the young person's difficulties and the challenges experienced by those caring for them. Safety and the attitude of PACE enable us to be curious about and actively embrace our diverse identities; in the process, we are able to deepen our relationship with each other and the children in our care. The DDP attitude of PACE provides a way of moving forward when there is anxiety about getting it wrong or causing offence. Questions that can feel uncomfortable to ask or answer can be tackled. With a focus on safety in relationships as the foundation, risks can be taken, and mistakes can be recognized, learned from, and used to motivate us to be better.

The importance of the non-verbal

Within the secure setting, it is not just what is seen or said that can highlight difference for the young person, but also what is felt at a multi-sensory level. The DDP model, with its focus on curiosity about the lived experience of the people we are relating to, reminds us to be aware of the unique needs of each child. This helps us to be mindful about the immediate day-to-day care needs, such as diet, skin, and/or haircare, and to ensure that young people have culturally sensitive options available to them on arrival. Young people have described experiencing a 'whitewash' on entering a very clinical environment. As an illustration, a young person of African-Caribbean heritage, who was used to hot and spicy flavours, found the food to be bland both in taste and scent. Meeting specific cultural needs with young people supports the development of the relationship we are seeking to establish in a low-key manner, with a lightness of touch that can transverse the formality of supervision, assessment, and intervention. For example, we connect with the young person's world through the intimacy of oiling and braiding their hair. Furthermore, frequently observed in the attachment relationships of young people with their carers who share a similar heritage are the cultural gestures that are known without knowing them. These gestures, such as a shrug or a flick of the eyebrows, provide a powerful, non-verbal relational connection that makes the young person feel 'at home' or safe in the familiarity of how 'we' are and what 'we' do.

What does DDP look like in practice?

Care staff

Care staff are the main vehicle for assisting the young people to develop trust. Trust in another is a fundamental developmental need, yet mistrust of others is part of the internal working model for most of the young people we care for. Some have learned to minimize their attachment needs and not to invest in relationships. Others have learned to keep others at a distance at all costs in order to keep themselves safe. Others have learned to escalate their attachment needs to ensure the availability of others. Others walk a tightrope on which they desperately need, want, and seek connection while, at the same time, inherently fear and therefore reject this, contributing to a chaotic and demanding push and pull in relationships.

DDP accepts the mistrust and honours the young person's experience with the development of mistrust as key to their survival in earlier relationships. It seeks to support the creation of a narrative that allows the young person to understand the impact of their experiences on their behaviours – often adaptive coping/survival strategies – and their relationships now. We are overt in our acceptance and acknowledgement of how difficult it is for the young person to trust us and that it is our responsibility to work hard to prove to them that we are trustworthy.

Hughes and colleagues note, however, that '[t]he child cannot be expected to address his most frightening and shameful experiences with any and all adults who are involved with his daily care' (2019, p. 247). Therefore, a DDP approach recommends that the child develops a few key relationships with staff we call 'key workers', with whom they begin to develop some security of attachment.

Let's return to Clayton:

Clayton did not agree with the system's concerns about his vulnerability and was resistant to accepting 'help'. At first, he fought what he perceived as unnecessary restrictions. He was aggressive to the care team that maintained the rules and held a boundary to his demands. He did not feel that he was being looked after, he did not agree that he needed to be cared for, and he did not experience the restrictions upon him to be about his welfare but about coercion and control.

Clayton was precontemplative about change in relation to any of the behaviours that had precipitated his admission; he did not consider his behaviours to be a problem and was not interested in addressing the risks attached to them. He did agree to engage in a piece of work that would help others – both in the home and the wider system – to understand his point of view. This would support others to step into his shoes, and perhaps, at the same time, offer him the opportunity to pause and reflect on his identity, on what had happened to him, who he had become, and who he wanted to be. Mindful of saying anything incriminating and resolute that he would not explore his earlier childhood experiences in any detail, he nevertheless engaged thoughtfully in a powerful piece of narrative work that shared how he was determined not to be vulnerable ever again.

Clayton's narrative sent a clear message to others to 'back off', a more sanitized version of a threat perhaps. It was also tender, and generated empathy in those who read it. This piece of work supported others to make sense of the needs, feelings, and perceptions underneath his behaviour, while also helping him to understand himself and his needs better.

Clayton was never in agreement with the decision to place him in a secure children's home. This challenged so many aspects of his identity, not just the loss of control and choice. Being powerful and not vulnerable was a central tenet of his life lesson about how to survive. He decided to do what he had to in order to 'get out'. For example, involvement with the youth offending services. He was an engaging young man who, when he felt he was being respected, was charming, sociable, and engaging, but who could easily be triggered by interactions that he felt were disrespectful. At these times, he would suddenly and unpredictably become violent towards others.

Clayton initially wondered whether he might feel more at home in a prison, where, in his idealized but not wholly unrealistic view, he would be surrounded by people 'more like me'. By the time he left, he had a more realistic appraisal about how being deprived of liberty felt and what the challenges would be, even more so in a prison environment in which multiple others might also be vying for power and control. He expressed a determination not to end up in the justice system. On the other hand, Clayton was honest about the likelihood that he would return to some of the risk-taking behaviours that had precipitated his admission. He had some sense of an alternative future in which he would engage in less illegal activity, decreasing the risks of gang violence to his physical safety and of having his liberty deprived again. But, he said, only when he was ready!

Clayton left us after four months to move to a bespoke care setting which would support him until he was 16 years old. Clayton travelled to his new placement with two of the home's care workers with whom he had begun to establish some trust. A photo book crammed full of the activities he had been part of while at the secure children's home had been created for him. Most notable in this were the relationships that populated the pages alongside the activities – moments of genuine joint attention and intersubjectivity that communicated to him that he was liked. These activities met a developmental need of a younger-child part that had never been expressed. His traumatic experiences meant it had never been safe to express these younger needs.

Among the photos were personal handwritten messages to him from the staff and young people.

When he left, we hoped that, in addition to providing for some of Clayton's unmet developmental needs, we might have planted a few seeds that could flourish in the future. We hoped we offered him an alternative view of himself that might support a different developmental trajectory.

There are multiple cycles of rupture and repair with the staff in the home, and it is these that can provide the foundation for change. Without the development of relational trust, our work rests on fragile ground.

Here is an example of building relational trust with the attitude of PACE.

PACE IN ACTION: ANDY

Andy was a large, 16-year-old boy with learning difficulties who had experienced developmental trauma. He was accommodated due to concerns about his increasingly aggressive behaviour towards others. When Andy was agitated, he posed a physical threat to staff, many of whom he had assaulted. At the start of his placement with us, the risk assessment and associated care plan advised two members of care staff to support him at all times.

On one particular afternoon, he became irritated with the two staff members supporting him. Their adherence to the two-to-one supervision plan meant a delay in using the PlayStation because they couldn't leave him to get the key to the cupboard where the PlayStation and its controllers were kept. He reported that not all the staff adhered to this plan and demanded that one of them get the key immediately. He was furious about their intention to contact another member of the care team to bring the key, and became increasingly verbally abusive and physically threatening, aggressively pursuing, and seeking to punch, spit at, and kick them. He was not responsive to their support and a restraint was being planned to move him from the communal area to his room where he would continue to be supported to de-escalate if further aggression continued.

Alerted by a panic alarm, the manager of the home joined Andy and the care staff. Staff had directed Andy to his bedroom, but Andy was now sitting at the communal table, refusing to move as requested. He was breathing heavily, and making continued threats. The atmosphere was heightened emotionally.

The manager gestured to the staff, who were standing surrounding Andy, to sit on the sofa nearby and sat with them. The care team began to explain what was happening and were gently halted by the manager, who was mindful of the impact of shame on Andy. 'We'll get to that,' he said and sought to connect with Andy's feelings first. 'This must be really difficult for you, Andy, if some staff do and some staff don't, so hard for you – I would find this really difficult too – I'm here to talk to you if you want to talk to me... You have shown us before that we can get through things like this together.' The manager approached Andy, tapping him gently on the shoulder. 'It's okay,' he said, and then returned to sit on the sofa. Other staff who had been alerted by the panic alarm were gestured to leave. The manager continued, 'I think it's important to have some time out now, and I'll help you with that... it's not okay to hit, kick, or spit at the staff; you and we need to find another way to manage your feelings...I'll come and talk to you in your room.' After 15 minutes, Andy followed the manager and went to his room. Further aggression and physical restraint were avoided. After a period of 30 minutes with the manager and another supporting staff member, Andy rejoined the group and spontaneously sought to repair his relationship with the care staff he had threatened.

Hearing about this interaction in a subsequent handover, I was struck by how the manager's intervention illustrated Dan Hughes's two hands in practice. Hand one connected first with the young person's experience underlying their dysregulation. Hand two provided the boundary, structure, and consequence (Hughes *et al.*, 2019). For Andy, the experience of being understood and his feelings validated contributed to a reduction in arousal. With less threat and increased connection, Andy could co-operate with the request to move to his room where he could continue to be supported. The manager's presence and authoritative support meant that both hands were delivered with PACE and focused on re-establishing safety, for Andy and for the staff who had been threatened.

Dyadic work
DDP highlights the young person's evolutionary need to form a secure bond with their caregivers. Sessions with a therapist whose work is informed by the principles of DDP provide a powerful therapeutic

means of awakening and establishing these secure relationships. DDP therapy is most effective when key care staff attend the therapy session as an attachment person for the child. However, it can be challenging logistically to get the young person, key care staff member, and DDP therapist in the same room at the same time. There can be a narrow window of opportunity to offer planned therapy appointments. This is due to the combination of part-time hours for most of the health team, shift working for the social care team, and children attending education.

When working dyadically with the young person and a care worker is not possible pragmatically, individual work with the young person is always guided by a PACEful approach. Often the child receives a combination of both individual and dyadic work. Regular therapy sessions may be offered; however, a benefit of applying DDP in a secure setting is that there are ad hoc opportunities to support a young person when dysregulated day to day. The very nature of the difficulties precipitating the young person's accommodation means we (health, care, and educational staff) are presented with multiple opportunities for building connections, both in the calmer times when creating moments of joy can be prioritized and in the dysregulated times when there is an opportunity to be present and to provide comfort.

Relational difficulties are a frequent part of the challenges precipitating a secure admission. Every rupture offers an opportunity for repair, every disconnection, an opportunity for (re-)connection. The duration of our time together may be limited by the length of the secure order, but the intensity of our time together presents multiple golden opportunities. To realize the benefit of these opportunities, everybody caring for the young person is supported to develop a skill set appropriate to the needs of the complex young people we are working with. As Dr Karen Treisman says, '[e]very moment and interaction can be an intervention' (2020).

Deborah, in her role as a residential care worker, was able to change her approach to a young person when she received training in PACE.

MAGGIE

Maggie was a 14-year-old girl accommodated under a secure order following a series of significant attempts to take her own life, which was attributed to trauma rather than a mental illness.

Deborah, a residential care worker, attended a therapeutic parenting course. She reflected upon how adopting a PACEful approach had impacted positively on her relationship with Maggie. She observed that, before taking the course, she would have felt irritated by the repetitive 'tornado' of emotion and accusation that would cascade from Maggie when she was struggling. After the course, she changed her style. Deborah now adopted an attitude of 'sit in with' rather than 'sit it out' (for fear of being pulled into it again). She was actively more curious about Maggie's internal world, sticking with this rather than jumping to advice and problem solving, as might have been her tendency previously.

Also noteworthy was the intersubjective impact that Deborah's PACEfulness had on Maggie. Maggie's ever present internal dialogue of being bad, responsible, and deserving of death began to lose some of its power because of her relationships with key staff, both due to their comfort when she was vulnerable as well as from their shared moments of joy during her recovery. Instead, she spoke about a more helpful, internalized other, that of her key workers, who had worked hard to build trustworthy relationships with her. Maggie would connect with a mantra of 'what would Deborah say?' to steady herself during times of distress.

This young woman also had a high level of support from the wider health team and me, including regular therapeutic appointments for 14 months with ad hoc support at times of distress. When she left, she fed back how important these relationships had been and how she was sorry she had not taken up the offer of therapy. In fact, she had met with me willingly on most occasions. During these times, we had made sense together of her earlier experiences and how they had impacted on her sense of self and on her relationships with others. She learned how her challenging behaviours might be understood as coping strategies and as a way to meet her unmet needs. The work wasn't easy for her; she was often avoidant of the task, rearranging or cutting short our formal sessions, but an approach informed by the DDP model structured our work together. This made it safe for her to keep trying, to keep connecting with me and with her experiences. Most interestingly, on reflection, Maggie said this didn't feel like work (therapy) at all for her! Such is the power of relationships that are grounded in safety.

Maggie has kept in touch with us since leaving, thanking us for being there for her and noting that she doubted she would have made it to 18 without these relationships.

Despite the power of a DDP approach, within the secure residential environment, it is easy to find examples of how our services can retraumatize the young people we are wanting to support. For example, the impact of restrictive interventions, such as restraint, separation, searches, and lack of choice and control/agency. As we have learned from other chapters, the importance DDP places on the relationship – on transparency around intention and expectation, and on repair and re-connection – lessens the impact of these unavoidable insults and injuries to the young person's well-being. In fact, this approach sends the vital message that sturdy relationships don't avoid ruptures, they repair them. This approach must be led by adults who are able to stay regulated, reflective, and compassionate, not only for the young people but also for themselves and each other.

Staff support and training

The secure setting can be really hard for the day-to-day care staff, who may be, at times, relentlessly subjected to assault, threat, and rejection. This increases the risk of the staff moving into blocked care. Decisions can be made from a position of defence rather than curiosity, understanding, empathy, and reflection, with consequences becoming punitive. Here is where training and supporting staff to develop an attitude of PACE is so beneficial, not just towards the young person, but also towards themselves and, importantly, each other. Only when we can be PACEful towards one another can we be curious rather than critical of the decision-making processes by individuals and teams. As Casswell and colleagues note:

> Residential care is a complex emotional and social environment. Individuals in and between staff teams will, at times, disagree with each other about ways of supporting children and how to provide boundaries and consequences. Accepting that this is part of residential childcare, and modelling emotionally regulated ways of conflict resolution and repairing relationships is the DDP way. (2014, p. 23)

We support staff to be PACEful by modelling this attitude in day-to-day interactions, and through the provision of a therapeutic 'parenting group', providing a regular opportunity for reflective practice as a group.

Level one DDP training has been a priority for the mental health clinicians in our service. This provides an essential foundation to support the integration and development of DDP throughout the day-to-day operations of the secure setting. For example, this training informs individual and dyadic work, consultation on site, reflective practice, the therapeutic parenting programme, and consultation with the external network about the young person's needs, supporting care planning on transition.

All residential care workers receive a comprehensive training in therapeutic parenting, the core of which is the DDP approach to parenting. There are two DDP-informed parenting programmes that have been successfully used in residential care settings: Foundations for Attachment and Therapeutic Parenting with PACE.[1] In this chapter, I explore how the Therapeutic Parenting with PACE has been adapted to meet the needs of the secure setting I work in.

The training programme supports the care workers to:

- understand the principles of attachment theory and the impact of developmental trauma on developing heart, body, and mind

- be mind-minded towards the young people, understanding without judging their inner experience of thoughts, feelings, beliefs, worries, fears, and wishes

- develop a PACEful way of being in their care of the young person, which supports the young person to move from a position of mistrust to trust in their new relationships

- explore their own attachment history and how this links to their choice of work and parenting of the young person; with greater self-awareness comes an increased capacity to stay present for the young person, but also, we hope, develops tolerance for each other

- contribute to the development of a relational culture, understanding why the young person might be behaving in the way they do, reducing their experience of oppositional controlling behaviour as a personal attack, and reducing conflict about how to work with the young person.

---

1   These programmes have associated books, which are listed in the References section. See Golding (2017b) and Page and Swann (2021).

In our therapeutic parenting training for care workers, we use an analogy of an iceberg – commonly used to understand the impact of developmental trauma – to make sense of complex presentations through an attachment and trauma lens (see Figure 9.1).

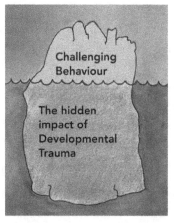

Figure 9.1: The Hidden Impact of Developmental Trauma
REPRODUCED FROM *THERAPEUTIC PARENTING WITH PACE* WITH THE PERMISSION OF PAVILION PUBLISHING AND MEDIA LTD.

The iceberg analogy highlights that the behaviour we see (above the surface) is only part of what is happening within the young person. If we respond to what we see only, we miss the bulk of what is driving their behaviour (the critical mass of the iceberg that lies hidden beneath the surface). For a young person who has experienced developmental trauma this could include:

- an overactive alarm system, which means they are easily triggered into not feeling safe

- limited ability to explore and learn about the world around them because they have had to prioritize survival at the expense of being able to focus on learning and skills development

- limited ability to explore and learn about (including regulation of) their inner world of thoughts, feelings, and perceptions

- an internalized view of themselves as bad and/or others as unsafe

- poor sensory development and integration

- numbing, dissociation, and trauma triggers.

Keeping our focus on what's going on both above and below the surface helps us to understand our young people better, to connect with them more, and to help them to recover from the impact of developmental trauma.

Thinking about how this analogy might support our day-to-day practice with the young people, one carer, Alice, observed that the handovers between shifts risked focusing on the event/content/detail of the challenging behaviour and less on understanding the underlying needs that were contributing to the behaviour. Hearing about the facts of an incident is important to an accurate assessment of risk which informs the day-to-day care plan for a young person. We are, however, more effective at preventing (not just containing) the young person's dysregulation if we also reflect on their underlying unmet needs and structure our interventions to address the factors that are driving their behaviour.

Within our training programme, we created the PACE submarine (see Figure 9.2) to help carers and those working in the young person's system to maintain a clear view of what's going on for the young person both above and below the surface of the iceberg.

At times, the submarine needs to surface and focus more on managing the behaviour. For example, the immediate safety of the aggressive young person and the staff being assaulted, or the young person who has tied a ligature. Other times, it dives deep into the hidden inner world of the young person. Mostly, though, it maintains a position where both aspects of the iceberg are fully in sight. Staff need to be supported to feel confident in the two hands of parenting (understanding and addressing behaviour), which are always delivered with a PACEful attitude. This is only possible to maintain if we anchor our practice with strategies that develop self-care, and self-reflection. The curiosity engendered in our commitment to making sense, collaboratively, with the young person about what happened (both in the present interactions within the home and in how these might relate to earlier experience, fears, and coping strategies) supports the service's commitment to becoming a more trauma-informed organization.

Figure 9.2: The PACE Submarine

REPRODUCED FROM *THERAPEUTIC PARENTING WITH PACE* WITH THE
PERMISSION OF PAVILION PUBLISHING AND MEDIA LTD.

The accompanying paradigm shifts the focus from 'what is wrong with this child?' to 'what has happened to this child?' (Perry & Winfrey, 2021). A PACEful attitude enables the adults and, given time, the young people to see the needs and strengths that underlie the distressed and challenging behaviour. It is also pivotal to the SECURE STAIRS focus on the centrality of formulation to the care and planning for children and young people in the secure estate (Taylor *et al.*, 2018).

The challenges
Stress and blocked care
As discussed above, the DDP model recognizes the level of stress that carers can experience when parenting young people with experiences of developmental trauma. This is acutely felt within the secure setting where, nationally, there are difficulties recruiting and retaining care staff. The relationships developed with the young people can be incredibly

rewarding for the staff working with them and life changing for the young person. Young people's difficulties with emotional regulation can be exacerbated by the secure environment both because it can trigger fear and anger associated with a loss of control and because it is one in which other means of regulation, for example self-harm or 'flight' (absconding), have been restricted. This can lead to young people being threatening and rejecting and staff at high risk of experiencing blocked care.

Evaluation

A level of stress for the care staff and organization as a whole can be fear of evaluation and judgement by those in authority, not only internal management, but also the external regulatory bodies that they are accountable to. Where the most severe deprivations of liberty of young people are concerned, there needs to be a high level of oversight and scrutiny over practice. Unfortunately, the media can contribute to the stress with its headlines that are quick to blame and shame social care provision. All of this can easily contribute to the replacement of curiosity with criticism and of understanding with polarized evaluation of right or wrong, not only for the young people but also for the self and each other.

Here is an example of how the shift from fear and polarization to self-awareness and curiosity can be made.

A particularly challenging time in the home occurred with the convergence of the COVID-19 pandemic and a cohort of particularly aggressive young people, the impact of which were frequent staff absences due to illness or injury. The atmosphere was tense. The staff group completing the therapeutic parenting group noted how much sense the theory made to them in the room but how challenged they were to put some of what they were learning into practice. Having spent time understanding the impact of danger on the young person's developing brain, their sensitivity to threat and the impact of this on regulation, the care staff noticed how their own brains could easily react from a position of defence. Staff noticed how they would catch the negative predictions of threat and danger pop into their mind as they were travelling to work and how they could feel the physical tension in their bodies as they entered the part of the home where the young people lived. While they did not 'flip their lids' with the young people (as described in Siegel's hand model of the brain, Siegel & Bryson, 2012, pp. 62–63), they had become hypersensitive to signs of danger, risk adverse, and had fallen into 'all or nothing' thinking in their evaluations of behaviour. At times, their creativity was shut down, and routines became more rigid. As facilitators of the group, we were able to validate their emotional experience and reframe their sense of having failed as suggestive of development in their skills. As their self-awareness of the challenges they faced grew, the care staff proactively recognized opportunities to ask for and receive support.

Cognitive challenges

We know when individuals (young persons or staff) and organizations feel unsafe, they go into survival mode and can find it much harder to think, explore, reflect, develop, regulate, and process information. They might use various coping strategies that can usually be understood as examples of fight, flight, and freeze/shutdown responses to danger. Understanding of the presence or absence of safety and trust is paramount to DDP upon which all other development and change is structured.

High staff turnover

As we have just seen, stresses of the work can make it challenging to recruit and maintain staff. The turnover of staff means constant training. This can feel like you know where you want to go but can't get there!

The reward system

The aim of the secure environment is ultimately to reduce the risks that precipitated a young person's admission to a secure setting, which is usually evidenced by a change in behaviour. Historically, there has been and still remains a behavioural focus with systems built on motivating change by the use of points systems. A points system that rewards adaptive social behaviour with increased privileges presents a dilemma for a relational approach. The reward system's inherent evaluation of the other threatens the relationships we are seeking to establish, especially when the evaluation is negative. Even positive rewards can provide cues of relational danger to a highly insecure young person. Therefore, staff may feel pressure to replace their relational approach with a behavioural reward system. It is important to recognize that this pressure may come from external agencies or regulations, or may be internal, through our acculturated beliefs about 'what is good for children'.

That said, I have observed that for some young people whose opinion of themselves and others is of so little worth there can be a lack of intrinsic motivation. If only initially, while we strive to offer them an alternative experience of others and the self, extrinsic rewards based on a points system can offer some impetus for change, but the privileges achievable in a secure setting, on their own, rarely create lasting change that reduces risk to the young person on discharge.

Pieces of work

When a young person enters the secure setting, there is often a list of interventions – pieces of 'work' – requested by the networks involved in their care. For example, 'anger management', 'a CSE (Child Sexual Exploitation) package', or 'gang work'. These requests are understandable given the level of risk and accompanying concern that has precipitated their admission. What can be easily missed is that many of these interventions require a level of reflection and cognitive insight on the part of the young person that is either not yet present developmentally or temporarily inaccessible while operating from a position of fear – fight, flight, and freeze. A pressure to be completing the 'work' misses the young person's primary need: a trusted relationship with a few key adults. As we have seen throughout this book, only once the young person has begun to build relationships of trust that can mediate the impact of trauma can they access the cognitive processes required to deal with strong emotions and understand the impact of their experiences. One has to crawl before walking, learn addition before multiplication.

Focusing on the specific packages of 'work' ignores the importance attached to the experience for the young person of the staff member who keeps turning up, being and staying with them during a moment of dysregulation, and thereafter having the time to make sense with them of what happened. Focusing on the package of 'work' minimizes the significance for the young person of the staff members' deep interest in them, all of them – not only the risks, but also what makes them laugh and feel good, and noticing their strengths. These are powerful interventions in and of themselves, providing opportunities for relational connection that may have been missed in their early experiences of developmental trauma. The relationship is the 'work' and makes a significant contribution to one of the key principles of trauma-informed work: that of the young person's experience of *being and doing with* rather than *done to*. As relationships become more secure, they provide a stable foundation from which specific aspects of the young person's behaviour can be addressed.

Conclusion

When I joined the health team in a secure environment to lead on the development of the Integrated Framework, DDP as an overarching model of relational care made intuitive sense to me as a DDP practitioner used to working with foster children and their carers. This model supports the 24/7 trauma-informed ethos of the integrated framework for the secure estate, supporting and developing carers and young people. My enthusiasm and passion for this approach may have contributed to some underestimation of the continued challenge in moving from working with the dyad and the team supporting them in the community to a system-wide approach in a highly complex social, emotional, secure, 'inpatient' environment. Four years on, I continue to believe in the power of this approach to support, not only the young people, but, importantly, the care team who are looking after the young people 24/7.

We are transitory figures in the life of the young people who come to stay with us. If we can keep ourselves anchored with the 'two hands' balanced and remain PACEful in our approach to the young people and each other, we have the opportunity to hold the young people we are caring for safely for a moment in time. In doing so, we provide a space for them to breathe, to pause, to begin to make some sense of what has happened to them and why they do the things they do, and to begin to believe in themselves. Some may continue with the high-risk behaviours that precipitated their admission when they leave us (and sustainability of change made in a secure environment is a substantial challenge facing the young people and those who care about them), but this is not so for all. Anecdotally, in the absence of any thorough national data tracking the progress of this complex cohort of young people through secure provision and into their future, the strength of an approach grounded in relational care and safety remains, for me, one of the most powerful ways to make a difference to this high-risk/high-vulnerability/high-need cohort of young people.

CHAPTER 10

The Cascade of PACE: A Culture of Support

Who Supports Whom to Stay Regulated and Reflective

The DDP approach values congruence between the way children and adults are cared for and taught. James P. Anglin, Professor Emeritus at the School of Child and Youth Care at the University of Victoria, has been writing and speaking about congruence in building and sustaining trauma-informed residential childcare organizations for 20 years. He defines congruence as '(in the service of the child's best interests) the need for core values and principles to be evident in action within each level and across all levels of an organization (extra-agency, management, supervision, line staff, clients)' (Anglin, 2015, slide 10). Anglin suggests that congruence flows 'from the top of the organization to the lower levels [and that] congruence is never fully achieved (perhaps 85%–90%+)' (2015, slide 10).

Likewise, Gillian Ruch argues that,

> for the potential of reflective practice to be fully realized, practitioners need settings which offer 'holistic containment'; settings where they feel valued and accepted, where managers offer empathic support and build safe relationships within which staff can engage in open and honest reflection about their practice and their relationships with children and colleagues. (2007, p. 660)

Within DDP, the congruence and containment provided is best enacted through the attitude of PACE. We might say that PACE is the surround sound for all relationships.

This chapter focuses on how to achieve a culture of support in which all relationships are surrounded by a way of being that is described as PACE. This is a top-to-bottom, side-to-side, bottom-to-top cascade which flows through the organization.

The cascade of PACE

It is important that the core attitude of PACE cascades down, through, and indeed beyond, the residential service. This supports all to be regulated, reflective, and proactive (see Figure 10.1).

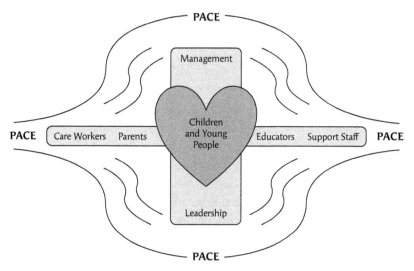

Figure 10.1: The Cascade of PACE

PACE is like a cascade of water: a series of small waterfalls descending over rocks interspersed with tiers of water pools. PACE flows down and through every tier of the organization. All can swim together in their tiered pools of PACE. As the Russian Olympic swimming gold medallist and world-record holder Alexander Popov said: 'The water is your friend. You don't have to fight with water, just share the same spirit as the water, and it will help you move' (Lohn, 2021, last paragraph).

Some people who join the organization know how to swim PACEfully and are confident on both the surface and diving under the water in order to explore. They are skilled navigating the rocks and boulders, coming up to breathe when they need to. Others learn, with support, to swim and then to dive relatively easily, but inevitably have a few bruises and skinned knees from the rocks! Yet others may want to swim but have to start by dipping their toes in the water until they begin to feel safe.

The children are invited and supported to join in the PACE toe-dipping and swimming, with the adults, with each other, and then independently. They learn to experience safety and success in the water. They learn to trust that, together with competent swimmers and when they are ready, they can explore under the water. They get skinned knees, stubbed toes, and bruises from the rocks, but have support to learn to navigate more confidently. They are offered comfort when they get hurt either swimming or diving.

The children's families, particularly their parents, are invited and encouraged to join the PACEful swimming. They dive with their children alongside a confident diver until they are competent to swim and dive alone or with their children.

Involving the children in the cascade of PACE

As we know, from the impact of developmental trauma many of the children in residential care are 'water averse'. They won't even want to put their toe in the water, never mind diving into its depths. They have no curiosity about what is under the water, or they may fear that the water is full of sharks – it feels too dangerous to enter. How can the adults make the water inviting? First, the child sees other children and adults enjoying dipping their toes in the water, then swimming and diving. They notice that when the child experiences cuts and scrapes adults are on hand to soothe and comfort.

As the adults hold the attitude of PACE, the child is allowed to join them as they feel ready. The adults additionally provide a gentle challenge within the limits of what the children can tolerate. With the messages 'we can do this together' and 'you won't be left alone', the child is encouraged to enter the water. Remembering that this may be the first time the child has entered the water, the adult accepts the child's reluctance while gently challenging them to take a first step with their support. The child gets an experience of PACE while feeling regulated and safe. In effect, the adults say to the child: 'I know this feels scary. It must be hard to trust me when I say that the water is safe. Hold my hand and let's stand on the edge until we are ready to dip our toes in, just for a minute. I know you can do this.'

The children watch how the adults relate to the other children and each other. They are making judgements about whether the adults are safe or not. They notice how comfort and joy are available to all.

In this way, the children are learning about themselves and others through the experience and understanding of PACE. The attitude of PACE supports children who consider themselves as unlikeable and unlovable to begin to consider the possibility that they might be likeable, they might be lovable.

There is an additional complexity when we consider the diversity that the children bring with them. All children living in residential care have experienced relational trauma. Trauma can also be experienced due to the inequities in power within an unequal society. Children may have previously lived in marginalized communities and/or absorbed attitudes towards such discriminated against populations. By marginalized communities we mean those communities who are discriminated against and oppressed because of their culture and identity. This includes race, sexuality and gender, religious beliefs, class, and disability.

The children bring power and inequality into the residential settings when they have experienced discrimination against them and/or learned to discriminate against others. Society's injustices become mirrored within the microclimate of the residential setting and become enacted in the peer relationships between the children and in the relationships that develop between children and adults. In addition, the children haven't chosen to live in residential care. The community within which they are now living is imposed on them. There is no opportunity to 'find your own community', which can be such a support to those living in the wider world with inequality and injustice. The children who are experiencing oppression or discrimination can find no respite from these daily threats. This is an additional challenge to the adults as they find ways to help children to feel safe within the residential setting.

This all creates many opportunities for additional turbulence. An important starting point in calming this turbulence is to acknowledge its existence. The adults need to reflect on their own experiences, acknowledging any conscious or unconscious biases which might lead them to ignore or overlook the turbulent waters created by inequality and social injustice. A climate of reflection allows adults to work together to notice the experiences of all the children in their care. The cascade of PACE needs to extend outwards to encompass this additional complexity.

In summary, healing relational trauma means supporting children to move from fear of relationships to trust in relationships. The adults adopting a DDP approach with a PACEful attitude support the change in the children's core beliefs lying at the heart of who they are. This must take into account the complexity and intersections of trauma that they have experienced.

Children need the cascade of PACE to provide them with the regulation and safety needed to take the risk to emotionally connect. This is the beginning of healing.

In the words of some of the children we have worked with:

- 'I learned how to be sad.'

- 'Most kids think they come here to feel better, but actually they come here to feel more.'

- 'For the first time in my life, you saw me.'

- 'This is really weird. You are talking to me differently…but I do quite like it.'

Involving care workers, support workers, and educators in the cascade of PACE: Horizontal working with each other

Having explored the cascade of PACE with the children at the heart of the organization, we are now going to explore the cascade of PACE in the horizontal (see Figure 10.1). By this we mean the adults whose day-to-day working lives is with the children. They are inhabiting the children's living and learning spaces. These adults are the teams around the children. They hold the attitude of PACE for themselves, with each other, and for the children. When they lose the attitude of PACE, they help each other to find their way back again.

Remember, as we explored above, the importance of the adults knowing themselves is integral to holding this attitude. Conscious and unconscious biases impacted by their own experience growing up are explored within a reflective culture so that the adults are in the best position to support the children in all their complexity.

Moving away from the water analogy, we would like to share a story with you to illustrate PACE in teamwork. This story also demonstrates the role a DDP consultant can take when providing support to a residential setting.

WORKING WITH RELATIONAL TRAUMA IN CHILDREN'S RESIDENTIAL CARE

THE BUTTERFLY STORY

Edwina was providing consultation to a residential team. The team were gathered in the upstairs lounge with the VELUX windows wide open to cool the impact of the sun streaming in. Edwina had just started the chat going with the team when a red admiral butterfly flew in the room. Delightful! However, she noticed Noah startle and look scared. In an instant, he had moved to the other side of the room. The other team members noticed, too, and laughed. To her shame, so did Edwina. 'You scared of a butterfly, Noah!' sniggered Wendy. 'What a wuss!' The butterfly flew out of the window. Edwina caught herself laughing at Noah's obvious fear and was mortified. She put her hands out in front of her in a gesture of 'stop'.

Edwina: Noah, I'm so, so sorry. We all laughed when you were clearly scared of the butterfly. We're here to talk about PACE, and I just did the exact opposite. So did we all.

Noah: (looking embarrassed) It's okay.

Edwina: No, it's not okay. We didn't acknowledge your feelings and we've embarrassed you. Noah, that was horrible for you. I think there must be a story behind butterflies. Am I right and are you okay to tell us the story?

Noah: Yes, there's a story. A good few years ago, my partner and I went on holiday to Indonesia. She was really keen to go and visit a butterfly forest, a tourist attraction. So you know how in the UK we have butterfly kingdoms, like a big glass house full of butterflies, and you get a small dish of some sweet stuff so they land on you and on the syrup? Well, my partner and I thought the butterfly forest would be like this, only outside in the forest. We arrived and got our dish of syrup. I should have suspected something then as the dish of syrupy stuff was pretty big! As soon as we walked in, I was surrounded by enormous butterflies – like a foot wide! They were on me, wings flapping. I froze. I wanted to bat them off, but I didn't want to kill them, so I just stood there – rabbit caught in the headlights. My partner was laughing at first and then she realized I was rooted to the spot. One of the staff had to remove the dish from my hand, take the butterflies off with a net, and lead me out of the forest. It was awful! I felt like such an idiot, but for me it was traumatic – I don't know why but it was! So now – I know it sounds daft, but – I am scared of butterflies, and I avoid them as much as possible.

Edwina: That's some story – thanks for telling us. Now I get why you were scared today, it's understandable.

Having heard the story, the other team members, looking a bit uncomfortable, apologized, too. They expressed their empathy for Noah and that traumatic experience.

Noah: Wait, wait – that's not the end of the story. My partner and I have a little girl now, Emily. She's six. She came home from school a couple of weeks ago and asked if I would take her to the butterfly kingdom, you know, the one near here. Some of her friends at school had been talking about it. The words 'yes, of course', were out of my mouth before I felt the dread. My partner offered to take Emily, but I decided to 'face my fears' as they say, and off Emily and I set that weekend. I had self-talked to prepare myself, saying 'I'll be fine, it's just little butterflies. Emily will love it and that will overcome the fear.' I was holding Emily's hand on the way up the ramp to the glass house. I was feeling chilled; then we were given the dishes of syrup. I could feel the anxiety coming up from my boots! My heart was racing, my palms sweating. I'm saying to myself, 'I can't go in; I have to go in for Emily.' Emily felt my fear and asked: 'Are you scared, Daddy?' 'Yes,' I said, 'I am a bit. Let me tell you why.' Emily and I stood to one side, and I told her the story of the butterfly forest – the children's version. I didn't want to terrify her! Telling the story helped me calm. Emily was surprised and a bit puzzled – her big, strong dad, scared? She said, 'It's okay Daddy, they are only little butterflies, like in our garden, and besides I'm here to hold your hand.' I did it, we did it! I'm still scared of butterflies, though, as you can see! (Noah and the team were laughing together now.)

Reflection
If you were Noah and Emily was your daughter, would you have acknowledged your fear or denied it?

What did this team learn about PACE within teamwork from this experience? They learned that sometimes playfulness can be misplaced, leading to judgement and a rupture in the relationship. Edwina modelled noticing and repairing this rupture with an attitude of PACE. This gave the team an opportunity to slow down, understand with curiosity, show acceptance and empathy, and thus repair the relationship with their colleague. This led everyone back to safe playfulness.

Returning to the water metaphor, what this example demonstrates is that teams can enter the water together. Sometimes, the water becomes stormy, whether because of misplaced banter, tensions and disagreements, or clashes of personality. PACE for self and others allows the team to navigate to calmer waters.

In the butterfly story, Noah was able to talk about his feelings and to acknowledge that he was scared, both to the team and to his daughter. When there is a reluctance in the adults to talk about and demonstrate their feelings with each other, PACE can get shut down. The cascade of PACE can dry up, reducing the healing environment for the child. Notice how Emily, Noah's daughter, had developed the capacity for PACE, most noticeably in her use of empathy. It is likely that this development was an outcome of living with a PACEful parent. Noah was able to be open about his feelings and be PACEful for himself in front of his daughter. This type of modelling enables all children to learn what their feelings are and how to express them. This is especially important for children with developmental trauma who have not experienced adults who can show their emotions in a regulated way.

Teams, therefore, need this cascade of PACE if they are to guide children into healthier ways of feeling, thinking, and being.

In the words of some of the adults we have worked with:

- 'PACE makes you cry, but in a good way.'

- 'One of the most important things I've learned is how to sit in the shit and to feel comfortable there.'

- 'PACE means I sit with the uncomfortable for longer than is comfortable.'

- 'Being PACEful gives you magic moments of connection.'

Involving children's parents in the cascade of PACE

Children have important parental figures who remain involved in their life, and it is important to include these adults in the cascade of PACE. These might be birth parents, foster carers, adopters, or other kin. Working with the parents as part of the horizontal support to the children (see Figure 10.1) is an important part of providing a healing environment.

The parents can be involved or not involved in a range of ways. Some parents are fully involved and want to play an active role in the child's life. Others are in contact, but direct involvement is limited. Unfortunately, there are also parents who have died. Other parents may not want to have contact, are not allowed to have contact, or have disappeared from view. All of these parents, regardless of their situation, have a central place within the emotional world of the child. The children are rooted in these relationships, for better or worse, and this continues to exert a major influence upon them.

When parents continue to be actively involved, they are supported to be part of the cascade of PACE. They are encouraged to enter the water with their children, whether lightly by dipping toes in, swimming, or even diving, always supported by the residential caregivers. The children experience their multiple parenting figures working together to support them.

Some parents are keen to experience the water; others, due to their own life experiences, show more reluctance, being water averse. These parents are involved in their children's life to a lesser degree while still maintaining some role. In these cases, the key adults in the child's residential life reach out to the parents at a pace and intensity that suits them and their child. They offer a life jacket to the parents, supporting them to be part of the cascade of PACE, while recognizing the difficulties this might present. Maintaining safety for child and parent is paramount.

When parents are absent, whether through choice or not, the key adults still have an important role in bringing memories of them into the cascade of PACE. This means helping the children make sense of why their parents are absent and reducing the sense of abandonment and responsibility for the loss that the children might hold. This often entails sitting with the uncomfortable to enable the children to have space to grieve these important losses. Sometimes, this is the first time that the children have been helped to find their voice in relation to the losses they have experienced. The offer of PACE, especially acceptance, empathy, and curiosity, can be a powerful way of enabling this to happen.

Holding a PACEful attitude for and with parents who have been responsible for the harm to their children can be complex and emotionally challenging. The adults need their own support to manage this successfully.

Let's remember that parents, too, come from different backgrounds and may have been marginalized and/or traumatized. A PACEful residential worker seeks to know the parent's story, including their unique successes and challenges.

We have explored the important role that parents have within the cascade of PACE, whether actively involved, peripherally involved, or indeed absent. The way the key adults talk with the parents and about the parents with the children is a key part of offering this cascade of PACE.

In the words of some of the parents we have known:

- 'I know my child needed to move into residential care, but I am and will always be his parent.'

- 'This is the first time that I've felt listened to rather than judged.'

- 'I didn't understand that the way I was brought up affected how I parented my children.'

- 'I know I relinquished my adopted children and understand I can't contact them, but please hold me positively in my children's minds.'

Bringing PACE in from the top: Top-down vertical support

Having explored the cascade of PACE in relation to the children and to the adults caring for and supporting them, we are now going to turn our attention to the cascade of PACE in the vertical (see Figure 10.1). By this we mean the senior managers, both strategic and operational, who create and sustain the DDP-informed culture within the residential setting.

Thinking about our cascade of PACE, it is a core management and leadership task to ensure the top tier of the cascade is infused and revitalized with PACE when necessary. Think back to the metaphor we introduced earlier of water cascading through a series of pools. We are now entering the top pool. It is the CEO's (or equivalent) and management team's responsibility to ensure that everything that happens within the organization is filtered through PACE, from vision, values, policy, systems, and procedures to practices.

This is no mean feat as the policy and procedures often flow against the cascade of PACE at the source. Imagine a river feeding the cascade of pools and the currents in the river creating turbulence. Policy and procedures can be prescriptive, corporate, rigid, and focused on the behaviour of the children and of the adults. These processes have good intentions; ultimately, there is a common desire for the children to be safe, to be healthy, and to thrive. However, there can be a lack of understanding about the length of time needed to help children who have experienced developmental trauma to trust in relationships before we might expect them to settle into adult's, and even society's, expectations of their behaviours.

When the children display behaviours which are challenging, and they are not settled or achieving, it can be easy to view this as a failure of the implementation of the policies and procedures by the adults. This is counter to the DDP-informed view of the need to slow down and give the children time and space to develop trust and to feel comfortable being supported and regulated by the adults caring for and educating them. Only then can the children develop the capacity to reflect, begin to believe in their essential goodness, and, ultimately, manage their behaviour in a prosocial way.

This, in essence, is what we mean by a trauma-informed approach, understanding, as it does, the necessity to support the needs of the children which have arisen because of their trauma. This is what the children need before we can expect them to settle and achieve. If the policies and procedures are aimed narrowly at demonstrating behavioural change, and the PACEful approach – informed by the DDP principles – is aimed at giving the children and adults time for relationship building, developing trust, and regulatory support, then we can see a basic incompatibility between the two goals. Ultimately, there is a need for a space for healing which can be lost in the shorter-term focus on behavioural change. Therefore, it can be difficult to implement a PACEful approach, which on first sight appears to be counter to what the policies and procedure are trying to achieve. Returning to our metaphor, there can be much turbulence created by this incompatibility. It requires skilful swimming and diving to maintain PACE in a way which also satisfies the requirements of the policies and procedures. This can be done when the policies and procedures are written with a DDP lens in place.

We have talked about the turbulence that can come from external drivers with respect to policies and procedures. The management and leadership teams are also managing the turbulence that comes from within the organization. These are the everyday conflicts, tensions, absences, and movement that occur in any residential setting. These can be complex to manage while also holding the child's needs in mind.

Creating and sustaining a staff team inevitably and helpfully involves proactively seeking and welcoming a diverse workforce. A diversity of culture and identity provides a wealth of experience that can enrich the overall culture of the organization. Relationships within the workforce and with the children benefit from a diverse and inclusive residential culture. There are many opportunities to learn from and model respect for each other. This also has the potential for more turbulence without careful nurturing and the cascade of PACE.

We have identified the need for a cascade of PACE within policies and procedures through nurturing the workforce and by fostering a culture of inclusivity. Let's think about how the management and leadership teams are supported to do this.

First and foremost, the management team are PACEful with each other, ensuring regular opportunities to reflect on how they are feeling as well as what they are doing. They celebrate successful swimming and diving as well as being honest about their own skimmed knees and bruises. They support each other to find the balance between the strength and empathy that is needed in leading the organization.

The management team, with this strong foundation, are able to model and encourage a PACE attitude throughout the organization. The challenge and complexity of doing this should not be underestimated. It requires a non-defensive, open, and engaged approach and the humility to acknowledge defensiveness and to repair. The management team work to maintain an open and engaged culture. The balance between strength and empathy is integral to achieving this.

If they are to swim and not to sink, the management team cannot be alone in this endeavour. They need their own support from external DDP consultants and adults who champion and model DDP from within the organization. With organizations in which there is accountability to a parent organization and/or to a board of trustees, the management team are greatly helped when DDP champions and modellers are on board. These consultants and champions truly understand and are committed to the DDP approach. The cascade of PACE is part of the whole organization and the structures within which it exists.

In the words of some of the managers we have worked with:

- 'We (the management team) need to be curious about issues

which make us want to fight, run away, or hide. It's hard, but unless *we* do this our staff will not.'

- 'I (the CEO) worry when you (DDP consultant) start a sentence with "I wonder…" because I know I have probably not given the issue we are talking about sufficient attention.'

- 'The pressure from outside the organization, and sometimes from within, "to do" rather than to think and do is immense.'

- 'There is a place for speedy decisions. However, we've learned, in general, to slow down, frustrating though it can be, as unless solutions are co-created PACEfully, they will not work.'

Involving external practitioners within the cascade of PACE

Although not directly represented within the cascade of PACE model (see Figure 10.1), there are also a range of people, external to the residential setting, who contribute to the cascade of PACE. It's important that social work, health, and education practitioners understand the DDP model that the residential setting is embedding. We want them to adopt the same attitude of PACE in their conversations with the children, parents, and with the team around the children. In addition to being given information about the residential setting, it is also modelled to the external practitioners in all their contact with the setting. This includes relationship repair when the attitude is inevitably lost due to the complexity of the work.

This collaborative working respects the individual experiences of the practitioners, including the beliefs, values, and practices that they hold. Sharing stories is an important part of finding mutually agreed ways forward.

In the words of some of the external practitioners we have worked with:

- 'As a principal psychologist, I had never experienced the depth of understanding of the impact of trauma that the residential team around the child demonstrated.'

- 'You persevered when others gave up.'

- 'This organization has a deep trust in process; by that I mean you know that children who have experienced relational harm can recover when their needs are met. It might take a lot of time and patience, but you know it will happen.'

- 'Thank you for the welcome we always have when we come here.'

PACE within the two hands of parenting: The cascade of PACE needs some containment

In our experience, it is not uncommon that when parenting figures are first introduced to PACE their enthusiasm for adopting this attitude means that they let go of structure, boundaries, and limits. The child experiences a lack of containment and safety, leading to a worsening of behaviour. The two hands of parenting emphasizes the importance of pairing the emotional connection, regulation, and co-creation enabled by PACE with the external support provided by supervision and emotionally connected discipline (see Figure 10.2).

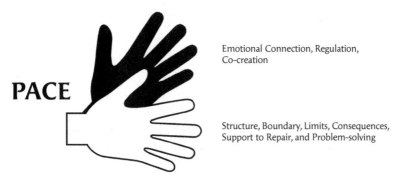

PACE

Emotional Connection, Regulation, Co-creation

Structure, Boundary, Limits, Consequences, Support to Repair, and Problem-solving

Figure 10.2: The Two Hands of Parenting

In a similar vein, it is helpful for the adult to move to some problem-solving as part of the second hand. Once the child feels connected with and understood, they are able to join in with the problem-solving, allowing consequences and reparative actions to be decided collaboratively. The DDP approach discourages early reassurance, which can be more about moving away from uncomfortable emotional experience, an invalidating experience. However, within a connected relationship, the carer can offer hope to the child that things can be different one day, saying such things as 'I believe you will be able to do this in the future' or 'We'll figure this out together'. The two hands of parenting provide both the emotional connection and the challenge to enable the child to gain the confidence to stretch and experience success.

Returning to our metaphor, the child learning to swim and dive in the pools needs the adult to hold them until they are ready to let go. The adult remains nearby, offering water wings to allow the child the freedom to explore, confident that they will return to them when asked. The two hands of parenting deepen safety and trust in relationships so that the child can respond to the guidance of the adult. Two hands are needed for the child to learn to trust in adult care, then to trust in adult authority, and, ultimately, to trust in self as they mature into confident, independent, and autonomous adults.

Conclusion

In this chapter, we have explored the metaphor of PACE as a cascade of water that is infused throughout and beyond the organization. PACE influences every aspect of practice: being with the children and their parents, within teams, and in leadership and management practices and policies. Within the DDP way, in which the building of safety and trust through relational and reflective practice is central, the attitude of PACE provides the holistic containment for living, loving, and learning.

CHAPTER 11

Living, Learning, and Loving in Residential Care

Bill's Story, Part 2

As we saw in Chapter 3, Bill is a seven-year-old boy who suffered from relational trauma during his first four years of life. After a year of foster care, he was placed with José, his newly discovered biological father. Bill continued to have symptoms of developmental trauma for the next two years with José, including shame-driven emotional dysregulation, a disorganized controlling attachment pattern, blocked trust, and an aversion to intersubjective experience. These conditions prevented him from making progress in his one-hour-a-week outpatient treatment and eventually caused enough dangerous behaviour to require placement in a residential level of care to keep him safe.

Here's an example of criteria from the US indicating when residential care is required to treat developmental trauma disorder:

> A child or youth (referred to here as 'child') needs a [Psychiatric Residential Treatment Facility] level of care when their psychiatric symptoms cause danger to themselves or others and intensive community services have failed to keep the child and others safe and have failed to improve their psychiatric condition or prevent regression. (Kansas Department for Aging and Disability Services, n.d., p. 1)

Bill met these criteria. When he got dysregulated and ran out of the house and across the street, he was in an impulsive state that prevented him from accessing the executive functions of his frontal lobes. He could get hit by a car if the driver didn't see him, resulting in a severe injury or even death. Already his disorganized attachment led him to do strange and potentially dangerous things, like run off the porch to hit the woman walking by or to stand over his father while he slept, contemplating who knows what. Therefore, he met the standard of posing a chronic risk of causing substantial harm to himself or another.

Bill's inability to trust posed a serious impediment to outpatient treatment. As described in Chapter 2, his stress response system was activated and on alert for signs of danger, even when a therapist or caregiver had benign intentions. His nervous system prioritized self-defence over social engagement, making him hypervigilant and controlling rather than curious or able to explore. He related to his father, therapist, and case manager with mistrust, certain that they intended to harm him. He kept himself safe by being constantly on guard and attempting to control the interactions. For these reasons, Bill's condition would not get better in outpatient treatment.

As we will see, Bill also met the third criterion for admission: residential care was expected to help improve his condition.

ADMISSION TO A RESIDENTIAL SETTING

We now pick up Bill's story as he is admitted to a residential setting where many of the staff had trained in Dyadic Developmental Practice and most of the therapists had trained in Dyadic Developmental Psychotherapy. They were all fairly comfortable with children and adolescents who had experienced developmental trauma. The staff were mostly people in their 20s who were drawn to work with children who had rough early lives. Some had studied psychology or related fields in college, while some had practical experience working with children instead of more formal training. At this point, the staff knew how to work with children who were mistrusting, controlling, and easily dysregulated by shame or terror. They knew to utilize an intersubjective approach designed to build trust and co-create new and healthier narratives. Bill was assigned to a unit with seven other preadolescents. Montrelle, the lead staff on the unit, welcomed Bill and showed him and José around, introducing them to the other staff and kids. Bill put his things in his room and revealed little emotion when he said goodbye to José. Montrelle told Bill, 'I'm sure it will take you some time to get used to this place. We don't expect you to understand it right away. I didn't get it at first either.' When he saw Bill paying attention to what he was saying, he continued, saying, 'One more thing. We are all new people for you. We get that you won't trust us at first. That makes sense. We do hope that as you get to know us, you might start to trust us a little. Sometimes, we'll need to tell you that you can't do something you want to do. It'd be much better if we could just get to know each other before we had to tell you these things, but I'm afraid we're going to have to say these things before you know us well. We'll try to remember how hard that is for you.'

Montrelle, a 28-year-old Black man, hadn't always known to say these things. When he arrived at the residential setting six years prior, he knew he wanted to help kids who had experienced some of the trauma he had experienced growing up, like watching his father, who was incarcerated on minor drug charges, get more and more time added to his sentence because the white guards didn't like the way he looked at them. At the time, Montrelle felt he understood the kids he worked with well enough. He had good instincts for what helped and had a good mentor who liked working with enthusiastic, good-hearted young people who were drawn to this work. When Montrelle did something counterproductive, his mentor gently guided him to a new way of thinking about the kids and new ways of working with them. When he did something helpful, his mentor would point out why that intervention had worked. From this supervision, the regular training he received, and extra reading that he did, Montrelle steadily progressed in his ability to build trust with kids like Bill and to help them calm down when they became upset.

For the first few weeks, Bill was somewhat shy and reserved. On the inside he felt numb and disoriented. 'What is this place?' he wondered. 'What's happening? Will I see José again?' He walked through his days in a bit of a stupor. Gradually, the numbness thawed a little, and he let himself play on the playground with a couple of the boys. They seemed okay at first, then they started getting on his nerves like the boys at his previous school. After a few weeks of what the staff called a honeymoon, he began having the same kinds of explosions he was having at home with José. The first one happened in school when he was given a worksheet with pictures of a cat, rat, hat, bat, and so on, and was asked to spell the words. He yelled at the teacher, 'I hate this stupid worksheet, and I hate you!' Another time, he hit a boy who had taken the truck he was playing with in the sandbox. Both times, he cowered in a ball, wondering what would happen to him after his explosion. He was worried because sometimes José would yell at him when he exploded. But so far, none of the staff had raised their voice.

The staff understood that these outbursts were a manifestation of the shame Bill experienced when something caused him to feel inadequate. They understood that when he was exploding, from the perspective of the polyvagal theory, he had gone into an activated state of fight-or-flight, causing stress hormones to course through his body. They recognized that when he curled into a ball, he had descended into a state of shutdown, which could cause lowering of the heart rate and blood pressure, along with a hazy and disconnected consciousness referred to as dissociation. They had studied and practised the PACE attitude, how a playful, accepting, curious, and empathic approach sent reassuring signals to the alarm centre, the amygdala, in the child's brain, that things were safe now, nothing was going to harm them, and they were secure. They knew that the PACE attitude was a key element of co-regulating a child's affective dysregulation and for building the trust that would be needed for them to get better.

The staff had learned a helpful phrase related to polyvagal neurophysiology (Dana, 2020):

- Socially engaged *connection* happens when a person neurocepts safety ('neurocepts safety' means their nervous system detects the signals of safe conditions).

- Fight-or-flight *protection* happens when a person neurocepts danger.

- A state of shutdown and *disconnection* are evoked by a neuroception of life threat.

Connection. Protection. Disconnection.

It was important to know which state a child was in because different things are helpful in each of these three states. When a child was connected, the staff could interact as they typically would, and they could be fairly confident that the child would understand what they were saying. When a child was protected in a state of fight-or-flight, they could co-regulate the child by using their PACE skills. When a child was disconnected, they would still use PACE skills, but would know that the child might not respond as quickly or with as large movements as they did at other times. The staff would go slowly, noticing the small gestures and tiny changes in facial expression that indicated the child was with them.

The staff tried to respond to Bill's outbursts with a PACEful attitude as often as they could, saying such things as: 'Aww, Bill, this is really tough for you. It really bothers you when that boy talks about your mum.' Bill looked at them like they were weird at first, then started to relax and nod, or say a few words in response to their comments, such as: 'Yeah, he shouldn't have said that. I hate it when he says that.' The staff didn't try to change Bill's experience, by saying, for example, 'Don't let that boy get to you.' That would be a non-accepting remark. The staff took what Bill was experiencing as what he was experiencing, an accepting attitude of 'it is what it is'. The staff's acceptance of what Bill was experiencing felt safe to Bill, and the staff noticed he would often let out a sigh when their empathy was on target. At that point, they knew that Bill would usually respond positively to their curious questions about what was going on for him. Accepting, curious, empathic. These three qualities demonstrated to Bill that the staff were interested in what was going on inside him, that his experiences were important, and he was worth getting to know.

The staff learned that matched affect, as discussed in Chapter 2, also has a calming effect on a child. When an adult matches the affect of a child, when they display the same embodied emotional energy that they perceive the child as having, there is a non-verbal communication of 'I get what you are feeling'. This demonstrates understanding of the child's state and has a soothing effect on the child. So, the staff would match the energy that Bill exhibited when he was distressed and agitated. Though they wouldn't feel agitated themselves, they would adopt a bit of a frenetic disposition, which they would tone down in step with Bill's calming.

DDP posits that you can't just tell a traumatized child (or a non-traumatized child for that matter) that they are valuable and have them internalize that perspective. It's the look in the caregiver's eyes, the tone of their voice, and the way the caregiver matches the child's affect that communicates that the child is worthy and valuable. In more typical, non-traumatic child development, these sorts of interactions happen thousands of times: the caregiver makes playful, accepting, curious, and empathic comments, and the child feels seen and valued. As a result of this repetition of positive interactions, the child builds an internal working model of a healthy relationship. This model includes qualities of shared experience, compassion, nurturing, care, and safety. The child comes to view themselves as valuable and worthy of good treatment.

Bill's internal working model said that he was not worth caring for, that he didn't matter to people, and that he would need to take care of himself if he wanted to survive. The staff recognized these inner self-representations through Bill's hyper-independent stance. He wouldn't ask for help with anything. He wouldn't ask for help with the worksheets at school, like the one that had caused the blow up. He wouldn't ask for help if he had a disagreement with another child. When he didn't know where his socks had gone, he just wore his shoes without socks. He picked up his chicken patty at dinner and took bites out of it when he was unable to cut it with his knife. He did these things the best he could alone.

Bill's hyper-independence extended to how he handled his episodes of dysregulation. When he was first admitted, he didn't respond when the staff spoke with him during an outburst. His eyes had a faraway look, staring at the staff without seeming to see them. Their words had little effect on his emotions and behaviour, and they concluded that these outbursts just needed to run their course. The staff continued to keep him safe, use a PACEful approach, match his affect, and be interested in what he was experiencing. They would debrief with Bill after each of these episodes, talking about what had gotten him upset, what had helped him calm down, and how he experienced each part of what happened.

After five months, the staff noticed that when Bill had an outburst, he stayed connected to them better. He seemed to hear them when they would tell him, 'You're so upset! This is such an upsetting thing for you.' He would turn his face toward them, and he appeared to be trying to calm himself down. They had a growing sense of working together with Bill to help regulate his emotions. Sometimes, they would say to each other, 'His heart didn't seem to be in it in that meltdown.' After another two months, Bill would calm down when the staff matched his affect, accepted his experience, and empathized with how hard he was working to learn new things. He was learning to trust them enough that he could allow them to co-regulate his affect. Co-regulation, as described in Chapters 1 and 2, helped Bill to develop a more secure attachment with the staff supporting him.

This arc of Bill's response in dysregulated states followed the neurophysiology the staff had learned about. They remembered the three states as:

1. socially engaged connection (in safety)

2. fight-or-flight protection (in danger)

3. neurophysiological shutdown and disconnection (in life-threat).

At first, when dysregulated, Bill was in a state of disconnected shutdown, and it took some time before an emotional storm would run its course. By the time he had been there for five months, he would go into a state of fight-or-flight protection during a torrent of intense feelings but didn't disconnect and dissociate as he had done before. Later, he could stay connected without pushing the adults away so much, even though his big feelings were surging. Until it had been pointed out to them, the staff didn't notice this progression. Afterwards, they used these changes as subtle guideposts to mark Bill's progress through treatment. They learned to look for other subtle markers of progress, such as when he started to allow them to cut his meat at dinner.

Around the time Bill was developing the ability to stay connected during outbursts, the staff noticed that he could let his guard down during happy times as well. He started to relax and enjoy himself, and the staff were right there with him, enjoying his enjoyment. There was more laughter and fewer tears. The staff remarked that Bill looked different too. When he first came to the facility, they thought he looked like a little man, with a serious expression all the time. More of the time now, he was just a boy, and they even saw him skipping to the playground one day.

José was doing well, too. José and Bill met weekly with the DDP therapist, Kiran, who saw kids on that unit. Kiran, a 32-year-old woman whose parents were born in India, would engage with Bill, talking about something lively that usually got Bill talking, too. One time, for example, she said, 'Bill, I heard you tell the other kids the best stories at bedtime. They always beg for more!' Bill became a bit shy, and Kiran continued, 'Keep that up, and you will need to practise taking a bow. Can you show us a little one now?' José marvelled at her energy and enthusiasm and the way she cared about what Bill was experiencing. Kiran explained to him that growing up as the child of immigrants had been painful. She felt she didn't belong in the world of her classmates at school and didn't really belong in her parents' world either. She told him she took a course in college on intersectionality, and described learning about how our various social categories, like ethnicity, race, gender, and sexuality, impacted how we saw ourselves and the world. She found she was fascinated by the unique emotions, viewpoints, hopes, and fears that each individual experienced, and, later on, discovered that practising Dyadic Developmental Psychotherapy matched her personality well.

One feature of this residential setting was that each child was assigned two staff members who were considered the child's 'key people'. The key person's job was to serve as the child's attachment figure and caregiver at the facility. They really get to know and understand the child, especially when the child had no caregiver they were returning to. They also made decisions about the child's limits. For example, one day when Bill was struggling more than usual, his key person made the decision that he wouldn't be allowed to go to the playground after lunch. He would stay inside, and they would have one-on-one time together until Bill felt more like himself again. It was important that Bill learned that the person who cared for and about him the most was also a person to govern his activities. Each therapy session, one of Bill's key people would come to the session with José and Bill. Kiran would help José and the staff member join in the conversation with Bill, and José was always surprised at the depth of feeling that the sessions would bring out in all of them.

José came to the parenting group regularly and learned more about the kind of relationship that could really help Bill with his issues. He learned the PACE acronym and practised adopting PACE as a way of being in role plays with other parents. The parents would often practise being PACEful with each other for 15 or 20 minutes at the start of the group session. This served several purposes. They could get feedback and practise their skills in being playful, accepting, curious, and empathic. It was also a chance for the parent who was talking to get something off their chest. The group leaders thought of this part of the session as a protective factor from blocked care. Chapter 2 described Hughes and Baylin's concept of blocked care (2012) as an exquisitely painful parental state which can occur when a child with developmental trauma disorder repeatedly rejects their parents' good-hearted efforts to connect. Blocked care represents a potentially serious impediment to parents accepting a child back home, so the group leaders paid particular attention to it.

After the parents paired to practise being PACEful with each other, they would come back and share challenges from their week, and the therapists would lead a discussion about the topics that had emerged organically. For example, in one session, the parents talked about feelings of shame and failure that often arose in learning to be helpful to their child. They wished they had learned about developmental trauma and PACE sooner and felt bad that they hadn't. The leaders pointed out that the parents were giving themselves a hard time instead of relating with self-compassion. The leaders wondered, 'What would it be like to say to yourselves, "Seeing my child struggle can be heart-wrenching. I wish we lived in a world where bad things didn't happen, or if they did, we got the help we needed right away"? What if we could say, "Well, at least I'm here with you, and I'm supported to feel both sad about my child's pain and good that we are learning these things now"?' This discussion, which had started out poignantly, gradually became more light-hearted as the parents' tender feelings were acknowledged and released. By the end of that session, the parents were playfully comparing notes on which inner critical voice had the best ways of putting the parent down and laughing as one critical voice bested another.

The group helped José improve in his skill at adopting the PACE attitude, and he also got a lot of practice in the sessions with Bill and Kiran. At the beginning of their work together, Bill's suffering made José want to run out of the room. Now he could stay connected to Bill and say, 'You were such a little fellow. It must have felt so sad that your parents left you alone.' José now felt he was a trust builder with Bill, and he could co-regulate Bill's shame more and more predictably. People at work commented that José was different there too – less distant, more connected, more interested in what they were thinking and feeling. They told José that, before, it seemed that he cared more about the produce than he did about them. Now they felt that, in José's eyes, they ranked right up there with the apples and summer squash.

Bill had been spending the night at home with José on the weekends, and the visits had mostly gone well. José found that Bill would let him into his world more than he had before he had come to the facility. He could tell José when he needed something and when he was upset. When Bill's upsets threatened to overwhelm him, José had the same success in co-regulating Bill's affect that he had in the therapy sessions. He could say things such as: 'You are so mad at me right now. You wish I understood how much you loved your Xbox. If I did, I wouldn't make you stop playing with it!' As José matched Bill's affect, Bill stayed connected and allowed José's attuned engagement to help him regain control of his emotions. José was proud of his success in using the two hands of parenting – on the one hand, he could set limits on Bill's videogame time, and, on the other hand, he could empathize with how hard it was for Bill to stop playing.

Even more importantly, José was able to repair the ruptures in their relationship when they occurred. Microruptures of attunement, as discussed in Chapter 2, are a part of healthy caregiver-child relationships and can't be avoided. Repairing these ruptures time and time again promotes development of a secure attachment. When ruptures aren't repaired, as in Bill's early life, an insecure attachment pattern develops to cope with the pain of misattunement. Bill's disorganized controlling attachment pattern was a response to the chaotic and harsh environment of his first four years. Though not a conscious decision, it's as if the child has decided that, if their caregiver doesn't provide the safety and nurture they need, they will get it by controlling the adults who surround them.

An early life of misattunement also leads a child to misunderstanding others' communications and motives. On one occasion, José told Bill how proud he was of the progress Bill had made. Bill took it to mean that, in the past, his problems had been a terrible burden on José. José recognized the misunderstanding and saw it as a rupture in their relationship. José was able to empathize with how bad that would feel and how much Bill wanted to make things better for José. Bill told José, 'That's right, I try hard not to be a problem, and nobody ever notices.' José accepted that as Bill's experience and was curious about it, asking, 'Aww, buddy, what are all the things you do that nobody notices when you are trying so hard not to be a problem?' After a bit, when Bill felt that José really understood how he was feeling – things that he hadn't ever told anyone before – Bill crawled up in José's lap and let José rock him to sleep. It was intimate moments like these, when José entered Bill's world and created a sense of togetherness, that were helping Bill move from a disorganized controlling pattern to a more secure attachment.

As Bill slept, José thought back to a psychological evaluation he read in the social services office three-and-a-half years earlier as he was in the process of bringing Bill home for the first time. The report said that Bill would hurt people, break their things, lie, and steal, and he showed no regret for the pain he had caused. As discussed in Chapter 7, the psychologist was concerned that Bill might be developing into a sociopath, someone who has no capacity to feel the remorse that comes from valuing others' experiences. If that was the case, Bill's future would be filled with legal infractions and contacts with the juvenile justice system. José knew now, especially after a conversation with Kiran, that Bill simply had experienced shame that he couldn't manage. When he was helped to regulate his shame sufficiently, Bill had a warm heart and was clearly sad about having hurt someone. When he was helped to move through his shame, Bill would often think of something he wanted to do to make up for the hurt, like drawing the person a special picture.

Nine months after Bill was admitted, the staff at the residential setting were feeling good about his progress. They recognized that Bill no longer got stopped by shame. He didn't get upset as often. He could trust them enough to let them co-regulate intense feelings when he started to get dysregulated. He would also let them co-create a story about what he was experiencing. One day, after Bill got upset about a new boy telling him he would never go back home, Montrelle talked with Bill about what the boy said, discovering in the interaction how Bill had actually learned to parent his sister, Olivia. Bill knew how to turn any place into a home, so the boy had been incorrect: Bill could *always* feel he was home. Montrelle and Bill agreed that the best home for Bill was with José, and he and José were working hard for him to be back there soon. This new narrative was quite different from the story Bill had told himself before, that he had no home because no one wanted him. As a result of co-creating a new narrative, Bill felt a measure of pride that he did work hard to feel at home in different places and began to notice how he made the residential facility feel like home, too.

The gains Bill made were evident at José's house as well. Most of the time, Bill trusted José to guide him, set limits, and co-regulate his affect. He could better tolerate not knowing something in school and let his teacher co-regulate him as well. He got along relatively well with the other children on his unit as long as he could take a break if he started to get too annoyed with them. In addition, José felt he understood Bill a lot better than he did when Bill was admitted. So, after a discussion with José, the team began making discharge plans. Kiran would continue to see José and Bill for psychotherapy. José would continue coming to the parent group to improve his PACE and other Dyadic Developmental Parenting skills and to get support. The teacher from the residential facility had been in touch periodically with the teacher at Bill's community school. The teacher to whom Bill was returning understood some of what was helpful for Bill and planned for the school counsellor to take breaks with Bill when needed.

DISCHARGE FROM RESIDENTIAL CARE, THEN A SETBACK AT HOME

Bill did well after discharge. He would get agitated, but José was able to help him get regulated again. He ignored José's requests on occasion, and they could work through those times, too. When he returned to school, Bill was shy around the other kids. He liked his teacher and could tell her when he needed to take a break with the counsellor, whom he really liked as well. Several weeks after returning, he was playing much more freely with his classmates. His teacher could tell when he would start to get frustrated with an assignment or peer, and she was usually able to slip in and give him the support he needed. She and the school counsellor were amazed at the difference in Bill, and both started learning about Dyadic Developmental Practice themselves.

Things continued to improve for the next 14 months, with some minor ups and downs. José and Bill met with Kiran for therapy every two weeks. Kiran would meet with José first to see if José was doing okay, if he had been managing things with Bill well, or if he had gotten discouraged. If there were hard things that had happened in the past two weeks, Kiran would listen PACEfully until José began to relax, connect, and brighten up, indicating that he was in a state of social engagement. At that point, she asked José to tell her something good that had happened for Bill recently, so she could start the session with that. When she brought Bill into the session, she enthusiastically engaged Bill with the good news story, then, without breaking stride, she would ask about something that didn't go so well with the same high energy and animated tone of voice, called affective-reflective dialogue. This strategy helps a child to continue talking about even more difficult topics.

Sadly, as often happens with children who have experienced developmental trauma, Bill suffered a setback when there was a perfect storm of unfortunate events. José learned that the court had ordered Bill to have supervised visits with his biological mother, Adina, whom Bill hadn't seen since he was four. Adina had met the reintegration requirements for a number of months: going to counselling, remaining sober, and holding a steady job. This news was unsettling for José, who talked things through with Kiran. Despite their concerns, there was nothing they could do to change the court's decision, and together they told Bill the news. Bill got quite still and quiet, and the adults empathized with how he might be feeling. He swallowed hard and said it was okay. Kiran said she could tell Bill was putting on a brave face. There had been so many things Bill had had to be brave about in his life. She said that she knew other kids who had to put on a brave face while down deep inside they had sad, scared, or mad feelings. She helped José tell Bill that he was sure Bill had some big feelings. That made sense and it was okay. Though Bill listened to what they were saying, he hadn't come fully out of his shutdown state by the end of the session. José and Kiran decided to meet sooner than usual and scheduled for one week hence.

Over the next few days, Bill started wetting his pants at school. Other kids teased him about these accidents, and Bill punched one boy in the face. He was sent to the principal's office, and the principal called José to come and take Bill home. Even though Bill's teacher and the school counsellor understood that Bill's aggression was related to the prospect of visits with his mother, the school district had recently implemented a strict antiviolence policy, and Bill was suspended for a week. Bill's teacher and counsellor felt terrible about it, experiencing the kind of moral injury described in Chapter 8. Bill's shame for getting suspended compounded his shame about losing control of his bladder. His shield against shame was activated again, and he became much angrier as a result.

José was really set back by these events. The manager of the grocery store had scheduled to take a vacation the same week that Bill got suspended and had asked José to serve as acting manager in his absence. It was José's big chance to show he had the wherewithal to manage that level of responsibility. He was in a panic. How could he take care of Bill and the store? José's mother had happened to get admitted to the hospital a few days before Bill was suspended. Her foot had been infected, gotten worse, and now it looked like it might need to be amputated. José didn't have anyone else that he could trust with Bill. So, instead of showing the regional VP (vice-president) that he could manage the store, José had to inform him that he was going to need to stay home with Bill.

José knew that Bill couldn't help his reactions, but José couldn't help his reaction either. In his frustration with the situation, and in his worry about Bill and his mum, he lost it. He yelled at Bill, 'Why are you doing this to me! You are making my life so hard.' José immediately felt terrible about what he said, but, before he could apologize and make up, Bill ran out the front door, crossed traffic, and disappeared in the neighbour's backyard, just like he did before he was admitted to the residential facility. Just like before, José couldn't find him and called the police. José drove the neighbourhood looking for Bill, while a sick feeling grew in his stomach about how quickly things had turned bad. The police located Bill a few hours later, but he screamed at them, banged his head on the window of the police car, and rubbed his wrists raw with the handcuffs they felt they had to put on him. The officers were worried that Bill was going to hurt himself more seriously, so they took him to the hospital emergency department. The doctors there thought Bill needed hospitalization, and José agreed. Bill was admitted to the acute psychiatric inpatient unit where he had been admitted twice before, but the staff there were mostly new and didn't remember him.

The social worker at the inpatient unit felt that José's yelling might have been abusive to Bill, and, because the law mandated making a report when abuse was a possibility, she called child protective services. As a result, when Bill was released from the hospital, he went to an emergency foster home. José tried explaining the situation to anyone he could reach, but he was told that a hearing had been scheduled for a week later, and it could get sorted out then. Needless to say, by that time, Bill had resumed a lot of his old behaviours, and the worker from social services recommended that he return to a residential setting. The insurance company that oversaw Bill's case concluded that the first residential programme had been a failure, so they sent him to another facility across town.

————————

READMISSION TO RESIDENTIAL CARE

The child behavioural health and child welfare systems would be well advised to reconsider the care that children who have experienced developmental trauma require. No matter how robust the outpatient services are that surround a traumatized child, that child may need the safety and security of a residential setting for a few weeks or a few months, or maybe even longer. When a child has had a single episode of trauma, a few sessions of therapy may be helpful in mitigating the resulting sense of threat, avoidance, and re-experiencing that follow. When a child's whole environment has been traumatizing to them, it may take a therapeutic environment to treat the results of that kind of trauma. Therefore, residential care can be seen as an expected occurrence in the treatment of developmental trauma rather than a failure of outpatient treatment. If children with developmental trauma are admitted to a residential setting earlier in a cycle of crisis, the treatment course is likely to be shortened. Small fires are easier to put out than bigger fires.

In addition to being needed to treat a deterioration in functioning, a second admission to residential care can serve another purpose as well. During the first admission, the child and family may have had a limit to how much information they could absorb and to how much change they could make. A plateau in their progress is often a signal that maximum benefit has been reached and it is time for discharge. It is frequently counterproductive to continue residential care past that point. A second admission provides the opportunity for the child and family to make more gains than were made the first time around. The child and family not only recover to the level of functioning attained at the end of their first admission, but their improvement may also surpass their highest previous level of functioning as well. Unfortunately for Bill and José, the second admission did not start off well.

The facility where Bill was placed was a trauma-organized institution (Bloom, 2017), as described in Chapter 8. They contained children's dysregulation and rages by putting them in seclusion, locking them in a room alone until they calmed down. At that facility, the staff member would stand at the door and watch through the window to make sure that the child didn't get hurt. When Bill was placed in seclusion during his third day there, he got agitated, yelling at the top of his lungs and hurling himself against the door. Eventually, the nurse asked the doctor for approval to give Bill a sedative injection. Several staff members came into the seclusion room and held Bill down long enough for the nurse to give him the shot. Then they locked the door again. Bill fell asleep in about 15 minutes, curled in a ball on the mat. It goes without saying that this facility's approach didn't follow the guidelines of Dyadic Developmental Practice. When José learned what happened, he called Kiran, who reached the worker from social services. She was able to get José transferred back to the facility where Bill was admitted previously.

The time for the court hearing came, and, after persuasive pleas from José, Kiran, and José's attorney, the judge agreed to place Bill back in José's custody. The judge also ordered José to have his own therapy and set a follow-up hearing for three months.

Bill was glad to be back at the other facility, though he was still in shock from the events of the previous couple of weeks. He felt more at ease around people he knew, and the PACEful attitudes of the staff were comforting. He had no big blow ups. In therapy with Kiran, they talked about the recent events and how everyone had responded. Kiran helped Bill tell José how much it hurt his feelings when José yelled at him. Bill talked about how scared he had been at the foster home and how he worried that he would never see José again. José empathized with Bill's experiences, saying, 'You must have been so upset with me when I yelled at you. You probably thought, "How can you treat me like this? You know how bad my parents treated me!"' Bill agreed with José's guesses about how he was feeling and tearfully asked José quietly, 'How could you say those things to me?' Kiran helped José explain that sometimes grown-ups get overwhelmed with big feelings too. José didn't have his mum to rely on, and he had big pressures at work. It wasn't an excuse for how he yelled at Bill, he explained. But it was a clear message that he needed his own support, and José was going to start therapy of his own.

Even after the recent events, the judge insisted that Bill have supervised visits with Adina, and José and Kiran concluded that it would be best if the visits started while Bill was still at the facility. Kiran met with Adina several times and was pleasantly surprised to find a young woman who had been through her own tribulations, and who was now humbly taking respon-sibility for her life. Kiran taught Adina the PACE attitude and role-played conversations with Bill in which Adina accepted Bill's experience. Adina liked these sessions and agreed to be accepting, curious, and empathic toward any experience that Bill wanted to share with her. In one role play, Kiran played Bill and said to Adina, 'I hate you. You ruined my life.' Adina responded to Kiran/Bill, 'Oh, Bill, I didn't give you what you needed and deserved. I made your life so hard. No wonder you feel like I ruined your life. I'd feel the same way, too.' Kiran felt that through these sessions Adina had learned enough for it to be safe for them to meet with Bill.

Around the same time, José and Bill talked with Kiran about how Bill had freaked out when he was locked in the seclusion room at the other facility. Bill recalled that sometimes Elijah and Adina would pass out with things still cooking in the kitchen. At three years old, he had gotten in the habit of turning off the stove to keep the place from catching fire. Bill realized, with help from José and Kiran, that when he was locked up, he felt panicked that he couldn't keep things safe. That's what happened when he was in seclusion – in his mind, Bill could see the place catching fire with him locked in that room.

Discussing the terrifying memory Bill had recalled unlocked the door to a whole new set of impressions of his time with Adina and Elijah to which he had not had access during his first admission. Behind that door were clues to why Bill needed to be admitted to the residential facility in the first place. Because Kiran knew that each of the states described by polyvagal theory had their value, she helped Bill appreciate how the fight-or-flight hypervigilance that he exercised with the stove helped to keep him alive. That response was part of his body's wisdom that had served him well in many circumstances in the past. The problem now was that his nervous system hadn't learned to relax when things were actually safe.

In fact, these days when Bill had a sense that he was safe, he would begin to relax, but then, paradoxically, he would start to panic. He, Kiran, and José became aware that Bill's hypervigilance felt safe to him, and actual safety, along with the relaxation that naturally followed, felt dangerous. They put things together and understood that before Bill was admitted to residential care the first time, he had begun to feel safe with José, and that sense of safety felt dangerous to Bill. He needed to keep himself stirred up in order to protect himself from letting down his guard, and this agitation is what created the circumstances necessitating the first admission. This realization also defined a new goal in therapy – helping Bill to feel safe when he actually was safe.

Additionally, Bill had the sessions with Adina and Kiran. Bill had decided that he wanted to meet without José, but he did want his key person from the facility there as well. He was able to tell Adina how lonely he felt when she and Elijah had left him and Olivia alone in the apartment. He told her how worried he had been about all of them. He also told her that, when he heard about the visits with her, he had been really frightened that she was going to take him away from José. Adina said, 'Oh my, that's such a scary thought. You have been with José for years. He's your dad. It would be so upsetting to lose your dad.' Bill nodded but was silent, and Kiran asked Bill's permission to speak for him, saying, 'Yeah, I don't know what I'd do if I didn't have my dad. I love him so much.' Adina replied to Bill, 'I am so glad you have José. And I am glad he has you. You guys are so good together.' After that session, Bill didn't lose control of his bladder anymore.

José found a therapist for himself to comply with the judge's order. How he had responded during the whole fiasco had deeply unsettled him, and he wanted to explore his own sense of safety and how he connected with people. He worked on a feeling that something was missing in his life and the doubt that maybe it had been his fault that his father had left. He noticed that when he felt close to Bill, he would start to get anxious. So, he worked with the therapist about his fears of intimacy and losing himself if he got too close. The therapist knew that sometimes parents wouldn't work in therapy just to benefit themselves, but they would do it if they thought it would help their children. The therapist helped José decide that he would keep working on his own ability to connect in order to be a good model for Bill as he worked on the same thing.

Bill was discharged about two-and-a-half months after he was admitted to the facility for the second time. He was happier and more relaxed than he had been even at his first discharge. José had a newfound confidence as well, and interestingly, he had succeeded with a second chance as acting manager at the grocery store. José and Bill continued therapy with Kiran, but, because Bill was doing so well, they decreased the frequency of the sessions to once a month about four months after discharge. The sessions Kiran supervised between Bill and Adina also continued going well, and José joined at times, too. Bill did well in school, but still needed to take breaks with the counsellor about once a week.

Two years after discharge, Bill returned to the unit to visit the staff. After obtaining the appropriate permissions, they invited him to talk to the current children on the unit. With insight beyond his ten-and-a-half years of living, he told them what he had learned from his two times at the residential facility, saying, 'I learned a lot of things are okay. It's okay to be mad at people. It's okay to feel bad about things I did. It's okay to make things better. It's okay to be happy. And mostly I learned, it's okay to be me.'

References

Adair, J. (1983) *Effective Leadership*. Pan MacMillan.

Anglin, J. P. (2015) *Building a trauma-informed organization* [PowerPoint slides]. MCFD-FCSSBC Conference, Richmond, British Columbia: https://fcssbc.ca/wp-content/uploads/2015/06/2-JAnglin-Building-a-Trauma-Informed-Organization.pdf.

Arnett, J. J. (2008) 'The neglected 95%: Why American psychology needs to become less American.' American Psychologist, 63, 7, 602–614.

Axline, V. M. (1964) *Dibs in Search of Self*. Ballantine Books.

Baldwin, J. (1962, January 14). 'As much truth as one can bear.' The New York Times Book Review. https://www.nytimes.com/1962/01/14/archives/as-much-truth-as-one-can-bear-to-speak-out-about-the-world-as-it-is.html

Baylin, J., & Hughes, D. A. (2016) *The Neurobiology of Attachment-Focused Therapy: Enhancing Connection and Trust in the Treatment of Children and Adolescents (Norton Series on Interpersonal Neurobiology)*. W. W. Norton & Company.

Berry, O. O., Londoño Tobón, A., & Njoroge, W. F. (2021) 'Social determinants of health: The impact of racism on early childhood mental health.' Current Psychiatry Reports, 23, 1–10.

Bloom, S. L. (1994) 'The Sanctuary Model: Developing Generic Inpatient Programs for the Treatment of Psychological Trauma.' In M. B. Williams & J. F. Sommer (eds) *Handbook of Post-Traumatic Therapy: A Practical Guide to Intervention, Treatment, and Research* (pp. 474–491). Greenwood Publishing.

Bloom, S. L. (2013) *Creating Sanctuary: Toward the Evolution of Sane Societies* (second ed.). Routledge.

Bloom, S. L. (2017) 'The Sanctuary Model: Through the Lens of Moral Safety.' In S. N. Gold (ed.) *APA Handbook of Trauma Psychology: Trauma Practice* (pp. 499–513). American Psychological Association. https://doi.org/10.1037/0000020-024

Bloom, S. L., & Farragher, B. (2013) *Restoring Sanctuary: A New Operating System for Trauma-Informed Systems of Care*. Oxford University Press.

Bowlby, J. (1998) *A Secure Base: Clinical Applications of Attachment Theory*. Routledge.

Bureau, J. F., Ann Easlerbrooks, M., & Lyons-Ruth, K. (2009) 'Attachment disorganization and controlling behavior in middle childhood: Maternal and child precursors and correlates.' Attachment & Human Development, 11, 3, 265–284. https://doi.org/10.1080/14616730902814788

Casswell, G., Golding, K. S., Grant, E., Hudson, J., & Tower, P. (2014) 'Dyadic developmental practice (DDP): A framework for therapeutic intervention and parenting.' The Child and Family Clinical Psychology Review, 2, 19–27.

Children Act 1989, Section 25 (United Kingdom). https://www.legislation.gov.uk/ukpga/1989/41/section/25

Cook, A., Spinazzola, J., Ford, J., Lanktree, C., *et al.* (2005) 'Complex trauma in children and adolescents.' Psychiatric Annals, 35, 5, 390–398.

Cozolino, L. (2016) *Why Therapy Works: Using Our Minds to Change Our Brains (Norton Series on Interpersonal Neurobiology).* W.W. Norton & Company.

Dana, D. (2020) *Polyvagal Flip Chart: Understanding the Science of Safety (Norton Series on Interpersonal Neurobiology).* W.W. Norton & Company.

Diessner, R., Rust, T., Solom, R. C., Frost, N., & Parsons, L. (2006) 'Beauty and hope: A moral beauty intervention.' Journal of Moral Education, 35, 3, 301–317.

Dozier, M. (2003) 'Attachment-based treatment for vulnerable children.' Attachment & Human Development, 5, 3, 253–257.

Emond, R., & Burns, A. (2022, June) *Everyday Care: What Makes it Therapeutic for Children in Residential Care?* The Sir Halley Stewart Trust. Available on the DDP website (DDPnetwork.org).

Emond, R., Steckley, L., & Roesch-Marsh, A. (2016) *A Guide to Therapeutic Child Care: What You Need to Know to Create a Healing Home.* Jessica Kingsley Publishers.

Fejo-King, C. (2017) *Practice Live. Attachment and Culture. Understanding Attachment.* Attachment and Culture (nsw.gov.au).

Field, T. (2007) *The Amazing Infant.* Blackwell Publishing.

Figley, C. R. (1995) 'Compassion Fatigue as Secondary Traumatic Stress Disorder: An Overview.' In C. R. Figley (ed.) *Compassion Fatigue: Coping with Secondary Traumatic Stress Disorder in Those Who Treat the Traumatized (Brunner/Mazel Psychosocial Stress Series)* (pp. 1–20). Routledge.

Fonagy, P., Luyten, P., Allison, E., & Campbell, C. (2016) 'Reconciling Psychoanalytic Ideas With Attachment Theory.' In J. Cassidy & P. R. Shaver (eds) *Handbook of Attachment* (3rd ed, pp. 780–804). Guilford Press.

Fosha, D. (ed.) (2021) Undoing aloneness and the transformation of suffering into flourishing: AEDP 2.0. American Psychological Association.

Geoffrion, S., Morselli, C., & Guay, S. (2016) 'Rethinking compassion fatigue through the lens of professional identity: The case of child-protection workers.' Trauma, Violence, & Abuse, 17, 3, 270–283.

Golding, K. S. (2017a) *Everyday Parenting with Security and Love: Using PACE to Provide Foundations for Attachment.* Jessica Kingsley Publishers.

Golding, K. S. (2017b) *Foundations for Attachment Training Resource: The Six-Session Programme for Parents of Traumatized Children.* Jessica Kingsley Publishers.

Golding, K. S., & Hughes, D. A. (2012) *Creating Loving Attachments: Parenting with PACE to Nurture Confidence and Security in the Troubled Child.* Jessica Kingsley Publishers.

Golding, K. S., Phillips, S., & Bombèr, L. M. (2021) *Working with Relational Trauma in Schools: An Educator's Guide to Using Dyadic Developmental Practice.* Jessica Kingsley Publishers.

Griffin, B. J., Purcell, N., Burkman, K., Litz, B. T., *et al.* (2019) 'Moral injury: An integrative review.' Journal of Traumatic Stress, 32, 3, 350–362.

Groopman, J. (2004) *The Anatomy of Hope: How People Prevail in the Face of Illness.* Random House.

Gunnar, M. R., Hostinar, C. E., Sanchez, M. M., Tottenham, N., & Sullivan, R. S. (2015) 'Parental buffering of fear and stress neurobiology: Reviewing parallels across rodent, monkey, and human models.' Social Neuroscience, 10, 5, 474–478. https://doi.org/10.1080/17470919.2015.1070198

Haidt, J. (2003) 'Elevation and the Positive Psychology of Morality.' In C. L. M. Keyes & J. Haidt (eds) *Flourishing: Positive Psychology and the Life Well-Lived* (pp. 275–289). American Psychological Association.

Haight, W., Sugrue, E. P., & Calhoun, M. (2017) 'Moral injury among child protection professionals: Implications for the ethical treatment and retention of workers.' Children and Youth Services Review, 82, 27–41.

Harwood, R. L., Miller, J. G., & Irizarry, N. L. (1995) *Culture and Attachment: Perceptions of the Child in Context*. Guilford Press.

Hatzenbuehler, M. L., & Link, B. G. (2014) 'Introduction to the special issue on structural stigma and health.' Social Science & Medicine, 103, 1–6. https://doi.org/10.1016/j.socscimed.2013.12.017

Henrich, J. (2021) *The Weirdest People in the World: How the West Became Psychologically Peculiar and Particularly Prosperous*. Penguin Random House.

Henrich, J., Heine, S. J., & Norenzayan, A. (2010) 'Most people are not WEIRD.' Nature, 466, 7302, 29–29.

Holmes, L., Neagu, M., Sanders-Ellis, D., & Harrison, N. (2020) *Lifelong Links: Evaluation Report*. UK Department for Education. https://assets.publishing.service.gov.uk/government/uploads/system/uploads/attachment_data/file/955953/Lifelong_Links_evaluation_report.pdf

Hughes, D. A. (2007) *Attachment-Focused Family Therapy*. W. W. Norton & Company.

Hughes, D. A. (2009) *Attachment-Focused Parenting*. W. W. Norton & Company.

Hughes, D. A. (2011) *Attachment-Focused Family Therapy Workbook*. W. W. Norton & Company.

Hughes, D. A. (2017) *Building the Bonds of Attachment: Awakening Love in Deeply Traumatized Children* (3rd ed.). Rowman & Littlefield.

Hughes, D. A., & Baylin, J. (2012) *Brain-Based Parenting: The Neuroscience of Caregiving for Healthy Attachment (Norton Series on Interpersonal Neurobiology)*. W. W. Norton & Company.

Hughes, D. A., & Golding, K. S. (2024) *Healing Relational Trauma Workbook: Dyadic Developmental Psychotherapy in Practice*. W. W. Norton & Company.

Hughes, D. A., Golding, K. S., & Hudson, J. (2019) *Healing Relational Trauma with Attachment-Focused Interventions: Dyadic Developmental Psychotherapy with Children and Families*. W. W. Norton & Company.

Kansas Department for Aging and Disability Services. (n.d.) Kansas Psychiatric Residential Treatment Facility (PRTF) Medical Necessity Criteria. https://kdads.ks.gov/docs/librariesprovider17/survey-certification-and-credentialing-commission/behavioral-health-licensing/prtfs/medical-necessity-criteria.pdf

Keller, H. (2022) *The Myth of Attachment Theory: A Critical Understanding for Multicultural Societies*. Routledge.

Keltner, D. (2023) *Awe: The New Science of Everyday Wonder and How it Can Transform Your Life*. Penguin Press.

Kikusui, T., Winslow, J. T., & Mori, Y. (2006) 'Social buffering: Relief from stress and anxiety.' Philosophical Transactions of the Royal Society B: Biological Sciences, 361, 1476, 2215–2228.

Kinouani, G. (2021) *Living While Black: The Essential Guide to Overcoming Racial Trauma*. Penguin Random House.

Kircanski, K., Lieberman, M. D., & Craske, M. G. (2012) 'Feelings into words: Contributions of language to exposure therapy.' Psychological Science, 23, 10, 1086–1091.

Lancy, D. F. (2017) Raising Children: Surprising Insights from Other Cultures. Cambridge University Press.

Lieberman, M. D., Eisenberger, N. I., Crockett, M. J., Tom, S. M., et al. (2007) 'Putting feelings into words.' Psychological Science, 18, 5, 421–428. https://www.scn.ucla.edu/pdf/AL(2007).pdf

Lohn, J. (2021, September 6) 'How the tsar, Alexander Popov, claimed the sprint throne.' Swimming World Magazine. https://www.swimmingworldmagazine.com/news/how-the-tsar-alexander-popov-claimed-the-sprint-throne

NHS England. (2018, September) The Children and Young People's Secure Estate National Partnership Agreement [Report]. HM Government. https://www.england.nhs.uk/long-read/health-and-justice-children-programme-national-partnership-agreement-2023-25

Osofsky, J. D., Putnam, F. W., & Lederman, J. C. S. (2008) 'How to maintain emotional health when working with trauma.' Juvenile and Family Court Journal 59, 4, 91–102.

Page, D., & Swann, R. (2021) Therapeutic Parenting with PACE: An Attachment, Trauma and DDP Informed Group Programme and Training Resource. Pavilion Publishing and Media Ltd.

Perry, B. D., & Winfrey, O. (2021) What Happened to You? Conversations on Trauma, Resilience, and Healing. Flatiron Books: An Oprah Book.

Pirelli, G., Formon, D. L., & Maloney, K. (2020, February 10) 'Preventing vicarious trauma (VT), compassion fatigue (CF), and burnout (BO) in forensic mental health: Forensic psychology as exemplar.' Professional Psychology: Research and Practice. Advance online publication.

Pope, A. (1709) An Essay on Criticism [eBook]. The Project Gutenberg. https://www.gutenberg.org/files/7409/7409-h/7409-h.htm

Porges, S. W. (2017) The Pocket Guide to the Polyvagal Theory: The Transformative Power of Feeling Safe (Norton Series on Interpersonal Neurobiology). W. W. Norton & Company.

Porges, S. W. & Dana, D. (eds) (2018) Clinical Applications of the Polyvagal Theory: The Emergence of Polyvagal-Informed Therapies. W.W. Norton & Company.

The Promise Scotland Ltd. (2023) The Promise Scotland. www.thepromise.scot

Rose, R. (2012) Life Story Therapy with Traumatized Children: A Model for Practice. Jessica Kingsley Publishers.

Ruch, G. (2007) 'Reflective practice in contemporary child-care social work: The role of containment.' British Journal of Social Work, 37, 4, 659–680.

Sanders, M. R., & Thompson, G. S. (2022) Polyvagal Theory and the Developing Child: Systems of Care for Strengthening Kids, Families, and Communities (Norton Series on Interpersonal Neurobiology). W. W. Norton & Company.

Schore, A. N. (2002) 'Dysregulation of the right brain: A fundamental mechanism of traumatic attachment and the psychopathogenesis of posttraumatic stress disorder.' Australian & New Zealand Journal of Psychiatry, 36, 1, 9–30.

Schore, A. N. (2012) The Science and Art of Psychotherapy (Norton Series on Interpersonal Neurobiology). W. W. Norton & Company.

Schore, J. R., & Schore, A. N. (2014) 'Regulation theory and affect regulation psychotherapy: A clinical primer.' Smith College Studies in Social Work, 84, 2–3, 178–195.

Siegel, D. J. (1999) The Developing Mind: Toward a Neurobiology of Interpersonal Experience. Guilford Press.

Siegel, D. J., & Bryson, T. P. (2012) *The Whole-Brain Child: 12 Proven Strategies to Nurture Your Child's Developing Mind*. Constable & Robinson Ltd.

Stern, D. (2000) *The Interpersonal World of the Infant*. Basic Books.

Tangney, J. P., & Dearing, R. L. (2002) *Shame and Guilt*. Guilford Press.

Taylor, J., Shostak, L., Rogers, A., & Mitchell, P. (2018) 'Rethinking mental health provision in the secure estate for children and young people: A framework for integrated care (SECURE STAIRS).' Safer Communities, 17, 4, 193–201.

Tedeschi, R. G., & Calhoun, L. G. (1995) *Trauma and Transformation: Growing in the Aftermath of Suffering*. Sage Publications, Inc. https://doi.org/10.4135/9781483326931

Tedeschi, R. G., Calhoun, L. G., & Groleau, J. M. (2015) 'Clinical Applications of Post-Traumatic Growth.' In S. Joseph (ed.) *Positive Psychology in Practice: Promoting Human Flourishing in Work, Health, Education, and Everyday Life* (second ed., pp. 503–518). Wiley.

Treisman, K. (2016) *Working with Relational and Developmental Trauma in Children and Adolescents*. Routledge.

Treisman, K. [@dr_treisman]. (2020, January 7) *Every intervention is an intervention* [Tweet; attached information graphic]. Twitter. https://twitter.com/dr_treisman/status/1214661466932023296

Treisman, K., Paxton, E., Metcalfe, E., Terral, W., & Nosheen, S. (2021) *A Treasure Box for Creating Trauma-Informed Organizations: A Ready-to-Use Resource for Trauma, Adversity, and Culturally Informed, Infused and Responsive Systems (Therapeutic Treasures Collection)*. Jessica Kingsley Publishers.

Trevarthen, C. (2001) 'Intrinsic motives for companionship in understanding: Their origin, development, and significance for infant mental health.' Infant Mental Health Journal: Official Publication of the World Association for Infant Mental Health, 22, 1–2, 95–131.

Tronick, E. (2007) *The Neurobehavioural and Social-Emotional Development of Infants and Children*. W. W. Norton & Company.

Tronick, E., & DiCorcia, J. A. (2015) 'The everyday stress resilience hypothesis: A reparatory sensitivity and the development of coping and resilience.' Children Australia, 40, 2, 124–138. doi:10.1017/cha.2015.11

Turner-Halliday, F., Watson, N., Boyer, N. R. S., Boyd, K. A., & Minnis, H. (2014) 'The feasibility of a randomised controlled trial of Dyadic Developmental Psychotherapy.' BMC Psychiatry, 14, 347, 1–11.

van der Kolk, B. A. (2005) 'Developmental trauma disorder: Toward a rational diagnosis for children with complex trauma histories.' Psychiatric Annals, 35, 5, 401–408.

Van Sant, G. (dir.). (1997) *Good Will Hunting* [Film]. Be Gentlemen, Inc.

Williams, D. R., & Mohammed, S. A. (2013) 'Racism and health I: Pathways and scientific evidence.' American Behavioral Scientist, 57, 8, 1152–1173.

Wilson, C. (2018) *Grounded: Discovering the Missing Piece in the Puzzle of Children's Behaviour*. CHEW Initiatives.

Woodier, D. (2019) *Residential Child Care Workers Talk about the Impact of a Relational Way of Working with Young People* [Report]. Scottish Attachment in Action. https://ddpnetwork.org/backend/wp-content/uploads/2020/05/Residential-Child-Care-Workers-Talk-About-the-Impact-of-a-Relational-way-of-Working-with-Young-People.pdf

Zhang, M., Zhang, Y., & Kong, Y. (2019) 'Interaction between social pain and physical pain.' Brain Science Advances, 5, 4, 265–273. https://journals.sagepub.com/doi/full/10.26599/BSA.2019.9050023

Subject Index

Author Index